Genetically Modified Athlete

In a provocative analysis of sport ethics and human values, *Genetically Modified Athletes* imagines the brave new world of sport. Examining this new ethical issue at a crucial time in its theorisation, the book questions the very cornerstone of sporting and medical ethics, asking whether sporting authorities *can* or even *should* protect sport from genetic modification.

The book brings together sport studies and bioethics to challenge our understanding of the values that define sport. Without asserting that 'anything goes' in sports performance enhancement, *Genetically Modified Athletes* argues that being human matters in sport, but that genetic modification does not have to challenge this capacity.

Genetically Modified Athletes includes examinations of:

- The concept of 'good sport' and definitions of cheating.
- Privacy rights and using genetic data for sport.
- Notions of autonomy, dignity and personhood.
- The usefulness (or not) of the terms 'doping' and 'anti-doping'.

Dr. Andy Miah is Lecturer in Media, Bioethics, and Cyberculture at the University of Paisley, and Tutor of Ethics in Science and Medicine at the University of Glasgow. He is co-editor of *Sport Technology: History, Philosophy and Policy,* and is the author of numerous published academic papers on the subject of genetic modification and sport.

Ethics and Sport
Series Editors: Mike McNamee, *University of Wales Swansea* and
Jim Parry, *University of Leeds*

The Ethics and Sport series aims to encourage critical reflection on the practice
of sport, and to stimulate professional evaluation and development. Each volume
explores new work relating to philosophical ethics and the social and cultural
study of ethical issues. Each is different in scope, appeal, focus and treatment
but a balance is sought between local and international focus, perennial and
contemporary issues, level of audience, teaching and research application, and
variety of practical concerns.

Also available in this series:

Genetically Modified Athletes
Biomedical ethics, gene doping and sport

Andy Miah

Routledge
Taylor & Francis Group

LONDON AND NEW YORK

First published 2004 by Routledge
2 Park Square, Milton Park, Abingdon, Oxon, OX14 4RN
270 Madison Ave, New York 10016
Printed in Great Britain www.routledge.com

Reprinted 2005

© 2004 Andy Miah

Typeset in 10/12pt Goudy by Graphicraft Limited, Hong Kong
Printed and bound in Great Britain by TJ International Ltd,
Padstow, Cornwall

Every effort has been made to ensure that the advice and information in
this book is true and accurate at the time of going to press. However,
neither the publisher nor the authors can accept any legal responsibility
or liability for any errors or omissions that may be made. In the case of
drug administration, any medical procedure or the use of technical
equipment mentioned within this book, you are strongly advised to
consult the manufacturer's guidelines.

British Library Cataloguing in Publication Data
A catalogue record for this book is available from the British Library

Library of Congress Cataloging in Publication Data
A catalog record for this book has been requested

ISBN 0–415–29879–2 (hbk)
ISBN 0–415–29880–6 (pbk)

For my family

Contents

Series editors' foreword

Andy Miah's book takes as its theme an issue which is emerging as a central challenge for the development of elite sport: the genetic modification of athletes. It draws upon and illuminates key debates in bioethics and their implications for the practices and governance of sport. Many of the arguments that have been developed against doping apply also here, for genetic modification – it is frequently alleged – seeks unfair advantage, fails to honour the contract to contest, encourages and permits secrecy and deception as to conditions of preparation and competition, applying possibly harmful or deleterious technologies, uses 'unnatural' means, and leads to the exploitation of athletes.

Miah provides a state-of-the-art account of the various routes to enhancement potentially offered by genetic enhancement, and considers critically their ethical implications. He articulates and defends the radical and challenging view that the performance ethic underlying elite sport continually requires the fresh impetus of technological development, and that genetic technologies represent an inevitable and valuable extension of the means available to us for the further development of performance sport.

As well as the specific role of each chapter in informing us about the nature of the possibilities opened up by rapid developments in genetics and in challenging our ethical preconceptions, Miah's argument forces us to re-think our taken-for-granted views of the value of sport in human life and indeed the very notion of the 'human' in sports.

Jim Parry, University of Leeds
Mike McNamee, University of Swansea

Foreword

How should we think about genetically modified athletes? What seems at first to be a narrow and futuristic question transforms under the inquiring gaze of Andy Miah into a meditation on human nature, the meaning of sport, and the appropriate scope of human self-manipulation. Other readers may find, as I do, much to argue with in Miah's analysis. But they will also be challenged to think about the familiar in unfamiliar ways, to question many well-settled preconceptions. Miah is indisputably correct when he asserts that anti-doping policies by national and international sport organizations have lacked a thoughtful ethical and philosophical basis. I witnessed that firsthand in my own work with a national Olympic committee and later with WADA – the World Anti-Doping Agency. One of the early leaders of bioethics in the United States, K. Danner Closer, advised his philosophical colleagues who were interacting with the worlds of practice – with clinicians and policy makers – to do philosophy, but *only* when necessary. It is abundantly clear that the time has long since arrived when it is necessary to do creative, probing, and incisive philosophy now at the intersection of sport and the technologies of human manipulation.

Genetically Modified Athletes: Biomedical Ethics, Gene Doping and Sport is to my knowledge the first book-length philosophical study of genetic manipulation and sport. In passing, Miah comments on many controversies in ethics and sport, most especially how we should think in general about the use of enhancement technologies in sport such as drugs. Miah is well read in the scholarly literature on philosophy of sport and also well versed in contemporary disputes within sport. For readers unfamiliar with that literature and those disputes, the book will be a useful introduction. Whether familiar or not, readers will be engaged and challenged by this provocative book.

Thomas H. Murray, Ph.D.
The Hastings Center

Series preface

The Ethics and Sport series is the first of its kind in the world. Our central aims are to support and contribute to the development of the serious study of ethical issues in sport, and shape international debates on sports ethics in policy and practice, and indeed to the establishing of Sports Ethics as a legitimate discipline in its own right.

Whilst academics and devotees of sport have long debated ethical issues such as cheating, doping, violence, exploitation, inequality, the nature and demands of fair play, and so on, they have rarely been explored systematically in extended discussion.

Given the logical basis of ethics at the heart of sport as a practical activity, every important and topical issue in sport necessarily has an ethical dimension – and often the ethical dimension is of overwhelming significance. The series addresses a variety of both perennial and contemporary issues in this rapidly expanding field, aiming to engage the community of teachers, researchers and professionals, as well as the general reader.

Philosophical ethics may be seen both as a theoretical academic discipline and as an ordinary everyday activity contributing to conversation, journalism, and practical decision-making. The series aims to bridge that gap by addressing the shared interests that exist between these otherwise disparate communities. Academic disciplines will be brought to bear on the practical issues of the day, illuminating them and exploring strategies for problem-solving. A philosophical interest in ethical issues may also be complemented, broadened and/or challenged by research within related disciplines in the natural and social sciences and the humanities, and some volumes aim to make these links directly.

The series aims to encourage critical reflection on the practices of sport, and to stimulate professional evaluation and development. Each volume will explore new work relating to philosophical ethics and the study of ethical issues in the social and cultural context of sport. Each will be different in scope, appeal, focus and treatment, but a balance will be sought within the series between local and international focus, perennial and contemporary issues, levels of audience, teaching and research applications, and variety of practical and professional concerns.

In the first two edited volumes of this series, a range of issues was explored, addressing issues central to the philosophical exploration of sports ethics as a discipline while indicating the breadth of the field. Subsequent volumes develop individual themes in depth, as well as posing general questions about the evolving significance of sport in contemporary society.

Jim Parry, University of Leeds
Mike McNamee, University of Swansea

Preface

My interest in genetics and sport has grown along with a number of fascinations with what some authors have called posthuman or transhuman technologies. One of the most extraordinary experiences of my initial research on technology entailed witnessing the training session of a life-extension group. At their invitation, I was able to sit through a rehearsal for the procedure they would go through when one of the members of the group died. It was not dissimilar to other medical procedures, except that these people were not interested in delaying death, but preventing it entirely. For them, the science of cryonics provides a mechanism whereby it might be possible to preserve a body in a state of clinical death, so that they may, one day, be revived using new medical techniques. By preserving the body immediately after death, damage is minimised and the patient has the strongest chances of a healthy recovery, if the technology to reanimate the preserved body is ever realised. As one might expect, the financial cost for cryogenic preservation is very high indeed. Participants have the choice between 'head-only' or 'full-body' preservation, the former of which is more economical. For me, this technology captured something very interesting about being human and our relationship to technology, and this intrigue persists in my thoughts about the role of genetics in society.

There are strong links to be found between ethical studies of medicine and the sporting context. For many years, bioethicists have referred to sport in their discussions about genetic modification. It is possible to find references to sport in many authors' works, including articles by Susan Bordo, Dan Brock, Ruth Chadwick, Carl Elliott, Jonathon Glover, Eric Juengst, Fred Ledley, Maggie Little, Erik Parens and Tom Wilkie, to name a few. Indeed, the emergence of anti-doping and the medical concern which doping implies took place at the same time as the development of bioethics. My inquiry has led me to believe that sport offers something particularly rich about understanding what is uniquely complex about genetic technology. Yet, until recently, little has been published explicitly on the ethics of gene transfer technology in sport.

As is the case more broadly with genetics, a great deal of research and debate has taken place in the scientific domain. Yet it seems only in recent years that people have become morally or ethically concerned about this technology in sport. Significantly, the interest from the International Olympic Committee and the World Anti-Doping Agency has been important for raising the international profile of this new ethical issue. Yet more surprising has been to observe non-sporting organisations such as the United States President's Council on Bioethics and the Australian Law Reforms Commission, who acknowledge that this topic is now serious enough to warrant discussion. A number of countries are also beginning to initiate discussion on this topic, which is crucial given the diverse views on genetics in society and the global implications of gene doping.

Through this volume, I hope to demonstrate that sport offers a context to ethical discussions about human genetics, which reveals something interesting about what gives value to being human. For this reason, discussing genetic modification in sport can be uniquely helpful for us to understand what feels threatened by the prospect of genetic technology. In addition, I argue that the important aspects of sport can remain (and are even enhanced) in a genetically modified future. This does not mean that there are no serious ethical dilemmas arising from the prospect of genetic technology. Rather, the kinds of ethical problem are not the intuitive ones that continually frame negative reactions to genetic technology.

This year, the Olympic Summer Games returns to its home nation of Greece. Perhaps for the first time of any Olympics, speculations have been made about the possible presence of genetically modified athletes among the competitors. And so, as the origins of sport come full circle and the natural status of the human has become disputed through genetics, this seems an opportune moment to requestion what is valuable about the sporting performance.

To track this ongoing issue, which is still very embryonic in the world of sport, I have created a website which endeavours to provide a bibliography for the continual coverage and development of this topic in various contexts. This site may be found at http://www.GMathletes.net.

Acknowledgements

A number of people have been important to the work and preparation of this book. First, my thanks go to the staff and fellows of The Hastings Center, where I spent a delightful summer writing a large part of this manuscript. I am particularly grateful to Thomas and Cynthia Murray and Angela Wasunna, first, for their generosity and friendship, but also for their critical comments on my work and engaging discussions that we continue to have about this subject. I feel privileged to have been present at the Hasting Center project meetings on Performance-enhancing Technologies during 2002 and 2003. My thanks also to members of that working group, particularly Don Catlin, Ted Friedmann, John Hoberman, Eric Juengst, Max Mehlman and Erik Parens, whose insightful observations and correspondence have challenged me to develop a more critical approach to my own arguments. My appreciation also goes to Jozef Glasa, who has been extraordinarily kind since we met at the Center.

I am also pleased to have been able to conduct a modest lecture tour while in New York during 2002 and would like to thank a number of people who made this possible. First, thanks to Nick Bostrom, Carol Pollard, Bonnie Kaplan, and other members of the Yale University Working Group for Artificial Intelligence, Transhumanism, and Nanotechnology: Ethics, Policy and Utopian Visions for their helpful comments on my work. My congratulations to them for holding such an excellent series of lectures and for pushing the envelope further on thinking about technology. Thanks also to colleagues and friends at State University of New York at Cortland for their hospitality, in particular to Kathy Russell and Ted Fay.

I have also enjoyed discussions and correspondence about genetics in sport with Andrew Courtwright, Francis Fukuyama, John Harris, Barrie Houlihan, Gordon Mellor, William J. Morgan, Christian Munthe, Gillian Patterson-Bartle and Claudio Tamburrini, all of whom have been instrumental to my thinking about this topic. I am also grateful to the kind support of Robin Downie, Carl Elliott, Simon Gardiner, Kostas Georgiadis, Vasilis Klissouras, Dave McArdle, John Nauright, Dawn Penny, Michael Shapiro and Trevor Slack, who have each been valued colleagues and friends since I have known them. In particular, I would like to thank Gunnar Breivik, Simon Eassom and Sigmund Loland who have been very close to my work in this area from the start.

I would also like to thank a number of organisations, which have made possible the research for this book and/or have allowed me opportunities to speak about my work. Specifically, I would like to acknowledge the University of Paisley, support from which has been given through Alex Gilkison and Neil Blain. My gratitude also goes to the Carnegie Trust for the Universities of Scotland, whose funding provided the means to carry out a significant part of this project, and to the British Academy, who have provided funds to disseminate this work. I would also like to thank the European College of Sport Science, the International Olympic Committee, the International Olympic Academy, the International Academy of Sport Science and Technology, the British Olympic Association, and Anglia Polytechnic University for inviting me repeatedly to speak on this topic over the past few years.

Thanks also to a number of people at Routledge, particularly Simon Whitmore who was responsible for commissioning this text, Samantha Grant for seeing it through to the end, and Mike McNamee and Jim Parry, editors of the book series and valued colleagues, for their continual interest in my work. My gratitude also goes to artist Daniel Lee for permission to reproduce 'Cheetah Man', the disturbingly familiar cover image on the book, and to Richard Twine for putting me in touch with Lee's work.

Finally, I would like to thank my partner Beatriz Garcia for her companionship throughout the writing of this book, which took place during an incredibly busy time for both of us, but particularly for her. Writing is easier with you around.

Andy Miah, PhD
Glasgow, January 2004

Part I

Anti-doping and performance enhancement

Introduction
Why genetics now?

While engaging in philosophical discussions about genetic manipulation was once mere speculation, the past decade has shown that societies are not always prepared for new technologies by the time they are in use. Genetic modification is no exception. The moratorium on the cloning of human beings, set in numerous countries including the United Kingdom, the United States of America and the European Union, seems indicative of this, though everybody does not share the sentiment. Numerous ethicists have recognised that there are not very many good arguments for banning human cloning, if such technology is safe to use. For example, Lady Mary Warnock, accomplished British philosopher and famed for her work in human fertility, considers that UK legislation in relation to cloning has been rushed through (cited in Connor, 2002). In part, she claims, this was due to threats from rebel scientists, such as the Raelians, Severino Antinori and Richard Seed, who spread moral panic when they claimed to be in the process of cloning humans. Thus cloning is one such example where the promise is often understood as peril, since it gives rise to great uncertainty and speculation about the future of humanity.

Today, after having seen the cloning of Dolly the sheep, pigs, ANDi the genetically modified rhesus monkey and horses (Galli *et al.*, 2003), there remains a lack of acceptance for human cloning. Moreover, this doubt is not solely in relation to cloning humans, but even to cloning our stem-cells, which are often referred to as the building blocks of life since these cells have the capacity to transform into any part of the body. However, the world is beginning to divide on this issue. Already, the United Kingdom has begun to permit the cloning of stem-cells for therapeutic and research purposes, though in the United States of America there is still a substantial degree of resistance to such research. If one were to prioritise ethical questions concerning genetics, then the modification of athletes would surely seem far too futuristic to be taken seriously. Yet, in July 2002, the US President's Council on Bioethics met to discuss the ethical implications of genetic enhancement in sport.

Recent controversies about genetic modification reveal a rich discourse of values, expectations and uncertainties. For example, the mid-1990s began a period of fear about the development of genetically modified food that still rages. Within the UK, this was made more acute by the food scares, such as foot-and-mouth, which preyed upon an established loss of trust in agriculture through the earlier Creutzfeldt-Jakob Disease (Mad Cow Disease) and Salmonella. Each case has contributed to a feeling of weakness in our management of biological life, which has resulted in serious loss of human life and the excessive destruction of sentient animals. The additional uncertainty about how genetic modification might somehow be irreversible has created a powerful incentive to avoid such technologies at all costs for fear that we might all be turned into disease-ridden chimeras.[1]

Cloning is an interesting example to compare with the present discussion about genetically modified athletes. Both instances of using genetic technology are similar in one important respect: neither is readily embraced by the medical community nor by the public at large. Currently, the medical community recognises the legitimate use of embryonic stem-cells for developing therapeutic medical techniques. Yet even those countries which restrict the applications of genetic research do so tentatively. Similarly, the genetic modification of athletes is highly undesirable or valuable from the perspective of most scientists. For both cases, there is a tendency to imbue such applications of genetic technology with the *Frankensteinian* metaphor, where even the well-intentioned scientist is perceived as a threat to some biological human essence or integrity (Anderson, 1998; Turney, 1998). The specific case of Dr Ian Wilmut's cloned sheep, Dolly (Wilmut *et al.*, 1997), did not seem such an ethical concern for many, save for the vague implications it presented for the possibility of cloning humans.[2]

For many medical ethicists, cloning is considered to be an ethically uncomplicated application of genetic technology, giving rise to many benefits at the expense of relatively few risks (Anderson, 1998; Harris, 1998). Indeed, cloning might not be conceptually very different from *in vitro* fertilisation (IVF), though its prohibition might violate other freedoms that we currently enjoy (Rhodes, 1995). Nevertheless, if applied to humans, some still argue that this would be an unacceptable or harmful level of tampering with the process of human evolution (Roberts, 1996). While Dolly seemed a rather media-friendly application of genetics, her creation brought into uncomfortably close proximity the ways in which genetic technology could be highly exploitative of life in general, but for non-humans in particular.

The very same ethical ambiguities arose in the spring of 2002 when headlines reported that Dolly had contracted the early signs of arthritis, a disease that led to her death on 14 February 2003. This breakthrough in mammalian cloning – Dolly the sheep – and the fantastic implications she might have for benefiting infertile couples, quickly became another reason for being cautious about the brave new world of genetics.

The way in which cloning has been dealt with by the media provides a useful comparator for our sporting case (see Wilkie and Graham, 1998). The rather careless manner with which both of these issues have been dealt by the media is not surprising, since the technology is conducive to particularly good newspaper headlines, invoking such phrases as 'The Frankenstein factor' or 'Playing God'. Indeed, the genetically modified athlete makes manifest many literary nightmares about the future of the world, typified by such works as Huxley's *Brave New World*.

These genetic discourses perpetuate the general distrust of science developed in the late twentieth century (Turney, 1998). Yet genetically modifying athletes differs from the cloning issue in one important respect. As yet, medical legislation does not embrace genetic manipulation for sport *at all*. In most instances, scientists speaking about genetic research in relation to sport are scientists who are working on medically therapeutic genetic research, the application of which may have some implications for producing humans who are more athletic. For this reason, little has been said about the ethical implications of such science, since the science itself is already in question. Instead, the discourse is an embodiment of the *Frankenstein factor* – the possibility that, through genetics, we might bring about a 'posthuman future' and transcend what Fukuyama (2002a) calls *Factor X*, the important aspect of our humanness.[3] Again, the discussions are comparable to cloning since they are much less about the consequences of applying genetics to sport than they are about how such trends to enhance humanity might detract from what is valued about being human.

Many scientists regard the genetic modification of athletes as nonsense and completely lacking scientific possibility. Indeed, there are good reasons to be sceptical, given how limited the success of gene transfer technology has been over the past twenty years. This is not to say that such research is not taking place, or that present research into, say, muscular disorders might not yield some meaningful insights for how it might be possible to boost athletic performance on a genetic level. Nevertheless, a common argument against such applications is that therapeutic genetics is, already, an unfruitful science. As such, the suggestion that genetic enhancement might be possible is, as UCL biologist Steve Jones noted, 'in the same ballpark as the babbling nonsense talked about a baldness cure based on gene therapy' (cited in Powell, 2001).

Yet genetic science is still in relatively early stages of development, and much remains unknown about complex gene disorders and our ability to do anything to manipulate genes with any degree of safety. A great deal of literature has emerged from biomedical ethics to address this new technology and its imminent reality is now being taken seriously on a global scale. Indeed, the 'globalness' of this issue is crucial to appreciating its ethical parameters, which have also not yet been considered within sport. While it is reasonable to suggest that therapeutic applications of genetics are considered to be most worthy of research funding, the concept of therapy is becoming increasingly confused in genetic research and experimental genetics is also considered to be valuable.

Thus the scientific community is divided about the prospects for genetically modifying athletic performance. Some geneticists argue that the application of genetics to sport is entirely conceivable and that there is nothing wrong with it, since elite sport is all about finding innovative ways of enhancing performance. Alternatively, some consider that such applications are impossible, since genes are far too complex to permit scientists to make specific sporting modifications. For this reason, such research would be considered unacceptable, as it would be a waste of resources on a trivial pursuit. Yet this conflict of views is also reflective of the discourse surrounding the genetic enhancement of *anything*. One might even argue that such views also exist in relation to *therapeutic* applications of genetics, for which some doubt there to be any credible medical benefit. For the present purposes, the important point is that the discussion of scientific possibilities often stifles the engagement with ethical issues arising from the application of such technology. There is little attempt to problematise the application of genetics within the context of sporting values or to address the broader questions about how genetic modification might challenge what it means to be human. For this reason, it is important to recognise that this inquiry into the use of genetic modification sport is both an ethical debate as well as an important philosophical inquiry into human value and our use of self-altering technologies.

Francis Fukuyama addresses this kind of topic in his recent publication *Our Posthuman Future: Consequences of the Biotechnology Revolution* (2002a), recognising that it is necessary to return to the debate about humanness in order to understand how technology threatens it. Such concerns are often absent from bioethical discussions, which focus on pragmatic decision making or applying medical ethical principles to genetic technologies. The lack of interest in sport from genetic scientists may not be surprising to many bioethicists who fail to see the importance of sport in any discussions about the ethics of genetics. Yet the sporting case provides a discussion about genetics specifically within a complex social context. Often, this approach to understanding how genetically modified humans might *fit* within society is neglected, or is addressed through very general moral concerns about social justice. In contrast, the sporting example can inform discussions about bioethics by discussing a particular case in depth and how it problematises human relationships and social structures. Such discussions are crucial to determining ethical conclusions, though they are rarely considered.

In this monograph, I wish to distance the discussion from the sensational headlines about how genetics might give rise to the creation of superhuman athletes. The prospect of creating a human who can sprint the one-hundred-metre race in five or six seconds is a ridiculous notion in our current (and near future) scientific climate. Equally, the possibility of creating an athlete who can have a non-depleting capacity for endurance is ludicrous. Yet the international sporting community has begun to take seriously the possibility that genetics may present ethical issues for elite sport and be used with some affect to performance (McCroy, 2003). In addition, genetic research has already begun in areas tangential to sport training technology (Sturbois *et al.*, 2002).

Yet perhaps the most important response to the question, *Why genes now?*, is that the international sporting authorities are already beginning to subsume these new technologies under the common term *doping*. As such, institutions are already rejecting the use of genetic technology in sport before it has even been theorised. Such an approach would be unforgivable in an international climate where genetics is increasingly valuable to society.

One important task in the course of this book will be to address whether it is still relevant to use the term 'doping' when we are referring to genetic alteration and whether 'anti-doping' should be our reaction to genetic modification in sport. Arguably, the term 'doping' implies a whole series of connotations, which limit the way in which new enhancement technologies can be seen. Potentially, it limits the way in which we can be critical about genetic technology and recognise it as a desirable method of human modification. A more useful approach might be to recognise how sport offers a context for bioethicists to better understand what is valuable about being human and how genetic modification might challenge this. Equally, bioethics offers a body of literature that can challenge taken-for-granted sporting values, which are implicit in anti-doping policies.

In this respect, while my interest is to address ethical issues about the use of genetics in sport and enhancement technologies in general, it is impossible to neglect the valuable applied philosophical debates that such an inquiry can yield, and which transcend the ethical concerns. While it may be argued that pursuing a satisfactory definition of humanness to assist with our ethical debate might be seen as whimsical, it is expected that the sporting context can at least advance our understanding of this term. Importantly then, my approach is to accept the possibility that genetic modification *might be* a desirable form of performance enhancement for athletes in competitive sport. Moreover, I will advocate this position as a departing premise for policy makers when discussing genetic modification in sport.

The genetically modified athlete is not somebody who can be straightfor-wardly labelled as a 'cheat', and it is crucial to accept this when beginning to discuss the ethical implications of this technology. After all, genetically modified athletes might not have altered themselves at all, but might have been brought about by the *knowledge* provided by genetics. Alternatively, if we are discussing whether or not a genetically modified athlete should be allowed to compete, it is important to recognise that we may be discussing the offspring of genetically modified humans. As such, we would only indirectly consider such a person to be genetically modified and the extent to which they could be labelled a cheat becomes far more complex, even if they have a competitive advantage in sport.

It is also possible that the genetically modified athlete is not genetically modified at all, but genetically *selected*, where genetic profiling is used to determine the next generation of elite athletes. This example is particularly interesting in the world of sport, since there is already a growing feeling that there are no ethical concerns about the use of such information. For example, the President of the International Olympic Committee Dr Jacques Rogge stated that there is nothing wrong with using genetic information to seek out genetically superior humans for elite sport (Clarey, 2001). Again, interesting parallels arise between sport and broader bioethical debates about the use of genetics. Thus the use of genetic information is one of the key priorities of national bioethical committees and advisory councils, such as the UK Human Genetics Council. The lack of awareness for the ethical issues arising from the use of genetic information in sport reinforces the lack of appreciation for bioethical research trends and the isolatedness of sporting debates from broader medical ethics discussions.

For these reasons it is necessary to think carefully about the way in which ethical issues are theorised in relation to genetics and sport, and to begin by questioning some taken-for-granted conditions of what it means to be 'doping', 'cheating' or 'enhancing' oneself for sport. Indeed, it is useful for sports ethicists to look at the development of bioethics for a variety of reasons. The very manner in which ethics is done is central to this point and some of my concerns require questioning fundamental principles in medical ethics, which might typically underpin the rationale behind 'anti-doping' and the approach to genetic modification in sport.

In recent years, some medical ethicists have become critical of principle-based approaches, because they seem to overstate the general to the expense of the particular case. Thus principle-based ethics – the process of applying moral principles to guide conduct in specific contexts – is criticised for being too prescriptive and vague, departing from contested ideals that lack any meaningful connection with specific cases. As such, it has been thought necessary to embrace a more casuistic approach to ethics, although there remains a substantial commitment to the value of principles in bioethical discussions. Thus casuistry – literally the study of cases – is sometimes criticised for arbitrariness and particularity.

Neither of these ways of doing ethics is considered wholly satisfactory by everybody, and adopting a casuistic approach to bioethics does not necessitate that one eliminates a variety of ethical theories and principles to help understand the moral goodness or badness of genetics. At most, one might argue that the realm of casuistry has appeal, since it has provoked critical questions about how ethics is theorised, which have yet fully to be explored. As Carter (1998: html) explains:

> In place of moral theory and the application of universal principles of moral action or agency, methods of bioethical inquiry from these perspectives include narrative and interpretation, case study and casuistry, and procedural decision-making by consensus, as occurs in many bioethics committees and commissions.

A further reason why bioethics as a branch of applied ethics is a useful model for sports ethicists to recognise in dealing with genetic modification in sport has to do with how bioethics has evolved as a discipline. Bioethics now has a substantial presence within philosophical literature. Moreover, the rise of bioethics has been noticeable through the emergence of national bioethical committees, such as the UK Nuffield Council on Bioethics, the US National Bioethics Advisory Committee, and international committees, such as Unesco's International Bioethics Committee, to name a few. It is useful to be aware of these debates when discussing sport, since they provide helpful parallels to the way in which discussions about genetics in sport could proceed. For example, the tension between setting policy about genetics and the theoretical ethics that underpins such policy is often difficult to reconcile, though there is a clear dialogue between ethicists and policy makers in relationship to genetics. Within sport, it does not seem that the links are quite so strong and sport ethics as an academic discourse remains marginal to applied policy discussions, significantly so in relation to doping. Methodological criticisms may also be made in relation to how doping and performance enhancement in general has been handled by both anti-doping policy makers and sport ethicists. While a significant amount of literature has discussed the ethical implications of drug use and other methods of 'doping', there has been only a limited attempt to distinguish between different forms of performance enhancement (Busch, 1998; Gardner, 1989; Gelberg, 1998; Miah, 2000). Even more limited is the amount of ethical discussion about non-drug-like methods of performance modification, such as sport technology, or advances in engineering (Miah and Eassom, 2002).

Only a narrow number of bioethical issues will be addressed here, which will not do justice to the literature. For example, recent bioethical concerns about the patenting of DNA and ownership of life are not given due consideration here, despite the possible implications for sport. If geneticists were able to isolate a particular performance gene, then such a commodity could be a particularly important discovery from the perspective of designing athletes. However, engaging with the broad bioethical concerns about such matters would distract too much from the present context. Instead, the approach will be to focus on broad categories of genetic modification and the immediate ethical issues arising from the use of genetic information from the athlete's perspective. Instead, the priority for this monograph is the ethical implications of human genetics in sport. I have chosen to use the phrase 'biomedical ethics' to characterise this interest, as my argument has considerable implications for how we understand the role of medicine in society. Nevertheless, one might also describe the broad range of issues dealt within this book as bioethics, philosophy of medicine, or even a concern for healthcare ethics. I am interested in the set of norms that draws medicine together to determine what is ethically un/ acceptable and to transpose this on to sport in such a way that we might reveal some inconsistencies with the approach from a humanistic perspective.

Importantly, it is not possible to sever the links between bioethics and applied ethics as an established subdiscipline of moral inquiry. Like many kinds of subdiscipline within moral philosophy, applied ethics draws upon a substantial amount of what some might term mainstream philosophy. In addition, the use of the term 'bioethics' has a relatively short and specific history, emerging out of the USA in the mid-1960s, though globally as a post-war reaction to the atrocious manner in which humans were exploited under dictatorial regimes during the twentieth century. In this context, the word 'bioethics' is partially misleading, since it must also be understood as related to 'medical ethics' and even the 'philosophy of medicine', which has been used extensively in the United Kingdom to describe similar interests to bioethicists. For this reason, a further caveat to this has to do with the relationship of bioethics with medical ethics. Some would consider that the former is increasingly replacing the latter and that bioethics presupposes medical ethics conceptually and in relation to its constitutive literature. However, perhaps a further question to ask is whether the more significant ethical questions in medicine are entirely (or largely) related to biomedicine. Indeed, one might consider that the emergence of healthcare ethics has been some reaction to this trend, where medical ethics has fragmented into bioethics and healthcare ethics, even though the two disciplines continue to inform each other theoretically.

For the present purposes, these distinctions are far less important than the fact that these varying ethical concerns draw upon similar sources of theorising. Many perspectives related to medical ethics continue to utilise long-established ethical principles, developed in Tom Beauchamp and James Childress' (1994) classical *Principles of Biomedical Ethics*, now in its fifth edition (originally published in 1979), and which continue to underpin ethical codes of conduct and human subjects' research codes of ethics. As noted above, in recent years, this principle-based biomedical ethics has received much criticism about whether it approaches medical ethical issues in a way that is useful. Yet it is not possible to reject the importance given to principles or guidelines in ethical codes of conduct, which continue to underpin research protocols.

One of the reasons for stressing the relationship between sport and biomedical ethics is because this principled approach to sport ethics also appears in anti-doping policy and discussions about morality in sport. For example, arguments have sought reasons for rejecting doping from sport on the basis of harm. Its bioethical equivalent here would be to invoke a principle of non-maleficence – do no harm – as an underlying ethical norm in medical practice. Yet sports are rather odd practices, within which harm often seems integral to the activity. Consequently, what we actually see as ethical in sport is a modification of the harm principle. The result is an ethical premise that states no *unnecessary harm* should be embraced in sport. This condition of necessity allows for tolerating harm that might accrue by virtue of participation in sport.

One of the interesting aspects of this discussion is the apparent interrelatedness of bioethics and sports ethics in relation to genetics. For, as long as genetic technology is perceived as a medicinal technology, its ethical status continues to be underpinned by medical codes of conduct. For example, a physician cannot simply prescribe a course of genetic enhancement for an athlete – if it were possible – because their decision would not be informed by an interest in the athlete's health. The very suggestion that a physician is part of the decision-making process gives reason to question whether this is an appropriate model. In part, it is surprising that the links between the respective literature of sport and bioethics have not been explored much before, since they would seem to be reciprocally informative.

To conclude, there are a number of reasons why genetic modification is suddenly important in sporting circles. Some of the explanation has to do with the progress of science and the scientisation of sport. Yet it is also important to recognise the theoretical development of sport ethics and bioethics to understand why it is that these two disciplines can provide a meaningful discussion on the issue of genetics and sport. Importantly, the approach throughout this text should be seen also as a philosophical inquiry into enhancement technologies.

For many, the prospect of *genetically modified athletes* conjures up highly dystopian ideals, which the sporting examples ground in potential and detailed contexts. Thus the use of performance enhancement in sport brings into question the role of humans in the natural order and reflects a curiosity for testing humanity in a manner comparable to, say, life extension. This is why it is important to recognise that *genetically modified athletes* are but one stage further on from the use of other technological means, which are slowly augmenting what humans can do. In some respects then, to reject or feel unsettled about genetic modification is really to encounter a broader, primordial sense of what humans should not attempt. This book will explore a number of these ethical issues concerning genetics in sport, and will attempt to reveal the synergies between bioethics and sport ethics. Such discussions can inform decisions about genetics in sport specifically, but also more broadly in relation to human genetics.

1 Why not dope?

It's still about the health

One of the initial questions asked about the prospect of genetic manipulation in sport is whether it is conceptually different from drug use or other forms of doping. Even though genetic modification for sport has yet to be firmly realised as a practice of performance enhancement, and even though the technology has not yet been formally conceptualised by sporting authorities, it is already being treated as a form of doping. It is on this basis that genetic modification is currently being rejected by a number of international sporting organisations and becoming part of anti-doping policies. Most recently, the World Anti-Doping Agency (WADA) and the International Olympic Committee (IOC) have each written into their anti-doping codes a note about genetic modification, stipulating that its use is unacceptable, except when therapeutic. The IOC convened a working group that met in June 2001, and concluded the following:

> Gene therapy holds great promise for all people including athletes competing in Olympic sports. We endorse the development and application of gene therapy for the prevention and treatment of human disease. However, we are aware that there is the potential for abuse of gene therapy medicines and we shall begin to establish procedures and state-of-the-art testing methods for identifying athletes who might misuse such technology. This will require investment in modern detection methods including antigen detection, gene chip and proteomic analysis which are now becoming available. We are confident that we shall be able to adequately monitor abuses and establish the procedures for doing so using ethically acceptable methods. We call upon other sports, medical and scientific organisations to endorse our position.
>
> (IOC, 2001: html)

However, the development of anti-doping policy has recently reached a watershed, which should prevent such clear comparisons from being made between other methods of doping and genetic modification. The new anti-doping Code, drafted by WADA, has committed to ensuring that there is a process of rationalisation in respect of varying methods of performance modification. For the first time, the Code now distinguishes between substances or methods that enhance the body – such as steroids – and those that do not – such as nasal decongestants. For this reason, it is reasonable to expect that subsequent versions of the Code will be more rigorous in making distinctions surrounding genetic modification in sport.

A subsequent question – which often quickly follows the previous one – is whether anti-doping policies can be sustained in an era of genetic modification. Some would argue that the possibility of detecting genetic manipulation, together with the cost in time and money that such testing would require, is too big a burden for sport to bear. For this reason, enforcing anti-doping policy would become impossible, and sporting communities would need to reappraise the value of enhancement and, perhaps, ignore the fact that pharmacological enhancements are constitutive of an athlete's performance.

The ability to make meaningful contributions to this discussion will depend largely upon the way in which genetic modification in sport becomes conceptualised by sporting authorities. If genetic modification is treated like any other form of doping, then the ability to sustain anti-doping ambitions will become very difficult, since, I suggest, the ethical issues arising from genetics are very different from other forms of enhancement technology in sport. Anti-doping policy makers need not end up in such a situation, though, in order to explain how this is so, it is necessary to outline the conceptual weaknesses of current anti-doping approaches.

In this context, I will first discuss the discourse surrounding the presentation and representation of performance enhancement in sport, exploring the way in which the media create the moral discourse surrounding so-called drug cheats. My interest is to understand the political context of anti-doping, as a basis for explaining the way in which genetic modification in sport might also be conceptualised. I will suggest that the condemnation of drug users and dopers in sport is manufactured largely by the media, but more specifically from inconsistent methods of reasoning about drugs, enhancement and sporting values. This perspective will be supported by a detailed clarification of the arguments against drug use in sport. I argue that there is currently no unobjectionable argument against many forms of doping and, collectively, such arguments also lack persuasiveness, if – and only if – the basis for rejection relies solely upon some ethical component of *sport*. This caveat is necessary, since there are many reasons why it is sufficient to reject doping on the basis of a concern for *health* alone. One of the key questions to answer is whether *sport ethics* offers anything more meaningful about the ethics of genetic modification in sport, beyond the *medical ethical* concern for health.

The media-political context of anti-doping

The media-political context of anti-doping refers to the varying institutions and forces operating to sustain an anti-doping agenda within sport. It is useful to explain why it is that anti-doping has such symbolic importance and why there is such strong support for believing that doping challenges sporting values. Moreover, it is important to recognise that this is an *explanation* rather than a *justification* for why doping is undesirable. Such ideas reveal very little about the coherence of such perspectives, which will be addressed later in this chapter.

To appreciate the rational and ethical basis for rejecting doping, it is necessary to acknowledge both the culture of doping *and* the culture of anti-doping in competitive sport. People are generally familiar with the former, which describes the problem of doping in cultural terms (Brewer, 2002). For example, one might refer to such a concept by discussing the overwhelming pressure on athletes to surpass human limits and how this creates a climate where there is a need to dope. In contrast, I refer to the *culture of anti-doping* as the overwhelming pressure to embrace international policy in anti-doping, which necessarily pervades sporting and other official organisations.[1]

Currently, it would seem that popular opinion about doping in sport is that it is morally undesirable. This may be a culturally biased perspective and caution may be necessary in making such claims given the varying meanings associated with doping, drug use, and even what constitutes a 'drug' between different cultures. However, within the industry of competitive sport, doping is internationally recognised as being undesirable, at least if one accepts that adherence to anti-doping codes is an indication of expressed values. This presents a very serious challenge to an ethicist who might reject this initial premise about performance enhancement.

One of the most familiar ways in which this perspective is reinforced is through the media, which repeatedly demonise drug-induced athletes. It also instils the idea that using such substances or doping methods is recognised as *cheating* and attributable to a flaw in the athlete's character; a character that should be otherwise (there is an expectation that athletes should uphold morally desirable behaviours). Measuring this alleged public contempt for drug use in sport is both problematic and highly imprecise, though some useful work may be found in Brian Denham's research on this issue (Denham, 1997, 1999, 2000).

Even if one accepts that the content of media productions is reflective of dominant social values, it is not possible to presume that there is a consensus about the ethics of drug use and doping in sport. Indeed, it is possible to identify characteristics of doping stories that suggest the need for caution in making clear conclusions about their relevance. After all, the typical *drug cheat story* has a number of elements that make it inherently interesting and engaging, even if the reader does not care (or know) much about sport. The athlete's endeavour is immersed in strong symbolic meaning related to a host of social values, such as national pride, meritocracy, hard work, talent, ethnicity and individualism. Arguably, it is this rhetoric of doping that sustains the public interest in the drug cheat, rather than it having to do with some coherent ethical or moral perspective. The contempt for drug users conveyed in the media has little to do with what such athletes have actually done to devalue sport. Rather, it is about engaging the public in stories about good and evil or right and wrong, as Denham suggests. Ridiculously, the drug cheat story is analogous to the narrative in such films as *Rocky IV* (or any of the Rocky films), where the naturally gifted and strong-willed athlete overcomes the evil, drug-enhanced, techno-athlete.[2]

Integral to media coverage, as a measure of why drug taking in sport is morally repugnant, is an 'expert' discourse given by *respected* individuals and organisations who regularly condemn drug use and doping through the formation of policy. Thus the IOC President, various governmental and non-governmental agencies such as United Nations Education, Scientific and Cultural Organisation (Unesco) or the Council of Europe, and the vast sporting federations networks, all publicly work towards a similar goal – the elimination of moral badness in sport (usually doping). It is unreasonable to claim that all these people and such trusted institutions have misplaced values or are acting without any morally credible imperative. Yet such claims cannot be taken for granted, and it is also unreasonable to conclude that improvements cannot be made to the way in which such institutions conceptualise performance enhancement. I have suggested that the mechanisms within international sport prevent this reconsideration about doping, which is detrimental to striving for ethical credibility.

In addition, support for anti-doping relies upon the voices of athletes who express their contempt for use of drugs and other forms of doping in sport. Determining whether this is a representative impression of athletes' feelings about doping specifically and performance enhancement more generally is difficult, since very few athletes receive media attention for what they want to say about such matters. It is unreasonable simply to assume that such athletes reflect the moral majority. Moreover, the very same athletes who criticise doping do not conduct their own training in a manner that reflects a coherent and consistent philosophy of sport or ethical view on performance enhancement. For example, athletes who claim erythropoietin (EPO) is wrong and that it should be banned from sport because it is dangerous and unfair, are also the same athletes who use such technologies as altitude chambers without any moral concerns, even though many athletes cannot have such advantages and even though there may be some dangerous health implications associated with the technology. In this context, while one would not criticise athletes for being inconsistent in their decisions about using different methods of performance enhancement, my point is that it is unreasonable to ignore the fact that this is a complex and difficult distinction to make. It is hard to rationalise the ethical difference between an altitude chamber and blood doping, or an aluminium baseball bat and a neoprene swimming costume. This is why it is important to requestion fundamental premises about anti-doping, since they appeal to some ethical view of sport that is incomplete and question begging.

It is naïve to assume that these various interest groups are apolitical or are acting wholly from a position of striving for moral purity in sport. However, the important point is that the public seems unlikely to suddenly change its opinions about the value of drug use in sport, even if such opinions are more emotive and politically motivated than philosophically grounded. Popular opinion is still very much against the use of drugs and any other kind of innovation in sport that leads to a perception of greater injustice. For this reason, it does not matter whether there is a justification for such arguments. The existence of a moral rejection of doping is sufficient for it to be taken seriously and given moral weight, even if the perspective is inconsistent and conceptually flawed.[3]

However, it has yet to be discerned whether these perspectives are conceptually coherent. I have merely suggested that there is a powerful moral discourse surrounding drug use, which influences the way in which the *doped athlete* is morally evaluated and that this might have nothing to do with what is ethically inappropriate for sports. Therefore, the task is to understand whether or not specific kinds of enhancement are unacceptable. It involves not being persuaded by the rhetoric found in media and politics.

These various discourses provide an explanation for why arguments encouraging the use of more forms of doping in sport are not met with sympathy from anti-doping policy makers. Even if it is desirable to approach performance enhancement in sport with an entirely blank page, there is no use in trying to remove the entire infrastructure of anti-doping policy, even if one is wholeheartedly against such work.[4] Thus it is no good to advocate the use of doping and drugs in sport based solely on the idea that the arguments supporting that perspective are inconsistent or weak. Nevertheless, an ethicist can, at least, attempt a systematic analysis of the arguments about a matter, in order to try and allow justifiable conclusions to surface and to reveal the weaknesses of inadequate argumentation and flawed conclusions.

While some moral weight may be ascribed to the outrage felt about the acceptance of drugs in sport, this does not constitute a sufficient basis for their rejection. As Tollefsen (2001) recognises, one may argue that a public outcry about a moral issue might have enough weight to make its tolerance impossible. Yet it is not clear that there is such a public outcry felt in relation to drug taking in sport, as might have once been said in the era of the Ben Johnson scandal. It is not even possible to give much credibility to intuitive appeals about the moral badness of drug use in sport. For example, it is common to hear as a defence against drug use that no parent would wish their child to end up a drug-enhanced athlete. Supposedly, the very fact that all parents are united against drug use in sport conveys some credibility to the weight of such arguments. Such appeals are not helpful if the task is to determine whether drugs, doping or any kind of performance modifier is ethically acceptable. While one can acknowledge that the parents of such children are sincere in their belief and wish to prevent their children from getting involved with performance-enhancing drugs, one cannot accept their testimony as a moral rationale to working towards ensuring that drug use is prohibited from sport. Indeed, such views reveal very little about what is valuable in sports.

If importance is given to these parental interests, or any party for that matter (as, indeed, it is), then it is necessary to determine what criteria may be used to conclude that these interests have moral weight. For this, it is necessary to define what constitutes a public outcry. Presumably it may involve protests, lobbying to government, demonstrations and so on. Yet there do not seem to be such protests about drugs in sport. These are the usual criteria for ascribing legal weight to an issue, and it is not that sporting communities are unable to levy such support. The blood sport of fox-hunting has recently caused controversy in the United Kingdom and an interest in this topic did provoke a significant amount of protest, demonstrations and a feeling of grief among the fox-hunting communities about the issue. Such strong feelings are not quite as apparent in respect of doping in sport. There is no public outcry about drugs in sport, aside from the rhetorical media articles and the accompanying institutional lobbying for keeping drugs out of sport. Moreover, even if this lobbying is sincere, it is more tied up with a social concern for drug use and harm deriving from it in general, than a concern for sporting values or performance enhancement. Spectators are, quite reasonably, not particularly concerned about athletes gaining an extra hundredth of a second on their performance by using a banned substance. People have been cajoled into feeling strongly about something that matters little in their lives through what Denham (1999) describes as agenda building.

Yet it is not possible to dismiss the anti-doping arguments so quickly. Most of what has just been said addresses the speculative claims about the public lack of appreciation for drugs. However, there has been an ethical discourse about drug use and doping for some years, even though it has been confined mostly to academic journals and the media. Consequently, it is incumbent to address some of the arguments that are used to sustain anti-doping ambitions. Importantly, it is often the case that many of the sophisticated arguments made within academic literature have had no place in informing anti-doping policy. Even accepting that there is a distinction between policy and ethics, it is still surprising to see the lack of appreciation for academic arguments that have endeavoured to reinforce anti-doping ideals.

The next section provides a detailed overview of these varying arguments against doping in sport, while Chapter 2 will address the interest to harmonise anti-doping policy, again elucidating some of the weaknesses of this approach. This latter part may be relatively specialised, though it has particular importance in international sport and anti-doping, where policy harmonisation is a main priority. As such, addressing the rational underpinnings of this concept can serve to advance the argument and succeed in questioning an aspect of anti-doping policy that is currently at its very core.

Why drugs have no place in sports

A useful articulation of the arguments concerning drug use in sport is provided by Schneider and Butcher's (2000) philosophical overview, which addresses the harms resulting from doping. Their synopsis brings together a number of overlapping perspectives that have been asserted during the past twenty years in the philosophy of sport literature and in anti-doping policy statements.[5] Schneider and Butcher (2000) separate their various arguments thus:

- Cheating and unfairness.
- Harm (to users, clean athletes, society and sport).
- Perversion of sport (against its nature).
- Unnaturalness and dehumanisation.

Their overview encompasses a number of sub-arguments that it is helpful to make more explicit, particularly since some of their advocates may not see them as fitting within the broader categories asserted by Schneider and Butcher. Indeed, I wish to suggest that there are some conceptual flaws with the manner in which Schneider and Butcher have derived these categories.[6] A different kind of categorisation may resemble the following:[7]

1 *Coercion*: The legalisation of drug would create an environment that forces athletes into choosing drugs to remain competitive, thus risking harm to their lives. For this reason, they are unethical since they force athletes to engage with practices they feel strongly against (Gardner, 1989; Lavin, 1987; Murray, 1984a, 1986a; Parry, 1987; Simon, 1991; Tamburrini, 2000a).

2 *Unfair*: Permitting drug use has some unfair consequences for either the participating athletes, other members of the sporting community or the sport itself (Gardner, 1989; Lavin, 1987; Parry, 1987; Schneider and Butcher, 2000; Simon, 1991; Tamburrini, 2000a).

3 *Health risk*: Permitting drug use entails a substantial risk to the biological constitution of an athlete, which is unnecessary and undesirable. As such it is unethical to permit drug use, since it would also imply creating circumstances where athletes are at a higher health risk (Brown, 1995; Holowchak, 2000; Lavin, 1987; Parry, 1987; Schneider and Butcher, 2000; Simon, 1991; Tamburrini, 2000a).

4 *Unnatural*: Drugs are unnatural and, for this reason, they are unethical, because sporting performances are valued as natural performances (Hoberman, 1992; Houlihan, 1999; Lavin, 1987; Perry, 1988; Schneider and Butcher, 2000; Tamburrini, 2000a).

5 *Rule breaking/Cheating/Respect*: Drug taking is unacceptable because it is against the rules. Breaking the rules is considered to be cheating and so the use of drugs is also cheating. Cheating is also unacceptable because it demonstrates a lack of respect for other participants and the sport (Arnold, 1997; Houlihan, 1999; Simon, 1985, 1991).

6 *Unearned advantage*: Because drugs make it possible to achieve better performances without additional training, they are unethical; sporting achievements should be earned by the athlete (Carr, 1999).

7 *Contrary to/Does not promote the internal goods of sport*: Sports are valued because of their unique, internal goods. The use of drugs does not contribute to, and is contrary to, such goods. As such, it is unethical (Schneider and Butcher, 1994).

8 *Contrary to the nature of sport*: Sport has an internal essence that is compromised by the use of drugs. As such, their use is unethical (Simon, 1991a; Tamburrini, 2000).

9   *Contract violation*: Entering sporting competition entails making a tacit contract with one's opponent to play under the same conditions. Failure to do this by using means of performance modification that are outside of the agreed means is unethical because it breaks this contract with other participants (Butcher and Schneider, 1998; Eassom, 1998; Feezell, 1986; Loland, 1998a; Morgan, 1994; Simon, 1991).

There are some clear overlaps between these nine arguments and Schneider and Butcher's four generic categories, though the reason for making the individual positions clearer is that reducing them to the four categories offered by Schneider and Butcher conflates a number of these quite different positions. For each of these arguments, there is no consensus about whether one or some of them can justify the prohibition of all forms of doping from sport. One of my main criticisms of the approach to ethical issues concerning doping and drug use so far is that it does not distinguish between different methods of performance enhancement, such as sports equipment, drug use, training or doping. Instead, as is common in many discussions concerning doping in sport, the philosophical literature has placed an emphasis upon analysing drugs as the primary method of doping. (Again, one might attribute this to the media-political influence, for which the drug stories have gained such attention.)

Examples of innovation such as blood doping, technological innovation or altitude chambers are not considered as explicit cases aside from their being labelled as methods of doping. It is not entirely surprising that drugs have been a priority. Certainly, blood doping and altitude chambers are quite recent innovations. Nevertheless, it is surprising that technological innovations have not been given much attention, particularly since there is substantial debate about their legitimacy. In addition, the rules are constantly shifting to include or exclude certain kinds of innovation and so they would be a rich source of examples, which could inform arguments about drugs or other methods of doping. However, drug use has been a high priority, largely, it would seem, because drugs are perceived to cause physical and mental harm to the athlete. I will not attempt to develop a theoretical framework for enhancements in sport, which I have anyway done elsewhere (Miah, 2002a), though it is perhaps important to recognise that virtually no overlap exists between the narrow ethical framework on doping and drug use and the similar concern in relationship to other methods of performance modification (Miah and Eassom, 2002).

There is one further conceptual limitation in Schneider and Butcher's (2000) categorisation, which is their interpretation of the concept *harm*. In their categorisation, harm refers to some physical or mental impairment incurred by the athlete, which results from doping or potential social harms that arise from promoting a culture of doping. The basis for Schneider and Butcher's argument is the idea that *only* living entities can be harmed. On such a view, because harm is something that must be felt, non-living entities cannot be harmed because they are incapable of perceiving such harm. In the context of medicine, Glannon (2001: 10) reflects a similar perspective, arguing that 'only beings with interests can be harmed, and having interests presupposes the capacity for

consciousness and other forms of mental life that defines persons'. Thus harm
to non-living or abstract entities is understood vicariously, where harm is experienced by entities that *perceive* harm is taking place. Consequently the harm is
indirect, but nevertheless has consequences for human beings. For this reason,
harm to non-living entities is separated from specific others by Schneider and
Butcher (2000).[8]

Yet Schneider and Butcher's admission that harm may also be incurred by
sport or society suggests that their view on harm is rather more complex. If they
are correct, then it does not make sense that cheating is considered as a separate
category from harm. Rather, it should form a subcategory within a broad category
of doping harm, where risk of harm is better understood more broadly to encompass harms that are *unrelated* to physical and mental impairment. As such, the
effect of doping to create *unfairness* or a *perversion of a sport's nature* can each be
understood as forms of harm. This clarification of the problem may be a relatively
trivial point, though it is significant because it develops a conceptualisation of
technologies in sport within which forms of doping can include other kinds of
technologies such as sports equipment.

Thus a more useful categorisation of arguments in relation to the ethics of
performance modification must encompass those that are made in Schneider
and Butcher's overview, along with a number of their other reasons for banning
doping within the general category of harm. The differences between the two
approaches may be seen in Table 1.1. On the left is Schneider and Butcher's
(2000) categorisation of harm, which falls within their broader conceptualisation

Table 1.1 A harms-based conceptualisation of arguments against doping and drug use
in sport

Schneider and Butcher's (2000) categorisation of harm	Present categorisation of harm
Cheating and unfairness	Harm to others:
Harm:	• athletes (users) – unfair advantage, health
• to athletes (users) • to (clean) athletes • to society • to the sporting community • caused by bans	• athletes (non-user): – unfair advantage, contract violation, coercion • members of the sporting community – expectation disappointment; role models
Perversion of sport's nature	Harm to society
Unnaturalness and dehumanisation	Harm to the nature of sport:
	• unfair advantage/de-skilling • rule breaking • compromise of internal goods • unnaturalness

of arguments against doping. In contrast, the present categorisation of harm reflects these 'other' arguments as also indicative of some form of harm.

Thus the category of harm used here includes harm to people, society and sports, within which Schneider and Butcher's other categories of argument against doping are included. For example, Schneider and Butcher's *cheating and unfairness* category appears in the form of a number of different kinds of harm in various sections of the proposed restructure. The revised framework also encompasses the nine specific arguments raised earlier. With this in mind, it is now possible to examine each of the arguments for why doping and drug use should be banned from sports.

Harm to others

Harm as risk of damage to health

One of the strongest claims about the problem of doping is that it causes unnecessary short-term and long-term harm to the athletes who use them (where necessary risk implies the risk required to accept in order to undertake the sport). For this reason, it is argued that such substances should not be allowed into sports, since they place athletes at *too much of* a risk. Given that this tends often to have been related to the use of drugs, there are additional fears about addiction and the socially debilitating effects of doping. Since such harms might overlap with the *harms to society*, this category will be specific to health-related harm to persons, rather than the social harm of doping, which tends more to be the social harm of drug use.[9]

Within this category, it is also possible to include the subcategory *harms of coercion*, which indirectly have moral weight due to the propensity of the coerced persons to be taking risks with their health as a consequence of being forced into a position of needing doping to remain competitive (Simon, 1984). One might also assert that coercion is problematic not because of the consequence, but because it is an infringement of liberty to be coerced into decisions (Houlihan, 1999). However, this argument does not have such strength in the context of sport, since sport is already a coercive environment. For example, one might protest at being coerced into training seven days a week as a requirement of being an elite athlete, yet have very little ethical concern for such coercion. These practices are deemed necessary if one seeks great achievements such as elite sporting status and are considered to be an integral, valued aspect of sport. Consequently, it cannot be coercion in itself that is problematic. Rather, it is the added condition that athletes are coerced into taking significant risks with their health by using banned methods of doping (Holowchak, 2000).

An important point of clarification is required about this argument in relation to the concept of *necessity*. A fairly typical pro-liberal response to doping is that sport is inherently risky. As such, if the basis for banning doping from sport is that it is too dangerous to an athlete's health, then one might question the practice of some sports at all, such as boxing or horse-racing, which are inherently dangerous, whether or not one dopes. On this view, there is no justification for doping on the basis of harm, if such sports as boxing and horse-racing are considered to present acceptable risks. For precisely this reason, the concept of 'unnecessary risk' serves to counter this perspective and assert that there are necessary risks in sport that cannot be removed without preventing or significantly altering the practice of the activity. Such risks, it is argued, must be tolerated. Nevertheless, this does not commit one to taking further risks, such as might be incurred by using drugs or doping.

In summarising the position, if a performance enhancement increases the risk an athlete accepts when competing, then it is likely that discussions will ensue about its ethical status. Yet this does not mean that if no additional risk is incurred, the technology will be ethically acceptable. Such circumstances have recently arisen in relation to altitude chambers and tents, which are argued as enhancing performance, but for which there has been little significant discussion in relation to their increased risk. Instead, the ethical debate about these technologies has been based upon their accessibility, largely because they are very expensive. Thus there are other characteristics of the performance enhancement that might make it unethical besides health risk, though if a performance enhancement is riskful to health, this is often sufficient to make it unethical. In such cases, it is important to recognise that this is a *medical* argument, rather than one which relies upon sporting values.

Harm as being unfairly disadvantaged

A concern for fair play dominates many sports' ethical discussions, and controversies surrounding performance enhancement are no exception. As a guiding normative principle, methods of performance enhancement that are unfair are unethical. However, the basis for determining what counts as 'unfair' is not straightforward to defend. Importantly, these methods of performance enhancement are to be contrasted with 'fair' disadvantages, which are ethical and desirable in sport (Gardner, 1989). The point then is that sport embraces performance enhancement, but only when it is regarded as fair. For example, if one discovers through training that, instead of building endurance capacity by running steadily for a very long time it is better to run at different speeds over a longer period of time, this would be regarded as a 'fair' means towards performance enhancement. Thus a fair advantage implies gaining some additional competitive edge in a competition by means that are considered to be legitimate. Thus, even though the means result in other competitors being disadvantaged, it is *desirable* disadvantage since they are legitimate means.

By articulating unfair disadvantage as a harm in sport, it is possible to identify two arguments that suggest how doping is unfair. The first may be understood as the *contract* argument; the second has to do with unfair disadvantage as failing to *respect* other competitors. Importantly, both arguments rely upon the doped athlete breaking the rules, though precisely what this entails is contested. Suits' (1973) seminal work on games and sport implies that it is sufficient to understand rule breaking precisely and only in terms of what is specified by the constitutive and regulative rules of the sport (see also Suits, 1978, 1988). It is possible to further apply this requirement of rule keeping to a broader 'ethos', which also entails rules that are tacitly understood, even if they are not written into any rule book (D'Agostino, 1981). For example, one might include within the accepted rules of soccer the understanding that, if the opposing team has a player injured on the pitch when one's own team has position, the ball will be kicked out of bounds rather than used to build an attack against the 'injured' team. Moreover, an accepted mode of practice would be for the 'injured' team to return the ball to the other team (who had possession), once the injured player had received treatment and was either removed from the pitch or back on her feet. This example of an underpinning ethos which extends the formal rules of a sport is also considered to be part of the ethical framework within that sport.

Regardless of where one decides to limit the articulation of rules, both perspectives (*formal rules* or *formal rules and ethos*) argue that failing to keep the rules entails failing to play the game (Arnold, 1997; Feezell, 1988; Loland and McNamee, 2000). If rules are not maintained in sports, then the objective of the contest becomes meaningless. For example, if it were acceptable to run a marathon by using a motorcycle or pole vault wearing anti-gravity boots, this would defeat the object of the competitions. The activities would cease to make sense as contests that try to evaluate a particular kind of performance.

Feezell (1986) argues that the sporting competition is analogous to a kind of contract, since competitors agree voluntarily upon the specific conditions in which they will compete. As Arnold (1992: 247) argues,

> when a person voluntarily chooses to enter a sport he or she makes a tacit commitment to abide by the rules that are applicable. To renege upon the agreement is rather like making a promise and then not keeping it.

In addition, Butcher and Schneider (1998: 7) suggest that fair play has meaning precisely because competition is such a contract. However, they also state that:

> Fair play as contract is open on the content of the agreement. On some versions of this view, the content of the contract is created solely by the rules. In other versions, it is the rules as practised and understood by the athletes.

This reinforces the idea that the specific content of the would-be sporting contract is not straightforward to articulate. Moreover, Wertz (1981) argues that the contract analogy is true only metaphorically and that, even if there is some kind of agreement between competitors, this does not constitute a contract between them.

Alternatively, unfairness may be seen as harmful, since it fails to give value to the interests of others. In short, it fails to *respect* them as ends in themselves, and instead treats them as means to the ends of others (Tuxill and Wigmore,

1998). This view takes its lead from the Kantian maxim to *treat others as ends in themselves, rather than as means to our own ends.* By accepting the former, we recognise individuals as rational agents with their own capacity for intelligence and own volitions. As such, doping and drug use would be considered unethical because it fails to take account of the interests of other athletes.

On each of these views, doping in sport is an instance of unfair play because it is an instance of rule breaking. However, the reason why rule breaking is harmful may be either because it entails breaking a contract or it demonstrates a failure to have respect for other competitors. A variety of people are harmed – conceived either as contract breaking or failing to respect – by doping just because they are placed in a more disadvantageous position than they would be if the doping method were prohibited. Most typically, attention is drawn to the non-users, the so-called *clean* athletes, who are disadvantaged because the *drug cheats* are gaining an advantage over them. However, even *users* could be disadvantaged, if the drugs they use do not confer the kind of enhancement they expect. For example, not all athletes using EPO will incur similar enhancements in their performance – some of the drug users will derive an advantage over other users. This argument is further supported by the claim that there is little certainty about the effects of specific substances – including possible side effects, which would further debilitate the user. Consequently, if our intention is to conclude that some athletes are harmed by the use of drugs in sport, then it cannot stop short of encompassing the drug-using athletes who may be using drugs in a way that is actually ineffective at performance enhancement. This would not be conceived typically as *unfair*, since the risk will have been undertaken voluntarily. Yet clearly the drug-induced athlete, who receives no benefit to his or her performance and, potentially, might be debilitated by using such substances, would also be harmed. Indeed, one might suggest that this consequence is (or should be) a genuine concern for anti-doping authorities.

A similar kind of claim may be made in relation to the non-using athlete who is also disadvantaged by the doped athlete. This is more typically the athlete for whom people have a moral concern – the *clean* athlete. For the non-user, the harms are rather more transparent. Initially, there is the obvious harm of being disadvantaged in competition as a consequence of the opponent using a performance enhancer that is not available to others. From an ethical perspective, the salience of this has been made clear in numerous cases in sport. Innovations are frequently banned on account of their not being available to the whole athletic community. For example, in the 1980s, the development of the fibreglass pole in pole vaulting led to circumstances where some athletes had the benefit of an enhanced pole while others did not. For this reason, the fibreglass pole was prohibited from use until such time that it was available to all competitors (Houlihan, 1999). A similar ruling was made in relation to the superman bicycle design, which assisted the ride by making the seating position more streamlined (Fotheringham, 1996a, 1996b). More recently, Speedo's FastSkin swim-suits raised similar controversies in the approach to the Sydney 2000 Olympic Games (Loland, 2002a; Magdalinski, 2000). All of these examples are cases where the technology was seen as ethically problematic by governing bodies largely because it was not available to all participants.

Underlying this judgement is the premise that a sporting contest *should* involve athletes who have an equal opportunity to win – no athlete should have access to means that others do not (Fraleigh, 1982, 1984b). Importantly, this is not to say that athletes should always use the *same* equipment, even though this is the case in some sports. Rather, it is to recognise that all athletes should have the opportunity to maximise their performance capabilities by having access to all legal methods of performance enhancement. In many cases, it might be that the same piece of equipment provides a similar advantage for all athletes. However, in sports such as skiing or even the FastSkin swim-suit, it is not necessarily beneficial for all athletes to have the same equipment, given the diversity of human body types, strategies and techniques. Consequently, the rules are such that some specifications of the skis can be altered to the needs of the individual, within a general framework of what is accepted by the governing bodies. Where such equal opportunities are not ensured, this is harmful because some athletes will be disadvantaged by something that is out of their control. Yet this alone is not sufficient to claim that the harm is unethical. After all, the *fair advantage* is something that gives value to sporting competitions. Consequently, while an advantage does create unequal competition, this kind of inequality is not sufficient to conclude that a performance enhancement is unethical, even if it might be a necessary characteristic for such a conclusion.

Each of these ideas is not without complications. The idea that cheating or rule breaking is determined solely by what is outside of the rules begs the question as to what ought to constitute the rules in the first place. As Brown (1980: 18) argues,

> Another question is if the use of drugs is ever unfair. Yes, if using them is cheating; if one contender uses them against the rules, but others do not. But why should we ever outlaw their use?

Why is it that drug taking is considered to be against the rules and, as such, a form of cheating at all? Presumably, if it were recognised as an acceptable method of performance enhancement, it would not be a form of cheating. Similarly, if all pole vaulters wore anti-gravity boots and such boots were legal, or if there were another event called the *anti-gravity boot pole vault*, then this would make it acceptable and it would neither be cheating nor unfair. Simon (1991: 87) goes even further, suggesting that by

> prohibiting athletes from using performance-enhancing drugs . . . we disrespect them as persons . . . we deny them the control over their own lives that ought to belong to any autonomous, intelligent, and competent individual.

However, Simon also recognises that the *voluntary* context of competitive sport means that athletes waive their right to such freedoms and accept that they will

be subject to certain individual restrictions. He also uses this as a basis for concluding why drug testing is not unethical, though more will be said about this later.

Harm to the nature of sport

Earlier in this chapter, I indicated that Schneider and Butcher also consider
there to be possible harm to sports, even though a sport is not a living entity,
and therefore cannot, literally, be harmed. Conceivably, this distinction might
be merely linguistic, but perhaps speaks more to different notions of harm. To
support Schneider and Butcher's analysis, it would be sufficient to consider that
persons are harmed indirectly by harm to sports. This leads Schneider and
Butcher (2000) to assert a further level of harm, which may be understood as
undermining the value of the sport itself. This is identified by Schneider and Butcher
as *gaining an advantage over the sport*, which they see as a more useful argument
to conclude why doping is unethical. For Schneider and Butcher, even if drugs
were legal in sports, they would still be unfair because they undermine the
challenge of the competition by providing levels of performance that are not
attributable to the athlete. In this sense, Carr (1999) argues that such performance enhancements *devalue* the competition because they do not merit praise
for the athlete.[10]

Again, Schneider and Butcher's conceptualisation – while inclusive of the
various arguments against doping – theorises its categories inappropriately. For
example, they include a separate category as *unnaturalness and dehumanisation*,
which, I suggest, should also be understood as a subcategory of the *harm to sport*
section. The arguments of naturalness and dehumanisation both assert that
there is something unethical about doping because it is unnatural or dehuman-
ising. However, underpinning this argument is an assumption that sport is an
activity that is valued because it involves the natural human athlete. The two
arguments assert a theory of sport, albeit rather briefly, arguing that doping
challenges some alleged essence of sport.

A different (but related) argument in relation to the concern for *harm to sport*
is the claim that doping challenges the prelusory goal of sports (Suits, 1973).
This also fits into the unfairness category and asserts that the purpose of sports
– the prelusory goal – no longer makes sense if certain means are used to
achieve that goal, as is suggested in the example of participating in the pole
vault event using anti-gravity boots. In such an activity, the challenge of pole
vaulting is to use the pole to vault as high as possible over a horizontal bar.
With anti-gravity boots, this challenge becomes simply a matter of how far the
boots will power the athlete into the air and requires very little challenge from
the athlete. In this sense, the challenge of the sport is made easier and less
valuable thereby (Simon, 1991). On this Suitsian perspective on performance,
enhancements are seen as unethical if they corrupt some inherent essence,
nature or prelusory goal of a sport (Gardner, 1989).

The challenge for each of these arguments based upon an alleged nature of
sport is to present an explanation of precisely what this essence or nature

entails, but also to provide some way of negotiating conflicting views on this essence. Importantly, this additional requirement of negotiation suggests that it is possible to construct different kinds of sport, each of which could be ethically justifiable (at least in relation to performance modification). Loland (2002a) challenges this idea. While recognising that different ethical views on perform-ance modification in sport can be asserted, he argues that they are not each comparably valuable. Specifically, Loland describes three theories of sport – the 'non-theory', 'thin theory' and 'thick theory'. The 'thin theory' argues that sport is valued largely because it is an enterprise concerned with pushing human limits and that this philosophy embraces the use of any kinds of performance enhancement. In contrast, Loland's 'thick theory' argues that sport is a complex social practice 'with its own characteristic norms, values and internal goods that ought to be protected and cultivated'. However, Loland accepts that there are various thick theories in the sport philosophy literature, which may be found in the work of Fraleigh (1984b), Simon (1991) and Morgan (1994). Loland's (2002a: 167) own thick theory asserts that:

> an athletic performance is a combination of talent and of cultivation of talent in terms of environmental influence in which our own efforts play the dominant role. Moreover, athletic performances ought to take place within a framework of non-exposure to unnecessary harm.

Clearly, further elaboration is necessary on such ideas as 'talent', 'environment', 'effort' and 'unnecessary harm', though this is a useful basis from which such ideas might be asserted. An argument to assist the *negotiation* of different ethical theories of using technology in sport is found in Alasdair MacIntyre's (1985) theory of social practices. This approach would also seem to satisfy Loland's requirement for considering sports as social practices.

In the context of sport, Brown (1990) argues that a feature of practices is reflected in the typical relationship of novice to master where becoming an expert necessarily requires a process that is not easily attainable and requires time and commitment. As such,

> the relationship is frequently between novice and coach and includes the transmission of skills and values through the careful application of stand-ards of excellence, which are the product of the sport's own history and the coach's prior experience. It is submission to this learning and the standards that govern it that is a prerequisite to mastery, just as it is the ability to extend and enrich the practice's techniques and goals that is the mark of achievement.
>
> (Brown, 1990: 73)

Moreover, it is only through this process that one realises the valued aspects of the practice, or, as MacIntyre phrases it, the 'internal goods' (1985: 188). It is on this basis that it can be claimed how sport might be harmed if the internal goods are challenged. Yet this perspective does not necessarily imply that performance modifiers that are currently banned contradict the internal goods of a sport. As Brown (1990: 77) argues,

> The constraints of the practice, including the internalising of the virtues are compatible with the use of performance enhancing drugs, novel and risky training regimes and biomedical or surgical treatments of modification or practitioners.

Nevertheless, it is possible to develop a critique of performance modifiers, such as drug use, based upon this argument. For example, one might argue that some enhancements are unethical since they prioritise individualistic values and because they do not foster the acquisition of internal goods, which derive mainly from skill-related abilities. However, it is not really accurate to suggest that methods of performance enhancement in sport necessarily make a practice easier. It might even allow an athlete to perform with greater competence and to enjoy a greater challenge. It must not be inferred, therefore, that the athlete need train any less to achieve such performances.

Harm to other members of the sporting community

Harm may also be incurred upon other members of the sporting community, not *clean athletes*, nor the sport itself, but people who simply care about sports; fans, spectators, enthusiasts. Such harms can be articulated from a number of perspectives, though clarification is needed first on what constitutes the sporting community to understand the limits of this category. Within sports, Morgan (1994) presents the notion of a sporting community in the form of a *practice community*. Defined in this way, a *practice community* draws upon a MacIntyrean concept of practices, which asserts that a practice is:

> any coherent and complex form of socially established co-operative human activity through which goods internal to that form of activity are realised in the course of trying to achieve those standards of excellence which are appropriate to, and partially definitive of, that form of activity, with the result that human powers to achieve excel, and human conceptions of the ends and goods involved, are systematically extended.
>
> (MacIntyre, 1985: 187)

Some confusion has arisen within sports ethics about the scope of MacIntyre's practice account, and how it is to be applied to sport (McNamee, 1995). Arnold (1997) considers that the concept may be used to encompass the practice of sport in general. Conversely, Eassom (1998) argues that the definition provided by MacIntyre delimits that a practice cannot be sport in general, but is reflective of specific sports. Instead, Eassom argues that sport is not a practice but *particular* sports, such as golf, soccer or basketball, are practices.

Returning to Morgan's concept of sporting practice communities, the problem of asserting the existence of a sporting community is more apparent. Accepting Eassom's position, it makes no sense to refer to a sporting *community*, since such an entity does not exist. Sports are far too diverse to lump them altogether as one single community. Doing so would be akin to referring to the community of human beings, who, by virtue of their sharing a species type, might be perceived to be a community. Morgan's practice community argument is useful, since it refers to those individuals who may be described as part of the sport's community, and thus have an interest in the state of their practice. This interest constitutes having a concern for the internal goods of the practice or those goods that are necessarily and exclusively tied to the practice.

Expectation disappointment

In the context of drug use (and doping in general), Schneider and Butcher (2000) describe how the sporting community has an expectation that athletes will be drug free. As such, one kind of harm incurred from athletes using drugs will be the realisation by the specific sporting community that athletes are not. Thus the harm derives from performances that are partly derivative of doping, which collapse the value that is placed into sport by members of the sporting community. A solution, they consider, is to remove the expectation and, consequently, to remove the harm. Yet Schneider and Butcher recognise that the majority of spectators want a drug-free sport and that removing the expectation (legalising the drugs) is not a solution to preserve the value that is invested into sport.

While one might attach moral weight to such a concern, the expectations of the sporting community are perhaps more difficult to discern, as there exist many examples of performance-enhancing technology that are ethically ambiguous. For example, the FastSkin swim-suit that raised controversy at the Sydney 2000 Olympic Games was neither clearly unacceptable nor acceptable. It could not reasonably be claimed that its use challenged spectators' expectations of the sport. Consequently, the basis for claiming that the swimming community would be harmed by the use of this technology is tenuous. In the case of drug use – accepting the media-political argument raised earlier – it might be reasonable to identify clearly defined community expectations, though even here caution is necessary, since it requires reconciling the importance of consensus as the basis for an ethical conclusion.

Role models

A further claim against doping in sport is that it sets a bad example for young children, encouraging the taking of risks with one's body in pursuit of unrealistic and ephemeral aspirations (Houlihan, 1999; Schneider and Butcher, 2000). However, although this may have strength in the context of drug use specifically, it is relatively weak in respect of other technologies. After all, it is not particularly alarming for a child to see that an athlete is using a titanium tennis racket rather than a wooden one. This comparison suggests that the particular theorisation of an innovation as a socially situated technology is what makes it potentially harmful for children to see their role models using it. In the case of drugs, parents are justifiably concerned about their children aspiring to be like the drug-enhanced athlete, specifically because drugs can be harmful in numerous antisocial and unhealthy ways (which, incidentally, also seems reflective of elite sport with or without drugs). Consequently, like the argument based upon a concern for coercion, this argument might be seen as being reflective of the *health risk* argument in disguise. After all, the conclusion that doping athletes sets a bad role model for children relies upon some negative connotation associated with the enhancement. As such, the onus must first be placed upon deciding whether the method of enhancing performance in question is morally problematic in itself. If the technology is not something that would set a bad example for children to follow, then it need not be harmful to children that athletes use such technology or that they also aspire to use it.

Harms to society

Finally, arguments against doping in sport focus upon the potential and actual harms to society. These are perhaps the most difficult harms to assess, largely because they rely upon many contingent facts about how society deals with social problems. Nevertheless, it is possible to make some attempt at describing such harms.

First, the media-political context of drug use and doping places strong emphasis upon the link between the use of drugs and doping inside sport and its use outside of it. Understandably, it is highly problematic for officials and organisations to speak out in favour of tolerating drug use in sport and, at the same time, vilify such use in society. Such a perspective would distort the circumstances within which doping in sport takes place. To suggest that there is no relationship between drug users in sport and outside grossly misrepresents the manner in which drugs are obtained.

As such, the use of specific kinds of drug provokes responses that doping results in significant social harm. However, one might ask why it is that the specific level of harm resulting from the use of some drugs in sport is considered more alarming than the harm resulting from, say, limiting personal freedoms by prohibiting such use (Tamburrini, 2000b). This specific argument has been raised in relation to the consumption of marijuana in the United Kingdom, where its use is currently illegal. Legalisation advocates draw attention to the inconsistency of the argument, using the legal examples of tobacco and alcohol as a basis for arguing that a concern for social harm cannot be the sole justification for prohibition. After all, these legalised drugs are also associated with significant social harms – violence, accidents, health problems and so on – yet they remain legal. While a stronger case may be made for the prohibition of such substances, there is greater strength in the legalisation of such drugs in favour of personal liberty.

Within sport, it is not that all forms of doping or drug use are anything like the examples of tobacco, alcohol or marijuana (although these substances do appear on some anti-doping lists of banned substances). There are specific substances for which there is reason to believe that they are more like hard drugs, insofar as they give rise to significant and life-threatening harms. In such cases, the argument from social harms is much stronger in respect of drug use. However, not all forms of performance enhancement are comparable to such hard drugs and there is a need for distinctions to be made – if, and only if, importance is attached to the health risk incurred by athletes.

Summary

Perhaps the strongest argument against doping in sport (and most used by anti-doping policy makers) remains the concern for the health of athletes and the interest to try to avoid a situation in elite sport where all athletes are taking unnecessary risks with their lives. Yet this argument alone does not tell us what is uniquely valuable about sport. Clearly there are concerns about, say, giving pole vaulters anti-gravity boots, which have nothing to do with health. Equally, it is unfortunate that some athletes deceive others in a way that neglects the value of competition and the assumption that all athletes adhere to a similar rule base. However, sport ethicists have contested such claims, arguing that athletes do not compete on an equal basis, even if all competitors adhere to the rules. Moreover, it is not necessarily the case that failing to maintain the rules implies deceiving competitors (Rosenberg, 1995; Wertz, 1981). If sports are seen as being undermined by a method of performance enhancement, then there might be a better argument for changing the kind of competition that is being tested.[11] Finally, it seems that both a concern for coercion and a concern for social harms only have moral weight when they are also a concern for health.

Each of these positions does not necessarily legitimate the prohibition of all methods of doping. In many situations, there is a reasonable case for arguing in favour of adapting the sport to create a new kind of competition, where performance enhancement is not simply associated with the emotive connotations of drug use. These arguments will be revisited again later in relation to the use of genetic modification for sport performance enhancement. For now, with this ethical context to doping in mind, it is necessary to turn to the philosophical underpinning of anti-doping policy, beyond the specific, ethical reasons for being against doping. The importance of this way of critiquing anti-doping is provoked by a lack of interest to question the manner in which anti-doping is approaching the problem. In addition, it derives from a perception of there being a pervading belief for anti-doping policy makers that there is an answer to the difficult task of making anti-doping a success: the ideology of *harmonisation*.

2 Forget drugs and the ideology of harmonisation

The idea of *harmonising* approaches to (anti)-doping has been associated with sport governance almost since its inception in the early 1960s, though it is only since the 1980s that there has been such enthusiasm for it. The harmonisation argument holding the most significant challenge to the success of anti-doping policy is the process of ensuring that the many sporting institutions are in agreement about methods of testing and sanctioning. Consequently, the most important ambition in anti-doping is ensuring that every institution is working to the same ends, rather than questioning the fundamental justification for prohibition or acceptance at all. As such, the process of philosophising about the acceptability of doping is beyond question; anti-doping is necessarily *anti*.

The theoretical basis of this harmonisation and what kinds of expectation may result from it have rarely been questioned. Houlihan (1999) asks what would actually count as 'harmonisation', and thus what kind of harmonisation is sought. Overwhelmingly, the message behind harmonisation is to ensure the equity of treatment for athletes and to prevent the continued undermining of policy by legal challenge. Consequently, the response to doping by federations and government must be consistent to prevent jeopardising the status of competition and its autonomy. While there is much more work to be done before federations and governments are sufficiently cooperative to allow successful harmonisation of anti-doping policy, Houlihan identifies the Council of Europe (CoE), among others, as endeavouring to achieve this.

As Houlihan (1999: 129) notes, 'A leading role in debates on doping policy has consistently been taken by the Council of Europe with bodies such as the European Union and Unesco, making occasional, but largely rhetorical, interventions.' The CoE has been proactive at raising the issue and framing it within a general ethical policy for sport. An early landmark in European anti-doping policy was the 1978 Conference for Ministers of Sport where the CoE formulated a recommendation to members of governments about doping. At this time, the CoE decided to focus less on the muddled problem of definition and move straight to implementation (Houlihan, 1999). In 1981, at the eleventh Olympic Congress at Baden-Baden, Unesco, the World Health Organisation (WHO) and the European Commission (EC) acknowledged an Anti-Doping

Charter. The CoE then re-designated its charter as a convention, which all members were required to sign, with non-members invited to give their support. Notably, this convention stressed the importance of *harmonising* policy, the new buzzword in anti-doping.

Presently, there are tensions within and between sports organisations and governments which preclude successful policy implementation. So too do there remain discrepancies between governments in what should be used as an overarching policy for sport. The reluctance of sports organisations to relinquish control over what takes place within their sport is matched only by the reluctance of governments to ignore the social implications of doping and sport more generally. Houlihan (1999) argues that the initial stages of policy development are coming to an end. Yet the successfulness of policy remains uncertain, while its objectives are still unclear; who should be targeted, when, and within which sports. This confusion is compounded further by the limited resources available. There is also much uncertainty about how testing should be administered and by which authorities. Moreover, there still exists a lack of commitment to prevention through education and an overwhelming amount of responsibility placed on the athlete, which overlooks the culture of doping in sport. Nevertheless, of key importance for anti-doping policy makers is how policy can attain uniformity.

The new driving force behind this harmonisation is the World Anti-Doping Agency (WADA), which has adopted the task of overseeing the harmonisation and development of anti-doping policy throughout the world.[1] WADA emerged in 1999, after a series of conferences about the state of doping in sport and the effectiveness of anti-doping agencies around the world. Notably, the delegation of the World Conference on Doping in Sport held in February 1999 at Lausanne, Switzerland, recognised the need to implement an international and independent anti-doping authority. The composition of this committee entailed the 'participation of representatives of governments, of inter-governmental and non-governmental organizations, of the International Olympic Committee (IOC), the International Sports Federations (ISFs), the National Olympic Committees (NOCs), and of the athletes' (Lausanne Declaration on Doping in Sport, see Delegation, 1999). Subsequently, in November of the same year, WADA was inaugurated.

WADA is a young organisation by anti-doping standards. With only four years of anti-doping experience behind it, it is a relative newcomer in the 'sporting drug war', though very much a force with which to be reckoned. It is placed in the most central position of anti-doping initiatives on a global scale, with the weight of the International Olympic Committee (IOC) behind it. There is an emerging expectation within international sport that WADA will provide the kind of *harmonisation* of anti-doping policies that is being sought on an international level in respect to anti-doping policy. Yet there remains a lack of clarity about WADA's priorities and, still, precisely what kind of harmonisation is sought. This does not imply that there must be some preliminary discussion about the value of anti-doping. Rather, it is to recognise the philosophical and ethical questions as integral components to policy discussions. Perhaps the main weakness of these discussions is that they are premised on a partial interpretation of the value of performance enhancement. Consequently, a useful place to start might be to revisit how doping fits into a broader conceptual framework about the ethics of performance.

Forget drugs

On account of the questionable status of anti-doping as a philosophically reliable enterprise, how might genetic modification become integral to this *anti* discourse? Is it possible for anti-doping programmes to be successful in an era of genetic modification, which will further challenge the possibility of reliable testing and effective detection of illicit enhancements? Indeed, the prospect of genetic manipulation will make testing for drug use seem like child's play, if, indeed, it is possible at all (Wadler, 1998). It is widely recognised that muscle biopsy may be the only way to detect some forms of genetic modification in sport, which would be a significant challenge for anti-doping policy given the invasiveness of such a procedure.

Coupled with emerging scientific research in this area, there is a case to be made for why sports authorities should be concerned about genetic technology. The ability of athletes to avoid doping test procedures by employing an enhancement technology which is far beyond that which can be tested is a worry for anti-doping advocates and jeopardises the entire rationale of anti-doping policies. Even with the new anti-doping code, there continue to be problems preventing the effectiveness and coherency of anti-doping policy. These problems may be categorised as (1) present drugs and doping methods, and (2) future 'doping' and technologies, which reveal the philosophical weakness of anti-doping as a basis for ethically consistent sports practices.

Present drugs and doping

There are a number of present doping methods, which are widely recognised as being problematic for anti-doping programmes to eradicate from competition. Athletes are, by and large, far more sophisticated in their drugs of choice in the current competitive climate than was previously the case. Currently, there exist two major methods of doping that are high on the anti-doping agenda: the hormones erythropoietin (EPO) and human growth hormone (hGH). Since the anabolic scandals of the mid-1980s during which Ben Johnson would become infamous for his Olympic 100m gold medal scandal, these two methods of doping have been the most elusive to detect. Currently, hGH still lacks an effective method of testing, despite having been around for over ten years. Only recently, on the approach to the Sydney 2000 Olympic Games, has there been a test for EPO, though there continue to be uncertainties about its effectiveness. There are rumours about a successful test for hGH by the Athens 2004 Olympic Games, though these are unclear at present.[2]

It would be misleading to claim that these two methods of doping are the only traumas for anti-doping agencies (or, indeed, that genetic modification is the immediate next problem). The recent past has seen celebrity performance enhancers occupy a significant amount of tabloid space. Amino acid, creatine, and the steroid nandrolone, have been particularly notorious between 2000 and 2002. In between these examples and genetics is a constant stream of new products that require new kinds of doping test.

New technology

A good example of new technology that is posing new problems for the formulation of anti-doping policy are hypobaric training systems, more commonly known as altitude chambers or altitude tents (Baker and Hopkins, 1998). This method of performance enhancement is particularly interesting for a number of reasons. First, altitude chambers have remained within the rules of international sport. Currently, there are no restrictions on their use for competition, except in Norway, where a ban exists. However, in 2002, a steady stream of newspaper articles following various international sporting events brought into question whether this would remain. For this reason, at the 2002 Tour de France, winner Lance Armstrong and a number of his team mates were using such tents. As well, England soccer player David Beckham used an altitude chamber in an attempt to promote the recovery of his injured foot prior to the 2002 Soccer World Cup.

Each of these instances of successful use has brought into focus whether such methods should be legal. Briefly, the value of these technologies is that they allow athletes from low altitudes to level the playing field when competing at countries of higher altitude, where the air is thinner and the capability for endurance is lessened for the low-altitude athletes. By using an altitude chamber, it is hypothesised that a low-altitude athlete can diminish the advantage of a high-altitude athlete. Previously, the science underpinning this technology was (and continues to be) applied to altitude training where athletes would physically move between locations in order to push themselves harder (Levine and Stray-Gunderson, 1997). The similarity between using a hypobaric chamber and conventional altitude training is often given as an ethical justification for the former. Moreover, each is regarded as being justifiable just because they purport to equalising the playing field. Otherwise it is thought that athletes who live at high altitude would have an oxygen-carrying advantage.

One of the inconsistencies with this defence is that athletes do actually use this technology in a manner that is different from athletes who simply live in countries of high altitude. Low-altitude athletes are increasingly training in low-altitude locations – where it is much easier to push the body harder – and sleeping in altitude chambers for maximum benefit. Nevertheless, the technology remains legal, though this would seem to be to the dissatisfaction of some key figures in international sport. IOC President Jacques Rogge suggested that this decision for altitude chambers to remain legal might need reconsideration. His concerns are largely intuitive, rather than being premised upon some coherent ethical argument. As Rogge states, 'I don't like the idea that people have to go into chambers, that's not my idea of sport, it is artificial, I don't like the idea' (cited in Magnay, 2002). Larry Bowers, senior managing director of the US Anti-Doping Agency, also considers their use unacceptable, stating that 'My position is that since [the devices] are artificial, and not everyone has access to them, they are unethical' (cited in De Simone, 2002). Notably, Bowers' argument has to do with access and equity and Rogge's seems more premised upon the potential for harm.

With these emerging voices, it seems imminent that altitude chambers will become illegal in more contexts. Yet from Rogge's and Bowers' articulation of why these innovations might be problematic, there is further reason to be concerned about the direction of anti-doping policy. From each of their statements the arguments resort to the kinds of perspectives most prevalent in the 1960s, where anti-doping policy was built on what is or is not (loosely termed) 'natural'. Nevertheless, Rogge's and Bowers' statements reveal one of the more problematic aspects of developing policy about performance modification. They each highlight one of the niggling facts about not condoning an *anything goes* attitude to performance enhancement in sport – that it matters how excellence in performance is achieved. When pressured for a justification of an ethical view on performance enhancement, it is common to hear appeals to founding concepts such as 'naturalness', 'integrity', 'essence' and so on. Yet this is precisely the kind of perspective that has proven quite insufficient to ensure a rigorous ethical evaluation of performance modifiers. Consequently, the challenge is to try to redevelop an ethical theory about performance modification in sport.

Given the difficulties of maintaining a coherent policy against doping, genetic modification would further complicate the problem. One of the main questions of the present issue is whether such attempts at removing the doped athletes from sport is at all justified or even worthwhile. Key questions need to be asked about the specific nature of genetic modification and how it is to be classified and evaluated; whether as a method of doping (illegal) or perhaps like altitude chambers (legal). In this respect, in order to address the ethical implications of genetics and the broader questions of anti-doping, there is a need to move beyond a sports policy discourse and even beyond a sports ethical perspective. Rather, it is necessary to situate the arguments explicitly within a moral discourse, which recognises that sporting values do not necessarily trump other kinds of values to which athletes may also make a legitimate claim. In short, a philosophy of harmonisation has very little value unless there is agreement about why such policies should exist in the first place.

It is this perspective which provokes the current chapter title 'Forget drugs'. The title intends to reflect the idea that genetics and other emerging technologies will present far greater (and perhaps insurmountable) challenges to doping policy in sport than any other forms of performance modification have thus far. It is also used to recognise that the arguments underpinning the rejection of doping in sport are premised upon highly contested terms. This would seem a rather confrontational statement given the strength of anti-doping efforts around the world, which command the attention of many important organisations. Yet this is not an argument which seeks the championing of sport without values. Neither should it be construed as a strictly 'pro-doping' argument, insofar as such a view would place no limitations on what an athlete should be allowed to do in order to compete in sport. It does not wish to suggest that sport is or should be treated as a practice that is without moral or ethical content. Rather, it makes the more tempered argument that the kind of values maintained by anti-doping campaigns – particularly those which could emerge in relation to genetic manipulation – require greater clarification.

Drugs (and doping in general) should be a secondary priority to broader discussions about performance enhancement, which genetic modification will make overwhelmingly apparent. This is why it is so important to consider the ethical implications of genetics and why anti-doping policy requires radical alteration in its rationale and implementation. If anti-doping policies continue to be developed from a basis of drug or substance use as its primary conceptual framework, then this will lead (and currently is leading) to an incoherent policy about genetics and other kinds of performance modifiers, as is typified in the disputes about altitude chambers.

Answering questions of the categorical distinctions concerning what is or is not an acceptable method of performance modification in sport requires first coming to terms with such questions as: What does it mean to be human? What constitutes human flourishing in sport? What are the moral limits of paternalism in sport? Questions about the 'natural', which continue to arise in arguments against technology in sport, are premised upon some unstated assumption about what it means to be human. Similarly, a concern for harm for athletes makes assumptions about the status of an athlete as a rational human being. Moreover, claims about the value of a performance as being largely determined by the athlete rely upon being able to identify that athlete in relation to their technology. For these reasons, it is upon the key concept of being human that our attention must focus. Consequently, the ensuing analysis deals specifically with genetic modification, drawing upon sport's ethical and bioethical perspectives in order to elaborate on these questions. Rather than appealing solely to sporting ideals and arguments, these questions will provide a framework within which to make decisions about new performance modifiers in sport and will elucidate broader ethical concerns about enhancement technology.

By drawing from literature in bioethics, it will be possible to respond to questions concerning our humanness and its value, which can be constructive in answering the difficult questions about what makes a sporting performance valuable. This is not to champion only a bioethical discourse on performance enhancement or even to present it as an isolated discourse. Rather, it is simply to notice that the kinds of questions arising from genetic modification in sport and other kinds of performance-enhancing techniques can borrow substantially from the mix of concepts problematised more frequently in bioethics than in sport, where issues concerning personhood, humanness, and distinctions between the normal and the enhanced have arisen.

Yet neither does this suggest that sport ethics will be informed solely by bioethics and philosophy of medicine. I suggest that, by considering the ethical issues arising from genetic modification in sport, it will be possible to better understand what might be unethical and alarming about the use of biotechnology in society more broadly. Thus discussions about genetics in sport will also lend strength to theorising about genetics in biomedical ethics. By trying to understand what it would be like to be a genetically modified human in sport, we will have a rich context in which it will be possible to see how genetically modified humans fit within social practices such as sport. From these conclusions it may be possible to infer how genetically modified people might function within other social contexts.

It is important to make explicit that my interest is in the ethical implications of *human* genetic modifications, as opposed to using genetics to engineer animals for sport. The subject of engineering animals is also highly topical, and there are useful and worthwhile comparisons to be made. For example, the genetic breeding of racehorses has become highly controversial, as has racehorse doping (Henderson, 2001). In addition, my concern will not be about the ethical issues arising from genetically modifying the sporting environment, as might be considered in relation to creating durable golf-courses. While it is important not to dismiss these kinds of examples which may be useful to clarify points of argument about the ethical status of genetically modifying humans, they will not be the focus of this book.

From drugs to genes

Neither WADA, nor any other anti-doping authority, has yet dealt with the many kinds of applications of genetics to sport. To date, WADA has given some time to considering the matter. In March 2002, WADA held a closed conference in Cold Spring Harbor, New York, focused specifically on addressing the implications of genetics for sport (WADA, 2002). In addition, the IOC Medical Commission held a meeting in June 2001, with an agenda to discuss the implications of genetics for sport (IOC, 2001). However, genetic modification is still not fully theorised in anti-doping policy. The 2004 World Anti-Doping Code makes the following reference to 'gene doping' prohibiting its use:

M3. GENE DOPING
Gene or cell doping is defined as the non-therapeutic use of genes, genetic elements and/or cells that have the capacity to enhance athletic performance.
(WADA, 2003)

Unlike with the doping issue in general, ethical decisions about genetic modification can be made *before* the technology is in place and is causing problems for sport. This provides a very useful opportunity to ensure that policy about the ethical status of genetics in sport is practicable and justified. Importantly, this does not imply deriving absolute ethical principles that can determine the value of genetics in sport. Rather, it is about ensuring a suitable forum for discussion and the re-evaluation of policy, which has been lacking so much in general anti-policy discourses. For genetics there is a possibility to be proactive, rather than reactive, as may be said of anti-doping policy since the 1960s.

Importantly, decisions concerning these technologies cannot (and should not) operate in isolation from broader bioethical policies of non-sporting organisations. This is also an important difference between doping and drug use generally and the use of genetic technology specifically. Sporting discussions will benefit immensely from the expertise within non-governmental organisations and governmental committees, which have invested considerably into discussing the broad ethical issues arising from genetics in society. Such international bodies as Unesco, the CoE and the EU may be seen as having developed into intergovernmental decision making in relation to genetics. For example, Unesco contains the International Bioethics Committee, within which there is a working party entitled the Inter-Governmental Bioethics Committee.[3]

These and other international organisations are working to develop policy in relation to biomedical ethics. Of course, Europe is not alone in this pursuit, though Europe has made considerable progress in its interest to consider intergovernmental policies and has a substantial variety of countries at various levels of development in genetics, which can make for a particularly fruitful future. Importantly, there continues to be a lack of links between mainstream bioethics and sport. The WADA conference in 2002 may be seen as some progress towards making these links. But there has yet to be any serious acknowledgement from non-sporting institutions, which are dealing with sport policy issues, that genetics is of serious concern. One of the few to make such links is the Australian Law Reforms Commission (ALRC). In 2001, the ALRC published a consultation paper about issues regarding the protection of genetic information, noting that sport is a context where this might give rise to serious legal and ethical concerns. In addition, the United States President's Council on Bioethics (2002) discussion offers quite different arguments concerning genetic enhancement in sport than may be found aired in anti-doping policy meetings.

Summary

The prospect of using gene transfer technology in sport presents a situation where the kind of harmonisation that may be sought by WADA or European anti-doping organisations is further complicated by the global context of this new technology. Policy about using genetic technologies in sport must also take into account the broader bioethical implications of such decisions, while in the past it has been able to isolate its own sporting reasons for rejecting doping.

There are very good reasons why anti-doping organisations should, first, look to the way in which governments are addressing the ethical issues relating to genetics, before seeking to enforce sporting ideals at a global level. While it may be argued that discussions about genetics are overly exclusive to richer, more scientifically oriented countries, it is not accurate to say that there are no concerns about the internationalisation of policy regarding the use of genetic technology. Recent events, such as renegade scientists fleeing to countries where regulation does not prevent their scientific investigation, presents a global social issue of great importance.[4] This, then, is a matter that must be discussed at an international, cross-cultural level, recognising the different kinds of value system between and within cultures. If discussion remains only at the sporting level, it is not clear that any such sensibilities will be acknowledged.

For this reason, I will suggest that anti-doping policy – if such a term is appropriate – can be best informed by revisiting its core assumptions about the meaning and value of performance enhancement. In order to attain the kind of harmonisation that is desirable, it is necessary that there is some basis for concluding that these are shared ambitions, though this is not an easy task. A discussion about the ethical status of various kinds of genetic modification can enrich that discussion because it is largely experimental and because it elucidates weaknesses in the consistency about anti-doping policy hitherto unseen. This is not an argument that requires all participating bodies to agree on a particular policy. Rather, it is about ensuring a process of deliberation, which allows the expression of diverse opinions.

Part II

Conceptualising genetics in sport

3   What is possible?

Imminent applications for the genetically modified athlete

If genetic modification is poised to make the application of anti-doping highly problematic, then it is pertinent to outline what are the specific and varied kinds of effects that might arise from such technology and how athletes might actually use genetics. It is also necessary to conceptualise genetics in relation to performance. A great deal has been written about the genetic basis of performance, often to answer questions about why some kinds of athletes perform with greater success than others (Entine, 2000; St Louis, 2003). Yet little has been discussed in relation to how this (mis)information might be used to modify performance and what it might require to effect such a change.

As was mentioned earlier, the possibilities of genetic science remain highly contested. Opinions range from a complete lack of faith in gene transfer technology to provide any meaningful alterations to the genome, to strong commitment in its capacity to make possible the creation of superhumans. While there has been no engineering of specific genes in order to enhance a person's physical capability beyond that which is humanly possible, some research suggests that specific genes are related to specific kinds of performance. Such claims are often of more interest to the tabloid press than to the serious scientific community, where associations between social behaviour and genetics are tenuous at best, though, more often, entirely rejected (Ho, 1998). Nevertheless, a substantial amount of research has begun to take place to explore these links, and the focus of this chapter will be to explore that research in depth. It is important to recognise that the phrase, *humanly possible*, is not necessarily the focus of our attention. Rather, it may be equally interesting to learn of genetic manipulation that has enhanced an individual beyond his or her own capabilities.

What are genes?[1]

The German monk, Gregor Mendel (1822–1884), is widely credited with having identified the basic rules of genetics and inheritance during the nineteenth century. His studies of pea plants revealed how molecular biology works, which would later inform scientific research on this topic (Mendel, 1866). The year 2003 celebrates the fiftieth anniversary since the description of the chemical called deoxyribonucleic acid by Francis Crick and James Watson, more commonly known as DNA.[2] Their paper, published in *Nature*, changed the way of understanding human biology, giving rise to the new discipline of molecular biology (Watson and Crick, 1953). A gene is a piece of information coded on a segment of DNA. It consists of a unique order of nucleotide bases, of which there are four standard types: adenine (A), thymine (T), guanine (G) and cytosine (C). These bases encode a number of different proteins (current estimates suggest approximately five kinds of protein per gene) and may be found in the chromosomes of all cells in all living organisms.[3]

While Crick and Watson are world renowned for having made a significant advancement in the science, it was Oswald Avery who first discovered in 1944 that DNA was the genetic material. Nevertheless, Crick and Watson's discovery, assisted by their colleagues Rosalind Franklin and Maurice Wilkins, would yield a great insight into how life works. Crick and Watson describe how the appearance of DNA resembles two chains wrapped around each other like strands in a rope – a double helix.

When occurring in various orders, the four-letter alphabet of bases communicates very subtle instructions to our bodies. It functions as a code or language which, when understood, is possible to explain how specific functions in the body operate and why dysfunctions might occur. As Bruce and Bruce (1998: 5) describe, 'It is the sequence of these bases, in different orders and combinations along the backbone, which makes up the genetic information – the genetic code.' The international scientific collaboration called the Human Genome Organisation (HUGO) has endeavoured to understand this language over the past thirteen years (since 1990) during which time it has been sequencing the human genome. In June 2000, HUGO announced it had completed its working draft of the human genome. At the same time, HUGO's competitor Celera Genomics, directed by estranged HUGO executive Craig Venter, announced that it had also completed its draft sequence of the entire genome. Seven months later, both organisations published analyses of their sequencing projects within a day of each other in different prestigious journals (the Celera Genomics Sequencing Team, 2001; the International Human Genome Sequencing Consortium, 2001).[4] In April 2003, HUGO announced the completion of its international project to map the human genome.[5]

In humans, there are forty-six chromosomes to DNA – or twenty-three base pairs – and around 30,000 genes. These genes are responsible for encoding a number of proteins, which are biological compounds, such as 'haemoglobin, the proteins that help protect us against invading microorganisms' (Reiss and Straughan, 1996: 15). Gene expression is the process by which a gene is transcribed into messenger ribonucleic acid (mRNA), which transmits information from DNA to the cytoplasm to control the chemical process in the cell.

How does genetic engineering take place?

Genetic engineering is the technique used where functioning genes are inserted into cells to correct a genetic error or to introduce new function to the cells. For some time, this was generally called *gene therapy*, though the preferred terminology is now *genetic transfer technology* since it is not always clear that such modifications will have a therapeutic intervention.

The method by which genetic engineering or modification can take place varies and has progressed as the science has become more refined.[6] For some time, it was widely recognised that the way of introducing new genes might be simply to blast them in using a type of gun, a biolistic or particle gun. This method of transmitting genes involves mixing DNA with tiny metal particles, which are then fired into a tissue culture of cells or into an organism itself. This method is described as *vectorless* since the uptake of the foreign material does not use a virus to 'infect' cells with the new DNA. Reiss and Straughan (1996) note that this method has not been particularly effective, as it can cause damage to cells and is relatively unsuccessful at promoting the update of foreign DNA. Vectorless transmission may also take place by injecting the new genetic material into the organism, which is more effective at ensuring that a high proportion of cells take up the foreign DNA. Finally, a further vectorless transmission involves using electroporation, where the cells to be genetically engineered are placed in a solution of the foreign DNA. This solution is then subjected to a sudden high-voltage electric field, which stimulates the integration of the new genetic material into the host cells.

A completely different method of genetic modification involves using a *viral vector* to infect the host DNA with the new genetic material. As Reiss and Straughan (1996: 37) explain, 'A vector is an organism that carries genetic material from one species (the donor species) to another (the genetically engineered species).' This can take place in two ways, as a *retrovirus* or an *adenovirus*. Each of these involves obtaining the desired piece of genetic material, inserting it into the vector species (the virus), and finally injecting the species (carrying the new genetic material) into the host. Once this has taken place, the virus begins to infect cells with the new DNA, thus transporting it throughout the organism. The way in which this can be done varies. Retroviruses can be delivered *ex vivo* (outside the body) and *in vivo* (inside the body). As Ho (1998: 212) explains, *ex vivo* entails:

> taking cells – such as bone marrow cells – from patients, transforming them in culture with the missing gene carried in a suitable gene transfer vector, and then returning the transformed cells to the patients.

Alternatively, *in vivo* retroviruses are injected directly into the organism. Yet each method of using a retrovirus is problematic, since they insert themselves at random, often causing cancers to form. Retroviruses achieve only limited success, since they only infect dividing cells (and there are many genetic disorders that are not caused by mutations in dividing cells). In addition, due to their random insertion, retroviruses are quite difficult to control. Potential consequences may entail merely a lack of effectiveness or, more seriously, insertion into tumour-suppressor genes, which help to prevent cancer (Reiss and Straughan, 1996).

A more successful method of gene delivery *in vivo* is using *adenoviruses*, which involves inserting functional copies of a gene. Adenoviruses permit a more efficient insertion rate, though this rapid uptake tends to decrease quickly with time and can often cause an inflammatory response in the host cells. While not every application of this technology relates to a human subject, the implication is that, if applied to humans, it might be ineffective and potentially very dangerous. Currently, it is considered that the retroviral vector is the most effective for *ex vivo* gene transfer and the adenoviral vector for *in vivo* gene transfer (Leiden, 2000).

Genetic science in sport

The application of genetic knowledge to sports tends to have been considered largely in relation to elite performers, where the benefits of knowledge about the genetic basis of performance are clearest. Hoberman (1992) discusses this imminent technology as a logical inevitability in performance-based sport. Some years later, studies are beginning to explore the ways in which genetic information may be used to augment the human athlete.

A succinct and comprehensive articulation of the varied kinds of application of genetic science relevant to sport is found in Munthe (2000). In Munthe's analysis of the various forms of gene technology that might be used to engineer sports champions, he considers four main categories, which are as follows:

1   Genomics (using genetic technology to improve methods of performance enhancement by creating more effective drugs and training techniques).
2   Somatic cell modification (altering the non-hereditary cells of the body, such as those specific to muscle tissue).
3   Germ-line modification (altering the hereditary cells of the body very early on in life).
4   Genetic pre-selection (using information of a person's genotype to conclude suitability for sport either at embryonic stage or infantile stage).

First, Munthe discusses the possibility of how information about genetic predispositions and their influence on the body might be used to fine-tune already established methods of training by manufacturing more effective drugs. Such information is comparable to how other scientific discoveries within sports medicine have yielded better ways of making training more efficient. The findings from the Human Genome Project would be of particular relevance here, though it is important to recognise that this application does not entail any genetic *modification* of the athlete at all. Rather, it is more a process of using knowledge about genetics to create more effective ways of enhancing performance by using drugs or optimising training methods.

Second, Munthe outlines the possibility of engineering the somatic cells of the body – the non-hereditary cells. Quite rightly, Munthe identifies these techniques of genetic modification as being most comparable to the ways in which athletes currently use other methods of doping. The procedure is performed upon already developed human beings (postnatal). A useful example of this is the possibility that somatic cell engineering could be used to develop genetically modified red blood cells to enhance endurance in a way that is comparable to the effects of erythropoietin (EPO) and blood doping.

The engineering of germ-line cells is Munthe's third category. Such engineering would most likely take place very early in life (within some days of conception), due to the complexity of engineering such genes. The effects of any modification are hereditary, and have the added ethical implication of affecting the genetic composition of subsequent generations.

Munthe's final category of genetic technology is its use for the pre-selection of athletes. Munthe suggests that this possibility, where prospective athletes could be chosen on the basis of their genetic predisposition for athletic capabilities, is not very different from coaches going to watch young athletes and selecting which is most deserving of investment. However, as 'ACE' gene scientist Hugh Montgomery argues,

> Screening by [observable characteristics] is always going to be more effective than genetic screening. . . . If you gave me £100,000 and said 'build a football team', I'd be much better off paying boys' clubs to give me first crack at their talented youngsters than spending it on genetic tests.
>
> (cited in Whitfield, 2001: html)

Tamburrini (2002) provides a similar categorisation to Munthe, with the additional distinction that the pre-selection of athletes could be made at the embryonic stages of human development and not only by testing infants and young children. As Tamburrini (2002: 254) argues, this would ensure that 'resources can be concentrated on those "good prognoses" who are in possession of the right physiological conditions to become top athletes.' The use of genetic pre-selection derives from the medical utility of screening for genetic dysfunction. The basic principle is to introduce a *probe* into the DNA molecule of the subject. This probe attaches itself to the subject's DNA to reveal disorders in the genetic make-up (Macer, 1990).

In addition, Tamburrini offers further detail on the process of germ-line genetic modification, which recognises that there are two methods of conducting such engineering. The first entails a similar process to engineering somatic cells, though the cells are then 'introduced into a blastocyst, thereby changing the germ-line of the future individual' (2002: 255). In addition, Tamburrini describes how 'the other procedure involves cloning. An adult somatic cell is genetically modified and, then, the DNA of this cell is introduced into an embryo by way of cloning, from which the new individual originates' (ibid.).

These categories offered by Munthe and Tamburrini provide a useful and broad account of the categories of genetic technology relevant to sport. Yet it is important to stress that neither Munthe nor Tamburrini group their applications based upon the ethical issues arising from each possibility. This is important, since it may be argued that different kinds of genetic technology give rise to similar ethical issues. Because of this, there is considerable overlap in the ethical analysis of each application. For example, the kinds of ethical issues arising from the development of genomics could be seen as conceptually similar to the modification of somatic cells, since each of these applications would involve the non-hereditary cells of the body. Indeed, each of these applications could be conceptualised in a similar way to current methods of drug taking and doping in sport.

In relation to the science, it is predominantly three categories that are of immediate importance to the world of science: genomics, somatic cell modification and genetic selection. Moreover, these applications are considered to be the most relevant to anti-doping policy makers for a variety of reasons, though partly because of their imminent use within science. In addition, this technology is most comparable to current methods of doping. In these categories, a number of researchers have begun to identify performance-related genes, though it is important to stress that this research remains contested. Broadly speaking, this research comprises work in relation to growth factors, such as insulin-like growth factor I (Barton-Davis *et al.*, 1998; Goldspink, 2001) and oxygen-carrying genes, such as the so-called ACE gene (Montgomery *et al.*, 1999; Taylor *et al.*, 1999).

Research on growth factors

Growth factors are involved with a variety of functions in organisms and are particularly relevant to sport, due to their capacity to help muscles grow and repair themselves when damaged. It is also possible to use growth factor to hasten the process of recovery after competitive injuries or training (American Association for the Advancement of Science, 2003). Examples of growth factor include 'basic fibroblast growth factor (bFGF), nerve growth factor (NGF), and insulin-like growth factor type 1 (IGF-1)' (Martinek *et al.*, 2000).

Of particular importance to sport is the use of genetic technology to boost muscle mass, which could provide a number of different functions for athletes. The present research demonstrating this link relies upon a synthetic version of the protein called insulin-like growth factor-1 (IGF-1). Various researchers are working with this protein to learn how to combat muscle-wasting diseases, such as muscular dystrophy, through genetic modification (Barton-Davis *et al.*, 1998; Goldspink, 2001). Although this research has yet to be applied to humans, the implications for sport are clear.

IGF-1 is produced naturally by the body and is stimulated by growth hormone. Thus a boost to human growth hormone would entail a boost to IGF-1, which would then provide a greater capacity for muscle strength. Lamsam *et al.* (1997) believe that such research could be used as a means to assist an athlete to recover from muscular injury, thus speeding up the process of recovery. Their work develops the pioneering research of John Huard, which has examined the possibility of regenerating muscle tissue using genetic technology.

In a similar vein, Lee Sweeney has researched the possibilities for using a synthetic form of IGF-1 to repair muscle tissue, which has demonstrated considerable enhancements in its application to mice (Barton-Davis *et al.*, 1998; Lee *et al.*, 2004). These findings are corroborated by further research with Sweeney's colleague Nadia Rosenthal when using IGF-1 with mice to halt depletion of muscle strength that comes with old age. As Rosenthal notes, 'Older mice increased their muscle strength by as much as 27 per cent in the experiment, which suggested possibilities for athletes as well as for preserving muscle strength in elderly people and increasing muscle power in those who suffer from muscular dystrophy' (cited in Longman, 2001: html). Goldspink (2001) makes similar findings by using a form of IGF-1 called mechano growth factor (MGF) with mice, which is used to treat muscle-wasting diseases such as muscular dystrophy. Goldspink's team was able to isolate muscle tissue and insert the MGF gene. The results showed an increase in muscle mass by approximately 20 per cent after two weeks (Goldspink, 2001).

Genetic science has also endeavoured to target specific genes that may be identified as determining biological characteristics, such as the capacity for endurance. Recently, research has begun to identify the effects of inserting genes into a virus to produce a specific bodily effect. Such research has taken place using erythropoietin (EPO) to increase endurance. For example, a research team led by Jeffrey Leiden used an adenovirus to deliver EPO to mice and monkeys, to observe whether it would provoke a change in biological capabilities (Aschwanden, 2000; Svensson *et al.*, 1997). By inserting the gene into a virus strand, it was subsequently transported throughout the body and did, indeed, have the effect of increasing the level of red blood cells that were being pumped around the body. In performance, this produces a similar effect to that of blood doping, which delays fatigue by reintroducing blood into the body to boost the amount of oxygen transportation around the body. Thus genetically inserting EPO into an athlete could increase the capacity for endurance when active, which would be useful for any long-distance event.

Other emerging research by Lin *et al.* (2002) has discovered a molecular switch that can convert fast-twitch muscle fibres into slow-twitch fibres, the latter of which are associated with more endurance-based activities. Known as PGC-1 $\propto$, this research could reveal information about an athlete's capacity to endure, though the research remains experimental and expectations are limited. Lin's research suggests that the addition of such genes to mice, on occasion, resulted in emaciation and sterilisation. Research by Yang *et al.* (2003) also shows how fast- and slow-twitch fibres have a genetic basis that can be linked to performance capacity.

Alternatively, variations in the ACE gene (angiotensin-converting enzyme) have been associated with endurance capacity and an anabolic response to intense exercise training (Brull *et al.*, 2001; Gayagay *et al.*, 1998; Montgomery *et al.*, 1998, 1999; Plata *et al.*, 2002; Taylor *et al.*, 1999).[7] Williams *et al.* (2000) study this enzyme by comparing two groups of athletes, one with a strong ACE presence and one with a low ACE presence. As Anderson (2000: html) explains:

The angiotensin-converting-enzyme story begins with a plasma protein called angiotensinogen, which is present in the blood of all human beings. Under certain conditions, kidney cells secrete a hormone called renin into the blood which cleaves a 10-amino-acid protein from angiotensinogen to form a compound called angiotensin I. The various physiological roles played by angiotensin I are not completely understood, but it is known that angiotensin-converting enzyme (ACE) can knock two amino acids off angiotensin I to form a compound called angiotensin II. Angiotensin II has a variety of functions, but for purposes of our discussion we can simply say that it directly increases blood pressure by constricting arteries, and it indirectly raises blood pressure and blood volume by stimulating thirst centres in the brain and directing the kidneys to conserve more minerals and water.

Finally, a quite different application of genetic science to sport might involve the manipulation of *Downstream Regulatory Element Antagonistic Modulator* (*DREAM*), which is being shown to affect the experiencing of pain (Cheng and Penninger, 2003; Cheng *et al.*, 2002).[8] DREAM makes a protein that suppresses the production of dynorphin, which is produced in response to pain or anxiety. In the absence of the gene, research has found more production of dynorphin and less sensitivity to pain. These findings could develop novel techniques of managing pain for patients through pharmaceuticals, though they may also suggest a way that athletes might try to inhibit the pain felt through intense training or injury. This application of genomics would be quite different from previous examples, which try to determine some link between genetics and performance. For DREAM, the value of the manipulation potentially creates far more complex discussions about the role and function of pain in being human and the necessity for pain as a critical part of being an athlete.

Collectively, these findings are providing a scientific basis for arguing why there are serious concerns about the ethical status of sport in the era of genetic modification. Research suggests that genes account for up to 50 per cent of variance in the performance of elite athletes (Bouchard *et al.*, 1997). For this reason, there seems to be an important rationale for sporting institutions to seek knowledge related to the genetic basis of performance. Yet much of the research in genetic science remains experimental and funded largely for non-sporting purposes. Consequently, even if such applications were possible and sufficiently safe for humans, it would not be straightforward to conclude that they could then be used to create elite athletes. This is because there is considerable uncertainty about what other changes might take place on the genetic level when altering one single gene. It is possible (and, for many, probable) that altering one gene would influence the function of other genes to the detriment of the individual's health (Harris, 1998). Within the immediate future, there is little reason to suppose one might engineer a specific gene without any imbalance occurring between other genes – a phenomenon known as *pleiotropy*. As such, it may be deemed too risky to do any kind of engineering for any kind of gene. Beyond engineering the 4,000 genes involved in single-gene disorders such as

Huntington's disease or muscular dystrophy, the possibilities of medical genetics are highly questionable (Appleyard, 1999).

A further reason for limited expectations about genetic modification is knowledge about the emerging science of proteomics (Fields, 2001). Proteomics – the study of proteins – is argued by many as crucial to understanding how it might be possible to alter human characteristics. Proteomics is considered by some as a more complex science, and more ethically alarming because the effect of tampering with proteins has such a direct bearing on an individual's capacities (Rabilloud, 2001). As was noted above, there might be at least five times the amount of proteins than genes. Thus while many aspirations have arisen as a consequence of mapping the human genome, proteomics suggests that the mapping of the human protein sequence may be even more important, though significantly more difficult.

Although the evidence is inconclusive in showing whether genetic manipulation could safely engineer genes with a view to a specific kind of enhancement, the research outlined above does provide some basis for expecting this to be possible. Indeed, it is in the context of such research that international sport authorities such as WADA are beginning to take this matter seriously. Furthermore, given the relative infancy of genetic research and what has already been achieved in this short amount of time, it would be naïve to ignore the possibility of experimental, therapeutic applications giving rise to enhancing ones. It is also important to recognise that the kinds of research currently taking place in genetic science are not exhaustive of all the possible applications that might produce sporting modifications. Consequently, to think through the ethical issues arising from genetic modification, it is necessary to discuss a broad range of possible applications and not only those that are reflective of current research findings.

In sum, while modest expectations are sensible in relation to genetically modifying athletes, there is a growing expectation that the science will soon make possible such alterations. The various techniques that might be used to achieve these alterations are growing in sophistication and the research underpinning such discoveries remains a high priority for governmental funding. It is in this context that various organisations and commentators are already beginning to make explicit their reaction to genetics in sport.

Chapter 4 will discuss a number of these interested parties and provide an analysis of the different kinds of ethical discussions that have already begun to emerge in sport and outside of it. It will not yet make any headway into an evaluation of these arguments. Instead, Chapter 4 gives an outline of the various arguments and ways of conceptualising genetic technology that have already begun. Understanding this diverse range of voices is, I suggest, crucial to appreciating the historical development of this matter.

4 Interests, politics and ways of reasoning

The prospect of genetic modification in sport has already begun to provoke a range of concerned voices within and outside of the sporting community to express their views on the subject. The diversity of these bodies is uniquely important to the discussion about doping in sport, just because this matter is already demonstrating that this is not only a sporting issue. Since 2000, there have been a number of academic and professional meetings that have devoted time to the consideration of genetic modification in sport. These include, but are not exhaustive of, the following:

- September 2000: Pre-Olympic World Congress of Sports Science and Medicine, Brisbane, Australia.
- September 2000: International Association for the Philosophy of Sport, Melbourne, Australia.
- March 2001: Playing the Game, Denmark.
- 6 June 2001: IOC Working Party.
- November 2001: Genes in Sport: A Seminar, School of Medicine at University College London and UK Sport, London, UK.
- July 2002: US President's Council on Bioethics.
- July 2003: European College of Sport Science Annual Meeting, Salzburg, Austria.
- October 2003: IOC Olympic World Congress of Sport Sciences, Athens, Greece.

Earlier, I also mentioned WADA's meeting at the Cold Spring Harbor Laboratories, which was originally scheduled for September 2001.[1] The meeting consisted of a number of experts within genetics and sport. Theodore Friedmann, member of WADA's medical research committee and active scholar in the promotion of awareness about the prospects of genetic modification in sport, stated that:

> The geneticist doesn't know a lot about the world of athletics, and the world of athletics doesn't know what is happening in the gene therapy world. As such, the meeting intended to provide an 'opportunity for both

camps to bring themselves up to date on the state of the art and what the potential dangers are in athletics through genetic manipulation'.

(Friedmann, cited in Wilson, 2001: n.p.)

The perspective of scientists outside of sport remains sceptical about the possibility of applying genetic technology to enhance sport performance. Currently, it is not clear that genetics will give rise to many effective therapeutic techniques at all. As such, University College London's eminent biologist Steve Jones argued at the Genes in Sport meeting hosted by UCL and UK Sport that:

There is a massive quantity of hype when it comes to gene therapy in sport. I put it in the same ballpark as the babbling nonsense talked about a baldness cure based on gene therapy.

(Jones, cited in Powell, 2001: n.p.)

One might take this response to be rather flippant, as Jones also adds that he wishes 'genetics had never been invented' (Jones, cited in Hamlyn, 2001: n.p.). Thus Jones' reaction suggests more a contempt for any of the speculations on how such information might be used, rather than directing his response specifically to the application of genetics to sport. Jones is not, however, alone. Thomas Murray, President of the ethical institute The Hastings Center, argues that isolating a gene for any characteristic, sporting or otherwise, is too simplistic a notion. He states that:

Those that believe you get simple effects from genetic manipulations see our genes as beans in a beanbag – you add or pull out a bean and get the effect you seek. . . . I see it as a complex ecosystem with each gene influencing and being influenced by others and the external environment.

(Murray, cited in Morgan, 2001: n.p.)

Consequently, the serious consideration of how such technology might be used for something so *trivial* as enhancing sporting prowess is regarded as being far-fetched by a considerable number of experts. Yet, scientific opinion is divided, since a number of geneticists see that there are possibilities to engineer genes for sport. Genetic research is already taking place in relation to sports performance and will be informed by other kinds of genetic research that can suggest ways in which therapeutic applications of genetics could be used to enhance performance, as discussed in Chapter 3. Moreover, a substantial amount of research has begun to claim links between genes and performance (Perusse *et al.*, 2003). Yet what is interesting about the scientific voices regarding gene doping is their dismissal of it as a valuable part of sport performances. Already, genetic modification in sport is being rejected on the basis of its being unethical.

These scientific commentaries and findings have been accompanied by a wealth of media attention from around the globe, reaching publications in medicine, science, ethics and sport. On many occasions, this attention has been sensationalistic and has sought to ground hysteria about the possibility for creating superhumans in sport. Indeed, one might attribute the rather dismissive response from scientists such as Steve Jones to the amount of bad press that has been written about genetics and sport.

Nevertheless, within the media, there have been responses given by the elite athletic community which provide some awareness and expressions of concern for genetic modification in sport. In general, these responses are from the usual key political figures, though they still offer some context for understanding the athletes' views. In particular, Johann Olav Koss, the 1994 Olympic speed-skating champion from Norway, member of the IOC and medical doctor, asserted that methods could have already started (Longman, 2001: html). Koss also claims that there is a need for aggressive strategies in the development of gene-doping policies:

> We have to do this in the early stages before any athlete starts using this. We need to act quickly to define the rules. I don't think sport has anything to benefit from having genetically enhanced athletes. This is not only an issue for sport, it's a broad ethical issue for human beings.
>
> (cited in Associated Press, 2001: html)

In addition, Sydney 2000 Olympic Gold Medal winner for the men's 100m, Maurice Greene, recognises the ethical issues arising from the potential for engineering germ-line genes, asking, 'What if you're born with something having been done to you. . . . You didn't have anything to do with it' (cited in Longman, 2001: html).

To reiterate the earlier concerns about the 'media-political' context of doping in sport, it matters that these key figures in the world of sport are making these particular claims, if our intention is to understand how doping and genetic modification are *becoming* evaluated. Understanding the way in which, for example, the character of Koss is 'made meaningful' through the press – in relation to his Olympic status and his medical knowledge – is crucial to understanding how the genetics issue is also beginning to be described. These details do not lend any weight to the credibility of the positions asserted by these people. However, they do help to explain how genetic technology and doping in sport are medicalised by the media through an evaluative discourse.

How sporting professionals would approach genetic technology remains highly uncertain, which punctuates its ambiguous ethical status. The US women's national team coach Harmut Buschbacher claims that it would be desirable to obtain the genetic profiles of young rowers:

> As a coach, I'm interested in performance . . . and if this information would give me a better opportunity to select the athletes for my team, I would like to use that. [That way] you're not going to waste so much time and energy on athletes who may not be as successful.
>
> (cited in Farrey, 2000: html)

A similar interest in genetic screening is offered by one of the US national team rowers, Amy Fuller, who says, 'I mean, my mom started me in ballet. . . . What a nightmare that was. Didn't have the grace gene, obviously' (ibid.). Despite this interest in using genetics to act as a more accurate way of focusing a child's sporting interests, Amy also admits an apprehension for having her future told to her at such an early age, revealing one of the alarming aspects of genetically selecting future athletes. To be told that one is not going to be an elite ballet dancer at such a young age, when having such an attraction for the activity, could be psychologically traumatic. Moreover, it may place too much of a burden on a young child, who might find success in their youth, but who might later decide not to become a professional athlete out of his or her own choice. Genetic selection would seem to prevent the many years of enjoyment that child might have had in youth, which seems unfortunate and unnecessary.

These quotations reveal an interest, awareness and concern for the prospect of genetic modification in sport and have contributed to the increasing attention this subject is currently receiving. They also serve to illustrate the strong moral discourse underpinning this issue. Most recent is Francis Fukuyama's (2002b) commentary in *The Economist: The World in 2003*, where he identifies the prospect of genetic modification in sport as being a strong prospect for being realised, and for allowing the discussion about genetics to become a truly open and global issue.

In addition to these various claims about gene doping, two of the most important political (and scientific) organisations are the International Olympic Committee (IOC) and the World Anti-Doping Agency (WADA), which have also begun to make their interests explicit in their own policy making. Each has created working groups to prepare for dealing with the problem of genetic modification, though the presence of ethical research to inform these discussions is unclear. Central members of these organisations such as IOC President Jacques Rogge and IOC Medical Director Patrick Schamasch have expressed a concern for how genetics might be abused for sporting purposes. Importantly, their reaction reveals a perspective of genetic modification as abuse rather than use. These two key individuals condemn any application sought within international sport that intends to enhance performance. As Rogge states, 'Genetic engineering in sport will foster not only a greater potential health risk for athletes than does conventional doping, but also a greater potential for performance enhancement' (cited in Longman, 2001: html).

Not surprisingly, there is a feeling in the IOC for wanting to be ahead of the 'cheaters', who might use this technology. As Schamasch states, 'for once, we want to be ahead, not behind' (ibid.). Statements by other key figures within international sport and medicine reinforce this sense of urgency. Arne Ljungqvist, IOC member and board member for WADA, says:

> The gene responsible for EPO has already been identified by the Human Genome Project and could, theoretically, be injected into the muscle. An EPO gene will promote the body's production of EPO and some people will

say this can never be detected. There may be other parameters we could identify that tell us whether a person has injected this gene.

(cited in Wallace, 2001: n.p.)

In addition, Bengt Saltin of Sweden gave a paper at the 2001 conference Play the Game, within which he states that the title of his paper, 'Gene Doping: Science Fiction or Impending Reality?' might already 'be outdated'. Saltin continues to assert:

> There is no doubt the medical technology is in place. Certain problems exist but they will be overcome. There are already possibilities for sportsmen. Within five years, commercial gene therapy will be available to everyone.
>
> (cited in Walsh, 2001: html)

Yet it is unclear whether this amount of time will be filled with the necessary philosophical and ethical considerations of the technology. Indeed, the depth of ethical issues that will arise from any kind of testing is of substantial concern. Even if the aspiration is to derive methods of testing for genetic modification, it is not clear whether such procedures will be ethically sound or possible to apply. As Peter Schjerling, senior genetic researcher from the Copenhagen Muscle Research Centre, a centre heavily involved with genetic research pertaining to sport, admits, 'A doping test based on taking pieces of the athlete's muscle is not likely to be ethically accepted' (cited in Powell, 2001: n.p.). Such a process would involve an invasive muscle biopsy for which no athlete is likely to provide consent. As Peter Hamlyn, consultant neurosurgeon at St Bartholomew's and the Royal London Hospital, notes, 'peeing in a pot is one thing, but having your legs cut open is another' (Hamlyn, 2001: html). Schjerling continues, explaining that:

> therefore gene doping can be arranged so that detection, in practice, will be impossible. . . . Artificial genes can, and most likely will, be abused by athletes as a means of doping. . . . Detection is extremely difficult since the artificial genes will produce proteins that are identical to those in the human body.
>
> (cited in Powell, 2001: n.p.)

Some sympathy for the need to pursue ethical and philosophical research into gene doping is voiced in the public statements of genetic scientist Theodore Friedmann, who questions the rationale behind genetic manipulation for sport (Friedmann and Koss, 2001). Friedmann's (Friedmann and Roblin, 1972) research has been crucial to the history of genetic science and he has been particularly active in raising the profile of this ethical issue in contexts such as the World Anti-Doping Agency (2002), the American Association for the Advancement of Science (2003) and the US President's Council on Bioethics (2002). In relation to sport, Friedmann asks:

> What are the endpoints of manipulation? . . . Is the hope to incrementally sneak up on the one-and-a-half-minute mile? Or six seconds for 100 meters?

Is the question, How fully can we engineer the human body to do physically impossible things? If it is, what do you have at the end of that? Something that looks like a human, but is so engineered, so tuned, that it's no longer going to do what the body is designed to do.

(cited in Longman, 2001: html)

Interestingly, though, Jacques Rogge considers genetic screening to have merits in the application to sport, though he draws the line at genetic modification (Clarey, 2001). While an explanation for this position is not clear, no special attention has been given to the ethical concerns arising from genetic screening. This is surprising given the considerable ethical discourse concerning the use of genetic information outside of the sporting context (see, e.g. Häyry and Lehto, 1998; Hendriks, 1997; Knoppers, 1999; McLean, 2002; Moore, 2000; Nuffield Council on Bioethics, 1993; Robertson and Savulescu, 2001; Savulescu, 2001).

For each of these institutions and individuals involved with the development of policy about genetics in sport, the approach is already beginning to replicate standard norms in medical ethics. Consequently, apart from Rogge's admission that genetic screening is ethically sound, the limits of what is ethically acceptable concern solely therapeutic (or medically prescribed) applications of genetic technology. Yet there has been no clear discussion about how medical ethical principles apply in response to applications that cannot strictly be called therapeutic. For example, a response about the use of gene therapy to repair muscle tissue has not been given specific consideration. Instead, statements tend to have been made only in respect of the general issue of genetic modification in sport. Such an approach is therefore highly simplistic and overly committed.

In response to these various statements of interests, some immediate criticisms are possible. Importantly, there is a greater need for *precautionary statements* regarding the use of genetic modification in sport though not only to their use, but also to their prohibition. Certainly, there is some merit for ensuring that a message is clear and straightforward and, in the case of genetics, it might serve a better purpose to make such a message one of prohibition and condemnation. For the IOC President to state publicly that some kinds of genetic modification *might* be acceptable would surely be harmful for ensuring that the abuse of genetic modification does not take place. Yet, in so doing, international sports organisations must be careful not simply to retreat into ideological perspectives about what sport should be and expect the perspective to be shared around the world. In the case of drug use, this seems to have happened. However, in the case of genetic modification, it is less likely to be a satisfactory justification of policy decisions just because of the vast number of legitimate applications genetics can have.

By not entering into a genuinely public debate about the ethical issues in sport arising from genetic modification, sports organisations are in danger of making similar mistakes as have arisen in respect of formulating policy about drug taking and doping. Genetic modification cannot be understood in the same way as other doping methods, due to its broader utility for medicine and society at large. In addition, observing the way in which governments around the world are addressing the use of genetics in society more generally, there is a realisation that the problem of genetics is not temporary. It is not sufficient simply to reject its utility and condemn all kinds of applications. Indeed, some kinds of genetic modification that might more typically be labelled 'enhancing' could have great benefits for various kinds of people. While the acceptance of these technologies in broader aspects of society is not, in itself, a justification for their use in sport or even in society, sport would appear noticeably inconsistent with broader policies, should it fail to adapt to changing values in medicine and society.

Currently, WADA has begun to initiate these discussions through the revision of the World Anti-Doping Code, the basic instrument for discriminating between different kinds of substances.[2] Thus the definitional work that needs to precede harmonisation (or, at least, to accompany it) is being addressed within anti-doping meetings. A similar process must ensue for the analysis of genetic modification in sport. It is also important that such discussions borrow from the kinds of discourses about medical ethics *outside* of sport. For example, there is considerable disenchantment with the applicability of the 'four principles' (Beauchamp and Childress, 1994; Gillon, 1994) of medical ethics (respect for autonomy, beneficence, non-maleficence and justice) in the light of new medical technologies. In particular, Jonsen (1991) and Jonsen and Toulmin (1988) develop a critique of principlism as a basis for ethical judgement in medicine. Jonsen and Toulmin (1988: 8) state that:

> once we move far enough away from the simple paradigmatic cases to which the chosen generalizations were tailored, it becomes clear that no rule can be entirely self-interpreting. . . . In dealing with real-life moral problems, which so often turn on conflicts and ambiguities of these two types, we are forced to go beyond the simple rules and principles themselves and see what underlies them.

Examples of attempts to highlight the need for a more critical approach to ethics in relation to genetic technology in sport can already be found. In the draft of its recently published report *Essentially Yours* (2003), the Australian Law Reforms Commission (ALRC) explains its concern about the potential for discrimination against athletes on the basis of their genetic disposition (ALRC, 2001). It states:

> Genetic testing may lead to discrimination against certain athletes. For example, an athlete with a susceptibility to a particular injury may never in fact develop the injury, but may be dropped from the team by management in an effort to avoid potential liability if the injury manifests. Alternatively, a sports co-ordination body may seek to impose certain conditions on players to minimise its own liability for any injuries they may suffer. For example, the Professional Boxing and Martial Arts Board (Vic) has proposed the genetic testing of all professional boxers in Victoria as a condition of their license to fight.

(html: Section 12.29)

The most recent institution to take an interest in genetic enhancement in sport has been the US President's Council on Bioethics (2002). On 11 July 2002 the Council met and received a paper from Ted Friedmann about the 'Potential for Genetic Enhancements in Sports'. The conclusions of this meeting varied significantly, from arguing that genetic modification threatens a 'romantic' view of sport, to claiming that genetic modification is integral to the 'technological rationality' of contemporary elite sport. More will be said about the content of these discussions later, though it is pertinent to recognise that they are not limited to the values of sport, as is often the case with ethical discussions within sporting institutions. Instead, the way in which these non-sporting organisations discuss the ethical issues arising from genetic technology in sport demonstrates a broader base of values, insofar as the sustainability of fair competition or 'ethical sport' is not their primary concern.

Individual interests: health-enhancing humans

Aside from these varied political interests and aspirations to develop policy about genetic modification in sport as soon as possible, it has yet to be considered what might be the interest of an individual to seek genetic modification. Moreover, it has yet to be discussed what would interest a prospective parent in genetically enhancing a prospective child. What would actually lead somebody to be interested in genetically modifying themselves or their children? It cannot be assumed that anybody would want to use genetic modification to alter their capacity to be an elite athlete, even if it might be obvious why a competitive athlete may wish to use such technology. This is because it is not clear whether a sporting modification would have any benefit to an individual outside of sport or, indeed, whether a sporting modification – let us say one that promotes the development of muscle mass – would be the most desirable modification that an individual could undertake. Understanding the context within which any such decision would be made can provide crucial information on how it is ethically evaluated. For example, in the same sense that abortion or euthanasia can be better evaluated in the context of the conditions related to anybody seeking to make such a decision, the use of genetic technology can similarly be better understood by exploring the specific circumstances where these modifications are to be used.

From a social scientific perspective, this aspiration may require surveying various kinds of individuals to understand their perspective and feelings about genetic modification. Alternatively, it may require in-depth interviewing to understand the contextual position of, for example, an athlete. However, the current approach will attempt to establish the conditions within which a person may decide that genetic modification is a beneficial or desirable choice. As was suggested above, it is less relevant whether people believe genetic modification is abhorrent, as this does not yield any insight into the value of such modifications. Rather, it merely reveals that people are socially situated and this is nothing surprising. Nevertheless, knowledge of these perspectives does provide some basis for exploring what kinds of concerns arise about the technology. For example, knowing that people feel strongly about who has access to their genetic information provides a basis for an ethical discussion about the ownership of genetic information (Miah, 2003b). In the context of such knowledge, I seek the logical and rational conditions that might lead someone to legitimately choose genetic modification, so as to understand what kinds of values this person holds and how genetic modification does or does not correspond with these values.

To answer the question about what might lead somebody to choose genetic modification, two conclusions must be asserted. First, it must be considered why anyone would seek to engineer themselves or their children at all. Second, it must be considered why, out of all the possible kinds of alterations that might be available, one would choose to engineer an embryo to become a super-athlete. After all, it is likely that enhanced capability for sport would be only one of a supermarket of genetic possibilities that could be chosen. What is it about sport that, as Fukuyama (2002b) notes, is particularly interesting or appealing? I suggest that it has something to do with the global reach of sports, but also the non-elitism of many sports, which appear to be an accessible opportunity to succeed and receive rewards, regardless of social class. To address the former issue initially, what is it that would lead parents to engineer their child?

For many, there might be something unnecessary about enhancing the genetic composition of a human embryo. Life is so precious that if one's child were born free from pain, discomfort or severe impairment, then to seek improvement upon this would be ungrateful to such good fortune. Furthermore, it might be considered immoral to genetically engineer such a child if there were a potential for jeopardising the baby's future health that might ensue by doing so (as might be the case for a long time to come given the experimental nature of genetic transfer technology). This is, of course, a concern that is necessarily tied to the possibility of health risk: if the modification creates any risk at all, then it is less appealing and a reason to reject genetic modification. Yet, as I outline in Chapter 1, the *health* risk argument is neither persuasive in and of itself – people take risks in all kinds of contexts elsewhere – and its use as a trump to other arguments circumvents the deeper ethical debate.

While it is possible to conclude that health risk might be sufficient to reject genetic modification, it is not the only condition on which people assert an aversion to this technology. As such, it is useful to ignore this medical (and largely egotistical and consequential) reason and to hypothesise a situation where health risk is *not* a concern. Thus the discussion requires that the technology is what I will call *sufficiently safe*, which is to say that it is no more dangerous than the kinds of risks people happily accept in their everyday lives. While this condition may be criticised for being overly abstract, it is a necessary assumption to proceed with the discussion. Admittedly, no medical intervention is without potential side effects (known and unknown) or potential complications. However, in itself, this is not a reason to reject experimental uses of medicine, nor do many scientists advocate this position. Perhaps a critique might be developed against using such experimental techniques in pursuit of something so trivial as sport, though this begs the question as to what would constitute a valuable application. To dismiss sport as being trivial so quickly is presumptuous at this stage, though it may be a conclusion to which it is necessary to return.

As such, it is useful to consider the hypothetical (though not inconceivable) prospect that the health risks would not be of significant concern. Moreover, if necessary, it might further be assumed that the health risks are non-existent and that engineering one's child would definitely not cause any harm to that child. In such circumstances, what then would be the individual's decision? It is conceivable that, still, parents would not wish to effect such fundamental changes to the genetic constitution of their child, and so the engineering would still not be particularly valuable. It might be that a parent would have concerns about the invasiveness of the technology. Yet we might further suppose that this need not be a concern, or at least that it would be no more invasive than contemporary medical interventions, which are widely tolerated and welcomed to enhance health and reduce suffering.

If there were still a reluctance to embrace such modifications, we might also imagine circumstances whereby a child with a genetic disorder – requiring some form of gene therapy – might also be made *better than well* and where this would pose no added risk. In such circumstances, the parents would be faced with the choice of making their child much more capable (or merely more resilient to disease) without it posing any greater risk to the child's health. In such circumstances there is no obvious reason why the parents would not wish to modify their child for the better (presuming that the child's health is the only concern), assuming that people are drawn to enhancing their current circumstances whenever possible, providing it is not at the cost of some greater value.

These circumstances describe conditions whereby a person would reasonably want to use genetic modification. Where the technology offers no greater risk and entails significant potential benefits; where the technology is not invasive; and where the technology is a necessity and using it can also be a means to greater health; all are reasonable choices. However, it is important to reiterate that this assumption relies upon the premise that *when no opposing reason presents itself and where there is no known or perceived cost, people are inclined to try and improve their lifestyle, particularly their biological capability or resistance to disease.* This assumption implies that people are bound to think consequentially about their health (and perhaps about their lives in general). Clearly, this is not the case for everybody or, at least, people do not always base ethical decisions on consequences. For example, some people would not use specific kinds of technology on the basis of it being an affront to religious beliefs that deem it to challenge the sanctity of being human or the role of humans in the natural course of evolution. Yet the condition of *no opposing reason* accommodates such perspectives and can allow us to assume that many people would seek genetic modification as a health enhancer.

The second and perhaps more difficult assumption to make would be to suggest that people would seek athletic enhancements instead of other characteristics. This matter requires some additional clarification about the science of genetic transfer technology, since the projected circumstances appear to be highly simplistic. As was identified above, genetic modification cannot entail the manufacturing of an elite athlete or, more absurdly, a particular athletic skill, such as high-jumping. It is more likely that it might be possible to alter specific biological capacities, such as endurance, strength or speed. As such, the choice facing a prospective modified athlete is not to select the modification to make him or her a good soccer player. It is not possible to engineer a good soccer player solely by altering his or her genetic constitution. Rather, it is more likely that one could engineer genes that promote the *capacity* for endurance, which, with training, would assist a soccer player's fitness or any athlete who requires high levels of endurance capacities. Consequently, the athlete (or non-athlete) might not specifically be choosing better genes for becoming a better athlete. It is more likely that the resultant greater capacity for athleticism would arise from modifying genes that are *health promoting*, and this is a much easier aspiration to understand.

Clarifying this conceptual model of a *genetically modified athlete* is important, as some ethical discussions about genetics have been criticised for being completely far-fetched to the point of not being genuine applied ethical issues. As renowned utilitarian Peter Singer argues, the claim to cloning elite athletes and other great historical figures is ridiculous, since it completely misunderstands the implications of the technology (Singer, 1999). This view is reiterated by de Melo-Martin (2002: 253) when discussing the prospect of a cloned Michael Jordan. The author notes that there is no assurance that a clone of Michael Jordan would be an exceptional basketball player. Michael Jordan's abilities as a basketball player depended not only on his genes, but also on the environment in which he developed and on the life choices he made. In contrast, the kinds of modification proposed here are those that could enhance the human capacity for athleticism. Thus it is not being claimed that it is possible to engineer an elite swimmer or football player. Rather (and at most), genetic modification could provide some basis for making humans better predisposed to being exceptional athletes by providing the genetic basis for elite performances in a broad sense.

On this basis, it is reasonable to assume that these opportunities would be of interest to some people, even if such motives were morally questionable. It is understandable that people would try to ensure a more fruitful future for themselves or their child by *safe* genetic engineering. Indeed, providing genetic enhancement may simply be construed as being akin to 'giving one's child a good education' (Ayabe and Tan, 1995: 463). With this concept of the *health-enhanced* human in mind, it is now necessary to consider the ethical implications of such choices for sport.

Part III

The ethical status of genetic modification in sport

5 Humanness, dignity and autonomy

This chapter will discuss how past literature has made sense of being human and how this is related to other ways in which being human has been challenged. Our present ambivalence about genetic modification in sport (and outside of it) can be informed by recognising how being human has been theorised against *otherness*, often explained in the context of new technologies. Moreover, the way of answering ethical questions about genetic modification must be understood in the context of the way in which humanness has been theorised in the past, particularly within medicine.

The ethical limits of using genetics in sport must begin with a consideration of what it means to be human. The importance of understanding humanness is expressed in a number of ethical discussions concerning performance modifiers in sport, where there is a lack of coherence about why some technologies are ethically permissible and others are not. Arguments against doping are, I suggest, persistently insufficient, because any such position relies upon a clearer articulation of what is valuable about being human. Thus an exploration of sporting values, such as fair play, sportspersonship and so on, logically depends upon a prior account of what gives value to being human. While anti-doping positions allude to the importance of humanness in the ethical discussion through such concepts as a concern for the 'natural' performance, they do not adopt the challenge of articulating it, nor has the history of anti-doping demonstrated problematisation of medical ethical principles.

The importance of understanding 'humanness' is reflected within the works of Schneider and Butcher (2000), and Loland (2000). Each of these authors recognises that defining the human has a bearing upon what kinds of technology are acceptable for use in sport, arguing that sporting value is inextricable from being human. The arguments highlight some form of ethical difference between performances that may be characterised as predominantly *human* (ethical) and those that may be said to be produced largely through *technological* means (unethical). Yet within sports ethics the concept of being human has rarely been tackled, nor fully articulated. McNamee (1992) makes some attempt to address this matter by articulating the importance of *demonstrating* personhood, so as to establish what counts as a valued sporting performance. This perspective will be explored later in the present analysis, though it is first necessary to clarify the logical connection between humanness and personhood. This is not least because the notion of humanness – mostly in the absence of a rigorous conceptualisation of personhood – underpins ethical assumptions in medicine through such concepts as human dignity.

In part, this lack of inquiry into the value and meaning of being human in sport is because humanness remains a highly contested concept. As Schneider and Butcher (2000: 196) recognise, there is not 'an agreed-upon conception of what it is to be human' and so, from their perspective, it is not possible to appeal to such a concept when deriving ethical conclusions. Yet some attempt must be made to elaborate on this important concept, which is so frequently the basis for drawing conclusions about the acceptability of human-altering technologies (Anderson, 1994; Fletcher, 1979; Ford, 1986; Gaylin, 1990).

Some authors have begun to talk about being human in sport in more detail. The importance of being human features in John Hoberman's *Mortal Engines: The Science of Performance and the Dehumanization of Sport* (1992). Hoberman's monograph is largely historical and articulates how a broad, social interest in the transgression of human limits and the pathological obsession with measuring and quantifying human performances was immersed in an age of calibration, of which sport became a part. Nevertheless, one can observe a moral discourse in Hoberman's writing from his account of the *dehumanisation* of sport through technology, which comes across as being highly undesirable. The issues raised in *Mortal Engines* beg the broader question about the ends of human existence and the degree to which human beings should strive continually for enhancement through technology. Hoberman presents the reader with a sense of *sport gone wrong* (or, at least, going wrong), where the culture of doping is so rife that the role of the human in sport is being made redundant. The human being – Hoberman's *Mortal Engine* – is dehuman, valued solely by its capacity to function mechanically, and capable of being engineered and manipulated to provide a functional and entertaining performance.

The difficulty is that Hoberman's metaphor reveals a sporting paradox: while it is accepted that sport without humans is not particularly interesting, the desire to witness an extraordinary performance is also acknowledged by most sports fans as a valued aspect of the practices. There is an aspiration for our athletes to be superhuman, just as there is an interest from many athletes to go beyond what is known as the limit of human performance. It is this tension between humanness and seeking to be superhuman that reflects the conflict in values about sport and that reveals the challenge to negotiate and requestion sporting values. Consequently, the central problem of this issue is establishing the aspects of humanness that give sport value and how genetic modification corresponds to or conflicts with these ideas.

At the end of *Mortal Engines*, Hoberman describes the possibility of genetically engineering athletes or breeding them as one might breed racehorses.[1] He suggests that this would be consistent with the logic of elite sport and would be the most efficient means of achieving the super-athletes that sporting values demand. This is not the first time such prophecies of super-athletes have arisen within academic literature. One of the early academic descriptions of modern sports tending towards the technologically absurd is found in Johnson (1976), who suggests that technology will become increasingly dominant in sports at the expense of the human being. Johnson explains a number of fantastical ideas about the future of sport that are increasingly representative of contemporary sport as greater sophistication in the technology available to sports is developed. Johnson (1976: 226) describes how:

> drugs will be sold openly at sporting-event concessions . . . hot dog of tomorrow will pack the same kick as the marijuana brownie of today . . . there will be only one discussion in boxing, the heavyweight, all others having vanished because of boredom or bankruptcy . . . ski boots will have sensors that release the binding if the stress on a leg bone approaches the breaking point . . . non-contact sports will be played in the nude . . . a round of golf will be played on one spot, by means of a computer and TV screen; and that ice hockey will be played on Teflon.

It is easy to be critical of any speculations and one cannot attribute much academic rigour to such claims. It is interesting to recognise that these prophecies were made twenty-five years ago and are quite reflective of present-day sport. Johnson (1976: 227–228) describes how:

> sport will continue to reflect the society in which it occurs . . . hockey and football will be more violent in the year 2000 because we may be such a sedentary society that we need some release for our emotions.

Johnson's prediction suggests that technological 'developments are likely to get piled upon one another, which will decrease the role of the human being' (1976: 230). Moreover, it is imagined that 'ridiculously super-fit athletes will occur as a result of random mating in an increasing population to bring together diversified genes, plus better nutrition and the absence of childhood diseases' (1976: 231). Again, it is reasonable to accept that Johnson had some foresight about the tendencies of elite sport. Yet the tension between performance and, perhaps, tradition is still present in sports, revealing ambivalence towards technological modification in sport.

Despite an interest in the technological sporting performances, there is still a sense of valuing the human in sport, for which genetics is seen as a challenge or refutation. There exist strong feelings about the technological modification of performances due to a belief that technological modification makes the human increasingly redundant. Yet to better understand this sense of affection for being non-technological humans, sport ethics becomes increasingly lacking. This may also be seen in relation to the present problem of understanding how genetic modification might challenge values in sport.

The challenge of being human

Philosophical articulations of the human demonstrate a tendency to answer the question 'What is human?' by contrasting it with other kinds of entity, such as animals, machines and automata. An early theme in philosophy, which reflects the attempt to distinguish humans from other entities, is found in relation to non-human animals. For example, Michel de Montaigne's (1533–1592) ideas about being human arise out of a frustration for understanding the place of humans in the natural order. Montaigne endeavours to explain humanness by contrasting the differences between humans and the differences between humans and animals. Arguing that beasts are more natural than humans and that there is a greater difference between humans and humans than between humans and animals, Montaigne claims that humans should aspire to be more like animals rather than to mark themselves off as being distinct and superior to non-human animals.

Subsequently, René Descartes (1596–1650) develops a philosophical approach to understanding the human being, rephrasing the question in the context of animal *intelligence*. Descartes places at the forefront of the discussion the ability of animals to reason, rather than their possession of souls. By identifying the perfection of animal actions, Descartes concludes that animals, unlike humans, do not have free will or the ability to determine actions. Whereas animals are perfect, humans have the ability to choose imperfection and to make mistakes, represented by the story of the Garden of Eden. In addition, humans must strive for perfection through reason and, from here, Descartes concludes that the method through which humans reason is *rational doubt*. Here, Descartes arrives at his canonical approach to philosophy, rational deductivism, and its resultant legacy, *cogito ergo sum*, more commonly translated as *I think, therefore I am*.

Distinguishing humans from animals is not the only way in which philosophers have attempted to reveal a coherent articulation of what it means to be human. Far from being a progression from the human–animal distinction, ideas have sought to distinguish between humans and non-living entities or automata. It is possible to see how this way of understanding humanness contributes a great deal to discussions about new technology and genetic modification. Mythical and fantastical ideas about human/machine hybrids are present from stories of Icarus and his wings, to Chinese, Greek and Arabic texts that are rich in the subject of automata (Mazlish, 1993). The mixing of fact and fiction is an important aspect of these discussions, and it plays an important role within the ethical consideration of new technologies. The ability to conceptualise the abstract being, the automata, the cyborg or the genetically engineered human are all useful ways to approach a clearer understanding of what constitutes the human and what might constitute desirable circumstances for the future of the human being.

An important part of this discourse is the sense of fear or anticipation about such changes. Often, fears are associated with the development of automata, and fictional literature has explained the sense of human insecurity arising from conceptualising the living machine or the cyborg. Automata are frequently represented as posing an irrational threat to human beings, calling into question their *identity* and powers of domination. These kinds of ideas are fundamental to explaining some of the concerns about genetic modification in sport, which constitute part of the ethical arguments against such technology. Literary examples abound on this topic, including Hans Christian Andersen's fairy-tale *The Nightingale*; Mary Shelley's *Frankenstein*; and more recently, Isaac Asimov's robot stories.

In each of these examples, there is a recurring narrative about how the new being creates a problem for the humans around it. Andersen's *Nightingale* tells the story of a mechanical nightingale that charms a Chinese Emperor far more than his *real* nightingale, even though the real bird had been with the Emperor for many years. The mechanical bird's greater beauty and more pleasant song results in the real nightingale being banished and fleeing from the Emperor's side. A year later the artificial bird breaks down and cannot be repaired, and the Emperor begins to die. Hearing of the news, the banished nightingale returns and the Emperor returns to good health once again. The story symbolises the conviction that it is biological life that endures, not machines, and is a part of our moral discourse on technology: being alive is good, being artificial is bad.

Other texts convey a similar message. In Shelley's *Frankenstein*, the monster is a human creation that is part biological and part mechanical (through its reanimation). Despite its human form, the resulting being is grotesque and alien to the human world, within which it soon becomes monstrous and violent. Importantly, the monster of Frankenstein becomes terrible only when it is rejected from human society. As such, the text reveals an ambiguity about this creation; its monstrosity is not a product of its creation, but a consequence of its lack of acceptance by other humans who fail to embrace it. On this point, Mazlish (1993: 44) argues that the story provokes the following warning about the future of the human species:

> if humans insist on their separateness and superiority in regard to machines (as well as other animals), viewing them as a threatening new 'species' rather than as a part of their own creation, will they, indeed, bring about the very state of alienation that they fear.

These stories of automata, cyborgs or robots all pose the same compulsive question: *How do humans differ from non-humans, or more simply, what does it mean to be human?* In its most recent incarnation, the classical period of the Enlightenment marks the triumph of humanism over theology, and many of the scientific discoveries of previous years are reworked and understood by scientists of this time. However, defining the human did not end during these times and new technologies provide the means for further kinds of discussions about the human being. The Industrial Revolution provoked a significant development in writing about the relationship between humans and other entities. The discourse reflects a scientific concern for automata and the Romantic revulsion against the mechanical Newtonian worldview. It illustrates the range of curiosities embodied in scientific inquiry and legends about the creation of life from inanimate material.

The subsequent years would see the works of some profound philosophers and scientists with a far more sophisticated sense of science than had existed before. This period of 'isms' (Transcendentalism, Idealism, Existentialism, Nihilism, Realism, Pragmatism, Socialism, Communism, Liberalism) included such icons of Western history as Charles Darwin, Karl Marx and Schopenhauer. The presence of machines in everyday life made the distinction between humans and non-living entities more acute, particularly during the late nineteenth and early twentieth centuries, where machines would be far more confrontational to a worker's life than ever before and, increasingly, within the family home.

The machine became an object of human interest, a means to an end, accentuating the role of the human being as a tool user. Tools were used to extend personal power and freedom, at the same time subjecting individuals to its impersonal organisation (Mazlish, 1993). Tools became the mediator for humans and the environment; an artificial skin separating humans from other animals.[2] The division of labour transformed the human into mere body parts and reduced workers' relationships with each other to functional, economic value. From here, it was a small conceptual step towards the computer revolution. The computer reflects the current articulation of machinic automation, extending human faculties as well as replacing humans and making humans more machine-like, both physically and cognitively.

Darwin's biological humanism allows the human to be reduced to a level of mechanics, a view that pervades contemporary understandings about being human. The classification of species and the survival of the fittest hypothesis reduces the complexity of life to neat and tidy relationships. However, it is here where the barriers between animals and humans collapse, identifying the difference between them as being one of degree, rather than of kind. Indeed, in Darwin's view, the most fundamental difference between humans and animals is that humans possess a developed sense of morality, or conscience, and religion. From here, the debate about whether humans are composed of mainly genetic, inherited qualities, or whether humans are more socially determined – the nature versus nurture debate – begins to ensue.

The move from modern to postmodern articulations of the human condition also plays an important role in understanding humanness, as it is articulated in present-day ethics. The underlying narratives of such classic texts as Huxley's (1932/94) *Brave New World* or George Orwell's *1984* (1949/83) recur frequently within contemporary discussions about the genetic revolution. The ideas within these works continue to haunt humanity, reminding us of how easily our acceptance of technology can lead to disaster.

This period of redefining the human condition as distinct from other entities is not limited to any specific technology. It encompasses biotechnologies, but also includes such innovations as artificial intelligence, virtual reality or life extension. Nevertheless, the symbiosis of the organic and machinic takes place in its most extreme form through the merging of humans with medical technology, allowing the transplantation of limbs and the reconstructing of life, which uses technology and biology.

It is in this vast historical context of conceptualising the human that we find arguments which challenge the importance of humanness as a fixed entity. The emerging (and varied) perspectives on cyborgism (Gray, 1995, 1997, 2002; Haraway, 1985), posthumanism (Fukuyama, 2002a; Hayles, 1999) or transhumanism (Bostrom, 1998) seek to reject humanness as a guiding normative concept. Each of these approaches to humanness resonates a strong twenty-first-century fetish for pondering the consequences of technological advancement.[3] For example, Katherine Hayles' *How We Became Posthuman* outlines a process towards disembodiment through cybernetics, where the human no longer has value as a fixed entity. Alternatively, Chris Hables Gray has repeatedly articulated our cyborgian identity in his co-edited *The Cyborg Handbook* and his most recent publication *Cyborg Citizen*. Each of these texts bases a critique of technology on the way in which it is changing humanity.

There is a remarkable lack of dialogue between these cultural critiques of humanness and contemporary ethical discussions about genetics (or bioethics), including the ways in which these different kinds of literature are engaging with the importance of humanness. For example, Francis Fukuyama's *Our Posthuman Future: Consequences of the Biotechnology Revolution* speaks more to the bioethical aspects of transcending humanness than to any literary or anthropological sense of being human. Nevertheless, Fukuyama's monograph is particularly interesting for our present purposes, precisely because it attempts to approach the concept of humanness that underpins ethical discussions about new medical technology. Even if Fukuyama's discourse on being human is relatively narrow, it is an attempt to readdress this important part of the bioethical discussion. *Our Posthuman Future* was originally published alongside Greg Stock's *Redesigning Humans: Choosing Our Children's Genes* (2002), which is a radical challenge to the present restrictions placed upon experimental medical technology. In it, Stock identifies that there is a lack of good reasons for being conservative about our use of genetic technology. In contrast, Fukuyama's conservatism aims to limit our use of human genetics by introducing Factor X, which is his special element of humanness that we are seeking to preserve.

There is no mistaking that the concern for both of these authors is the concept of humanness, even though the authors disagree on what this entails: Fukuyama's essentialism and Stock's pluralism. In response to this conflict, I suggest that, in principle, Fukuyama is right; there is some Factor X that requires greater articulation. Moreover, his approach to capture this within a discourse of human rights can serve as a starting point for greater elaboration on humanness. However, much more must be said about this concept in order to support Fukuyama's claim. It is not sufficient to frame the debate with the related concepts of individual rights and human dignity, since these terms are also in need of greater elaboration.

Fukuyama's (2002a) *Our Posthuman Future* highlights the 'blip' in philosophical history that has occurred over the past 200 years of theorising morality. Fukuyama argues that these past two centuries have failed to continue the discussion about humanness. His approach is important in an academic climate where constructivism is rarely appreciated and where *post* implies a rejection of grand theories and (in ethics) principle-based methodologies. One must, of course, manage constructivism carefully, since there are good reasons for this age of pluralist ethics, which have to do with the contestability of moral concepts.

While Fukuyama's argument does not satisfactorily explain what is valuable about being human, he is on the right track, which is to attempt the difficult task of articulating values. In contrast, Greg Stock appeals to liberalist autonomy with very little recourse to constraint, which gives far more importance to transcending human limitations – the theme in his earlier book *Metaman* (1993) – than to paternalism about technology.

Since the writing of the Nuremberg Code after the Second World War (Annas and Grodin, 1992) and later the Helsinki Declaration (World Medical Association, 2000), the human has become a subject of moral protection through the notion of individual human rights. This is not to say that what is implicitly protected by the discourse of rights is new. Indeed, wherever we find codes of ethics or morality throughout history, there is an interest to protect some human vulnerability. Yet the establishing of rights and the concept of a *moral dignity* intrinsic to all humans is a product of twentieth-century reactionism, rather than the well-laid plans of philosophers and ethicists. The ethical principles of autonomy, beneficence, non-maleficience and justice underpin modern, Western medicine and any research involving human subjects. As such, an initial conclusion to explaining what is valuable about being human may be found from such discussions about dignity and rights.

Humanness and dignity

The concept of *human dignity* is highly influential in debates about new technologies, and presupposes what is valuable about being human by ensuring that people are protected from having their dignity compromised. How it is understood and used is interesting to explain, though of far greater value is to understand what it is *supposed to mean and accomplish*. Human dignity is an elusive concept, the definition of which often entails divorcing it from the context to which it attempts to give value.[4] As Harris (1999: 66) notes, 'appeals to dignity are universally attractive and vague.' It has extensive applications and uses from broad philosophical to specific legal interpretations. Thus it would be inaccurate to present *human dignity* as a coherent set of beliefs, or even as having derived from a specific origin. Hailer and Ritschl (1996) outline four very different though overlapping origins to the concept, which consist of the following:

1   The Physis concept. Stoicist in origin,which stresses the interconnectedness of all things. This definition suggests that humans should live in accordance with the concept of physis (approximately, nature) and have respect for its place in the locus of all things.
2   Human dignity on the basis of the biblical tradition.

3   Human dignity by means of a treaty. Hobbes and Locke: The concept of dignity is tied to the state and its responsibility to protect.
4   'Never only as a means but always also as an end.' This view has a Kantian foundation, which rejects the theological argument. It asserts that human freedom indicates and guarantees a prominent and elevated status of the human being over and against nature. Moreover, it prioritises the autonomy of ethics and of the human being.

In each of these definitions, *dignity* has been used to explain some characteristic of humanness that gives it a special importance. In some instances this has been in the context of a species category, where the human is considered to be special by comparison to other animals, on account of some unique aspect of human origins. As Rendtorff (1998: html) describes:

> The principle of human dignity signifies that the human beings have a special position that places them over the natural and biological position in nature. As a moral being and because of its status as a human being the notion of 'dignitas' is contributed to its intrinsic value and place in the world. From the beginning it emphasized this out-standing position of the human being in the universe.

In Stoicism, the uniqueness of being human relies upon a perception of the place humans have in the natural order of the world. For some biblical interpretations, human dignity exists by virtue of humans having been made in the likeness of God. On Hobbes' and Locke's accounts, the existence of human dignity is tied to the need for the state to protect individuals from each other, either by contract or by legislation. Importantly, this does not necessitate an ethical system based on a concept of human rights, which contrasts thus with the way in which human dignity is protected in contemporary Western societies.

Finally, for the Kantian interpretation, human dignity is afforded by virtue of being able to reason morally as autonomous individuals. For Kant, this is the salient and inviolable characteristic of being human and necessitates his Golden Rule – that we should treat others as we should like to be treated ourselves, i.e. as ends in themselves, rather than exclusively as means to the ends of others. As such, the intended use of the concept is to recognise that being human has an inherent, objective value; it is not necessarily that humans regard themselves as special or distinct from other life, but that there exists some measure external to human judgement which also ascribes a special status to being human (Egonsson, 1998).

Yet even if this approach to understanding why humans have special value is appealing, the concept of dignity encounters difficulties when applied to many contexts, particularly in medicine. It continues to be used without much explanation or theorisation and, for this reason, begs the question as to quite what is protected when protecting human dignity. Some might argue that this is unavoidable, even necessary. On such a view, human dignity is not reducible, because it is a basic value (Rendtorff, 1998) or a self-evident principle, which gains moral weight through its specific and particular articulation each time it is used. Indeed, this is the interpretation of Hailer and Ritschl's (1996) articulation of the German equivalent of human dignity, *Menschenwürde* (a detailed explanation of *Menschenwürde* may be found in Bayertz and Engelhardt (1994), particularly Dieter Birnbacher's (1994) chapter). Birnbacher (1998) and Bayertz (1996) can also assist in relating this concept to the practical bioethical context. Thus, while we can recognise that human dignity implies something morally salient about the protection of human values, we can also recognise that the term cannot be used arbitrarily or without due reason. For example, even though we might assert autonomy as a particularly important aspect of human dignity, one cannot claim that any compromise to individual autonomy is an (important) affront to one's human dignity.

Hailer and Ritschl (1996) recognise that the various traditions of interpreting human dignity may be found in social documentation, such as the UN Declaration on Human Rights, the US Bill of Rights (through Thomas Jefferson's intervention), the Magna Carta and the UK Bill of Rights. In addition, the concept of human dignity plays a central part in Unesco's Universal Declaration on the Human Genome and Human Rights (1997). In each, the concept of human dignity is applied similarly, without much greater theorising than is found in the various philosophies outlined above. Hailer and Ritschl (1996) also note non-Anglo-Saxon traditions in such countries as Germany, where human dignity is used far less than the concept *Menschenwürde*, which has no literal translation into English.

Interestingly, where human dignity is used as a fundamental and over-powering argument to uphold an individual's claim to autonomy, the German interpretation does not tend to conceptualise it in this way. Recalling Robert Alexy's articulation, Hailer and Ritschl (1996: 112) note that it can be better understood as optimising offers 'of universal character, having precedence over rules, but which do not enjoy the definitive unambiguity of rules'. From this perspective, it is not that appeals to human dignity trump all other values or that individuals are entitled to use it in such a way. Instead, human dignity is used as a moral guide rather than as an absolute rule. It provides good reasons for being cautious about decisions, which seek some way of resolving balances between human values and individual autonomy.

It is important to remember that the tradition of understanding human dignity is not exclusively Anglo-Saxon and this value-laden term may not actually be the best descriptor of what makes being human valuable. Kant's work is critical to the historical development of conceptualising human dignity (Pullman, 2002). For Kant, recognising dignity implies having a *respect for persons* and this respect is now recognised as a fundamental human right. It is Kant's discourse that still underpins the way in which ethics is theorised in medicine and science, and so is instrumental to the way in which ethical issues are framed in discussions about the ethics of science and technology in sport. As Gaylin (1990: 5) argues:

Ultimately Kant's writings were to produce the most profound changes in modern thinking about ourselves and our nature. His rationale for, and definition of, human worth were to become his supporting pillars on which much of modern moral philosophy would be built. Kant's position was very clear. The dignity or the worth of the human being as distinguished from all other animals was based not on our special reasoning powers, although he acknowledged we were quite different from even our closest animal relatives in this way, but on our freedom, our autonomy.

Indeed, Bayertz (1996) notes that *rational autonomy* (Leist, 1996) is the key concept for Kant, through which dignity is most clearly expressed:

> Man in the system of nature is a being of slight importance . . . but man regarded as a person – that is as the subject of morally practical reason is exalted above any price. . . . Autonomy then is the basis of [human] dignity.
> (Kant, 1785: html)

Gaylin (1990: 7) also gives this importance to Kant, arguing that:

> after Kant, literature on autonomy flourished and the concept of dignity declined. 'Dignity' was to become an accepted term in modern writing without ever having been adequately analyzed, and it always implied the Kantian definition of autonomy. One supporting fact is that, in B.F. Skinner's Beyond Freedom and Dignity, the concept of dignity is never discussed. Even the word is not present.

The US tradition of medicine is perhaps the strongest example where autonomy is considered to be the hallmark of its value structure in medicine and scientific research (Wolpe, 1997). As Caplan (1992: html) notes:

> In American medicine, respecting autonomy is the core principle used to settle disputes about the ultimate goals that ought guide the provision of care. In situations where doubt as to the goal of care exists adherence to the principle of autonomy requires clinicians to defer to the wishes and preferences of those receiving care or their surrogates even when patient choice results in forgoing likely benefits.

This tradition is reinforced by the early period of bioethics in the 1960s, from which emerged the principle-based approach typified in the classic *Principles of Biomedical Ethics* by Tom Beauchamp and James Childress, now in its fifth edition (2001) (Beauchamp and Childress, 1994). Autonomy also underpins the rationale of *informed consent*, one of the most important instruments in medical ethics and scientific research. As Harris (1999: 88) explains in relation to cloning, the real issue underpinning human dignity in cloning has to do with 'whether or not people have rights to control their reproductive destiny', thus highlighting the importance of autonomy in ethical discussions about medical technologies. Harris goes further, claiming that 'failing to permit cloning might violate principles of dignity' (1999: 89), precisely because it undermines the importance of individual autonomy.

It is within this historical context that autonomy is given such importance in the discussion about what is valuable about being human. These ideas are made explicit in a wealth of legislation for individual freedoms where the capability of being moral is presupposed by the capacity of autonomy. For example, Harris (1999: 92) explains how the US Due Process Clause outlines that:

> matters involving the most intimate and personal choices a person may make in a lifetime, choices central to a person's dignity and autonomy, are central to the liberty protected by the Fourteenth Amendment.

Such conditions are also reflected in European Union laws, which stipulate that an infringement on individual autonomy would 'have to show that more was at stake than the fact that a majority found the ideas disturbing or even disgusting' (ibid.). This is a particularly interesting requirement when applied to sport. Certainly, the prospect of genetically modified athletes provokes a feeling of revulsion in many people. Indeed, the same may be said for stem-cell research or cloning. Yet Harris' utilitarian requirement necessitates that there must be more at stake than simply this reaction. If it can be shown as more important for individuals to be allowed the autonomy to enhance themselves than it is to ensure that there are no genetically modified athletes, then the current articulation of ethics through autonomy necessitates that athletes must be granted such permissions.

Yet we ought not to be so quick to conclude that individual autonomy is justified in such contexts. Indeed, Beauchamp and Childress (1994: 126) note that:

> Respect for *autonomy* . . . has only prima facie standing and can be overridden by competing moral considerations. . . . The principle of respect for autonomy does not by itself determine what, on balance, a person ought to be free to know or do or what counts as a valid justification for constraining autonomy.

Thus it would be much more persuasive to enrich our concept of autonomy before making such conclusions.[5] Kahn (1997: 119) defines autonomy as 'the indeterminability of the individual with respect to external human will' making links with the concept of human dignity. A closer examination of Kant also reveals that his use of the concept is grounded in human rationality. Our capacity for reflective thought, Kant suggests, is an indication of our capacity to have our own interests. However, this position is not without critique and some have argued (mistakenly) that it implies concluding that persons lacking the capacity for demonstrating autonomy are not to be valued as human, such as might be said of individuals in persistent vegetative states or newborns. This argument is mistaken, since it applies the following invalid logic:

Premise 1: Human dignity is afforded by the capacity for rational thought.
Premise 2: Individuals in vegetative states do not have the ability for rational thought.
Conclusion: Individuals in vegetative states do not have human dignity.

A number of comments are necessary in relation to this argument to summarise this chapter. First, it can be recognised that the interest in framing human values by a concern for being human arises out of an historical context, whereby philosophical questions concerning the place of the human species in the world have given rise to an interest to derive concepts such as human dignity. These concepts have become foundational to medical ethical principles, though the way in which they have been theorised is often unclear. Nevertheless, the absence of human dignity does not imply an absence of human worth. While human dignity is sufficient, it is not the *only* basis upon which value may be ascribed to humans (or any entity for that matter). Importantly, it is possible to value human lives for reasons other than the fact that they are human beings, just as it is possible to value non-human entities for reasons unrelated to humanness. Finally, it is necessary to correct the misconception that lacking the facility of rationality means not being human. To support this final assertion, it is necessary to introduce and explain a further characteristic of what gives being human value: the capacity for being a *person*.

6 Personhood, identity and the ethics of authenticity

Ideas stressing the importance of personhood may be found in recent sports ethical discussions concerned with understanding the nature of competition. To assert their *respect for persons* argument, Tuxill and Wigmore (1998) describe the Kantian and Lockean origins of personhood, which use notions of *rational will* and *self-determination*. Kantian ideas have informed a substantial amount of work in sports ethics with respect to understanding what may be considered as sporting moral obligations and duties (Fraleigh, 1984b). In the context of performance enhancement, Arnold (1997: 27) notes that drug use is alarming because it calls into question the 'participant's status as a person'. Simon (1984, 1991) goes further, arguing that drug use is morally wrong because it reduces athletic competition to competition between mechanised bodies rather than total thinking, feeling and acting persons.

The central claim about the importance of personhood in sport is that sport performances are a measure of individuals. As such, the demonstration of personhood through performance is crucial to understanding its value (McNamee, 1992). This reconceptualisation of humanness as personhood responds to Schneider and Butcher's (2000) conclusion that there is no such accepted articulation of humanness. Indeed, DeLattre (1975) and Bailey (1975) opt to develop an appreciation of personhood and agency that informs later debates about the notion of agency and its role in developing conclusions about the ethical status of performance-enhancing technologies. Thus an ethical framework for performance enhancement in sport relies upon understanding the aspects of personhood that give it value. Moreover, it is this capacity for personhood that makes being human in sport valuable. This approach is not shared among sports ethicists. The reasoning applied by Tuxhill and Wigmore (1998) is distinct from others in sports ethics, which have been restricted to addressing respect as an *attitude* to be held between individuals. Previously, Simon (1984) argued that the notion of personhood is best thought of by recognising the sporting attitude as a mutual *quest* for excellence through challenge, a term also used by MacIntyre (1985). This notion of a quest implies a level of agency that makes it insufficient to conclude that *only* the quantitative achievement of an athlete matters. Rather, the manner in which that achievement has taken place is crucial to how we give value to it. Simon uses this perspective to argue that drugs reduce the sense of humanness by making the body solely responsible for the performance, as opposed to being the consequence of the athlete's resolve.

This position has attracted a number of sports ethicists to cite the morality of athletes within a MacIntyrean understanding of how practices function. On such a view, it is considered that practices require leadership from the practice communities rather than from the institutions associated with the practice (Morgan, 1994). It is the practice community which is deemed to know best about what is required in order for the practice to flourish, because the persons concerned with the practice have access to the internal goods of the sport. In contrast, Morgan continues, the institutions deal only in the extrinsic attributes of a sport, such as its participation base, administration and so on. As such, the challenge becomes finding a way to allow members of the practice community to voice their concerns in a manner that allows the possibility for change to result from such opinions. This is seen as particularly difficult, since it tends to be the bureaucrats of the institutions who have such means, rather than the community members.

Again, these ideas concerning personhood can be placed into the context of bioethics, which has discussed the concept of personhood in respect of various medical technologies. As Goodman (1988) notes, while Kant did not formulate detailed ontological criteria for humanness, he did use the concept of *personhood* in his moral philosophy (Kant, 1785). In addition, Harris (1999) notes how Kantian notions of humanness and dignity can and should lead into a discussion about what gives personhood value. With respect to genetic technologies, Harris argues that the onus must be placed on demonstrating how human dignity is challenged by technology. A strict application of Kant's Golden Rule does not suffice in this respect, as this places too great a limit on interpersonal relationships. Thus the requirement to treat individuals as 'ends in themselves' – as valuable in themselves (Downie and Telfer, 1969) – is overly demanding. As Harris (1999: 70) argues:

> almost all commercial relations people have with one another are basically instrumental . . . there is a difference between treating someone as a mere thing and recognizing his or her humanity.

As such, if it is desirable to treat people as means to our own ends in some contexts, then Harris wishes to explore what conditions legitimise such actions. Yet Williams suggests that Harris' critique conflates two different ways in which we conceptualise people (and subsequently respect them). Specifically, Williams (1973: 236) makes a distinction:

> between regarding a man's life and character from an aesthetic or technical point of view, and regarding them from a point of view which is concerned primarily with what it is for him to live that life and do these actions in that character. . . . The technical or professional attitude is that which regards the man solely under that title as 'minor' or 'agricultural labourer' or 'junior

executive', the human approach that which regards him as *a man who has* that title (among others).

Williams' position suggests that, even if we treat some people instrumentally for specific functions, we do not (necessarily) deny them a minimal level of respect in their capacity as persons. This minimal level of respect is an appreciation of them by virtue of their being persons. Thus even if we employ a plumber to fix our heating, we do not treat that person without respect while he or she is completing the task. We might even provide some minimal hospitality when in our homes by offering a drink and so on. Alternative ways of describing such minimal respect might be courtesy or good manners. Nevertheless, one can infer that Kant's concern for 'respect for persons' presupposes an understanding of what it means to be human, which Kant avoids defining through invoking an ethics of reciprocity. Sympathy for this approach is also found in Mary Warnock's work, which argues that defining *personhood* can be avoided, as the relevance of the discussion is simply as a means to ensuring protection for individuals. As such, for Warnock (1987: 3), it is far more important to 'take the direct route forward and ask whether or not human embryos have rights', rather than stalling discussions through metaphysical deliberations about humanness, which often tend to create more problems than solve them.

Yet there are many who disagree with this approach or, at least, recognise that it takes the easier route through applied philosophy, by avoiding the metaphysical assumptions which guide ethical and moral conclusions. This is evident by the breadth of philosophy that has attempted to develop a theory of personhood and, for this, we must return to the Lockean underpinnings as a point of departure. For Locke, the interest is to base personhood on what might be termed largely biological characteristics. As such, a person is:

> a thinking intelligent being, that has reason and reflection, and can consider itself as itself, the same thinking thing, in different times and places; which it does only by that consciousness which is inseparable from thinking, and, as it seems to me, essential to it: it being impossible for any one to perceive without perceiving that he does perceive. When we see, hear, smell, taste, feel, meditate, or will anything, we know that we do so. Thus it is always as to our present sensations and perceptions: and by this every one is to himself that which he calls self.
>
> (Locke, 1690: html)

For Locke, citing personhood in the context of selfhood is crucial (Gordijn, 1999), and this observation informs Kant's notions of rationality and autonomy. Through this approach, Locke illustrates the implications of personhood on the basis of person-based rights. However, Honnefelder (1996: 42) contests that this is not possible on Locke's account of personhood, since he relies upon a speciesist definition of humanness:

Locke's concept of a person is not up to the practical task which he assigns to it: where he is concerned with the establishment of rights. . . . Locke does not refer to the concept of a person, but to that of a species, which, he claims, carries normative weight because of the associated notion of creation and of God's possession of his creatures.[1]

Honnefelder is doubtful of personhood as being anything more than a practical 'ascription, by which I identify myself and others as a moral subject. This identification implies the respect for the dignity of the moral subject' (1996: 156). Arguably, Locke's limitations steer Kant's formulation of humanness into the discourse of reciprocal relationships and seeking moral personhood in such boundaries. Nevertheless, Locke's line of argumentation is extended in the work of Peter Strawson. However, Ford (1986) recognises that Strawson gives far more salience to the *body* as an integral aspect of personhood than Locke ever did.[2]

These naturalist groundings to personhood are taken to task by the works of Peter Singer, Michael Tooley, John Harris and Mary Warnock, to name a few. Singer's (1993) concerns for the speciesist Lockean position led to identifying self-consciousness as being of significance for identifying what is unique about the human person.[3] For Singer, this ascription could still permit its application to non-human persons, such as higher apes or dolphins. Lockwood (1985) furthers this concept of self-consciousness through ideas about reflexivity and the possibility to reflect on one's self and one's values as more specific criteria of personhood. Therefore, the capacity for moral perception emerges as defining what is uniquely indicative of the human person. To this criterion, Harris adds being able to recognise one's self as an independent centre of consciousness, existing over time, and with a non-determined future, as fundamental to being a person.

As Ford (1986) notes, each of these positions – from Singer to Warnock – recognise that it is possible for there to exist humans that are not persons. This is made most explicit in Michael Tooley's (1983) arguments on abortion and infanticide. Tooley (1986: 64) argues that:

> an organism possesses a serious right to life only if it possesses the concept of a self as a continuous subject of experiences and other mental states, and believes that it is itself such a continuing entity.

While much is unsaid about what constitutes a 'serious' right to life, Tooley argues that neither foetuses nor infants have any such claim, despite the *prima facie* obligations that such lives would seem to demand. In addition, Tooley concludes that, on this basis, it is possible for some animals to have a serious basis from which to claim their right to life. As such, understanding the value of humanness becomes a matter of developing a theory of personhood, since the speciesist connotations of humanness are not important. Theoretically, one does not need to be a human to be a person, even if it is often the case that being human implies personhood. Similarly, being a person does not require one to be human, since we might attribute characteristics of personhood – the morally significant aspects of a life – to non-human animals as well.

Such an approach reveals a way of understanding personhood through necessary and sufficient criteria, which are then used to justify particular ways of ascribing moral value to humans (and non-humans). This metaphysical leap has attracted some criticism. For example, following Frankfurt (1971, 1988), Dennett (1976, 1988) questions this assumption and seeks to make explicit the connection between personhood and moral value. Moving through rationality, consciousness, intentionality, reciprocity, verbal communication, and finally to self-consciousness, Dennett bases his ideas about personhood upon Frankfurt's notion of *second-order intentionality* or 'desires of the second order' (1988: 132). Thus Dennett argues that it is not sufficient to consider simple volitions as a basis for identifying personhood; it is not enough simply to have desires and beliefs. Rather, one must have the capability to form a belief about a belief. As Frankfurt (1971, 1988: 135) explains:

> It is only because a person has volitions of the second order that he is capable both of enjoying and of lacking freedom of the will. The concept of the person is not only, then, the concept of a type of entity that has both first-order desires and volitions of the second order. It can also be construed as the concept of a type of entity for whom the freedom of its will may be a problem.[4]

These ideas imply that what gives meaning to being human is the capacity for second-order intentionality. In short, it is the capacity of moral agency that gives value to being human. However, more needs to be said about moral agency and personhood before clarifying precisely what is the content of such value.

The remaining characteristic to appear consistently in definitions of personhood is *continuity*. The way in which this term is used in relation to personhood also refers to the rationale behind identifying the capacity for second-order volitions as its basis. While I am sceptical about the value of this characteristic (for reasons I will outline below), it deserves explaining since it has a significant presence within the literature about personhood. For many of the arguments that I will go on to champion, it is a necessary aspect of defining personhood and I will endeavour to demonstrate how continuity may be used in a more constructive way to how it has emerged within literature on personhood and medicine.

Continuous persons

Tooley's (1986: 64) controversial papers on abortion and infanticide approach a definition of personhood (and a right to life) based upon possessing the 'concept of a self as a continuous subject of experiences and other mental states, and believes that it is itself such a continuing entity'. Tooley (1983) outlines four essential qualities of personhood: having a non-momentary interest, rationality, being an agent and self-consciousness. Tooley also considers that the use of the different concepts 'human' and 'person' in discussions about, for example, abortion have confused the ability to understand what are the characteristics of an entity that give it moral value. Tooley concludes by stating that 'an entity that lacks such a consciousness of itself as a continuing subject of mental states does not have a right to life' (1986: 69).[5] His perspective relates closely to Derek Parfit's articulation of personhood, which states that, to be a person, a being must be self-conscious; aware of its identity and its continued existence over time (Parfit, 1984: 202).

A reason for doubting this psychological connectedness approach to personhood is found in David Hume's work (Doran, 1989). Hume (1739) argues that identity cannot be grounded in any real psychological connectedness theory, since *real* identity does not exist. Thus the concept of continuity is, in fact, misleading. This might be seen to be a rather pedantic point, since Tooley (1983) and Parfit (1984) do not necessitate that any lived *reality* has to take place in order to conclude that a human is also a person. However, it does make explicit that the perception of continuity, which derives from *believing* that one's present beliefs have some identifiable link to one's past experiences, is misleading. At most, we can make such causal links between events – or, as Hume describes, as 'resemblance and causation' (1739: html) – but we cannot make any further claims to the overall connectedness of pasts and presents, since they are only discrete occurrences.[6] Bernard Williams (1970) is also sceptical about the *psychological continuity* or *complex view*, arguing that, even if there were a break in the psychological continuity of a person, this would not entail concluding that this person ceased to exist.

While the relevance of this to the ethical discussion about genetic modification in sport may not be immediately apparent, it becomes clearer when one aspires to appeal to the existence of moral agency on the presence of a continuous life narrative. The current discussions about genetics in sport do not necessitate further inquiry into such borderline cases outlined by Tooley (1986), since our concern is with individuals for whom their psychological or physical connectedness is not in question.

Instead, our approach questions the legitimacy of an identity, through enquiring into its sense of coherency, or authenticity. Thus the test of connectedness need not rely upon memory of past events, but – drawing upon the earlier notions of second-order intentionality – *consistency with moral evaluations*. Consequently, this fundamental metaphysical link is justified by requiring that a person has second-order volitions, or *beliefs about beliefs* (Frankfurt, 1971, 1988) or what both he and Dennett (1976, 1988) call *second-order* desires. It is not sufficient simply to have beliefs; one must also have beliefs about the nature of beliefs. As Frankfurt (1971, 1988: 135) notes:

> It is only because a person has volitions of the second order that he is capable both of enjoying and of lacking freedom of the will. The concept of

the person is not only, then, the concept of a type of entity that has both first-order desires and volitions of the second order. It can also be construed as the concept of a type of entity for whom the freedom of its will may be a problem.

In addition, personhood implies a degree of connectedness between past experiences and present memories of them. It is these characteristics that give value to being human and which, subsequently, give value to being human in sport. Yet, first, it is possible to say much more about these concepts and what they tell us about the ethical limits of genetic modification in sport.

Towards authenticity, via identity

Charles Taylor (1985) adapts the concept of *second-order desires* by requesting that personhood necessitates the capacity for making *strong evaluations*. Taylor's distinction between weak and strong evaluations asserts the latter to be defining of moral agency, where the former concerns outcomes and the latter the quality of evaluations. Emphasising why moral agency is most importantly constituted by strong evaluations, Taylor introduces the relationship between evaluation and identity. As Taylor (1985: 34) states:

> the concept of identity is bound up with that of certain strong evaluations which are inseparable from myself. This either because I identify myself by my strong evaluations, as someone who essentially has these convictions; or else because I see certain of my other properties as admitting of only one kind of strong evaluation by myself, because these properties so centrally touch what I am as an agent; that is, as a strong evaluator, that I cannot really repudiate them in the full sense. For I would be thereby repudiating myself, inwardly riven, and hence incapable of fully authentic evaluation.

Taylor is able to avoid the essentialist and idealistic connotations of authenticity by isolating it as a mode of strong evaluation.[7] For Taylor (1985), identity is intelligible only insofar as some things matter and other do not. It is this distinction that gives a context to identity for Taylor, which is why the term is so crucial to moral discourse. Taylor also explains why identity is necessarily a non-naturalist term, and therefore impossible to understand in any purely descriptive manner. Consequently, Taylor rejects the approach to personhood summarised earlier by Tooley, which is typified by the quest for necessary and sufficient conditions grounded in concepts of rationality, autonomy and consciousness.

Crucial to Taylor's argument is the importance of articulacy, though this should be seen as distinct from arguments claiming that language is defining of humans. Taylor's argument is for the *depth* of articulacy, not simply the capacity of verbalisation. Thus, in comparison with the weak evaluator, Taylor (1985: 24) states that:

the strong evaluator is not similarly inarticulate. There is the beginning of a language in which to express the superiority of one alternative, the language of higher and lower, noble and base, courageous and cowardly, integrated and fragmented, and so on. The strong evaluator can articulate superiority just because he has a language of contrastive characterization.

Moreover, Taylor (1991: 33) notes that 'I want to take "language" in a broad sense, covering not only the words we speak but also other modes of expression whereby we define ourselves, including the "languages" of art, of gesture, of love, and the life.' In short, personhood entails having the capacity to articulate qualitative differences between second-order desires, not simply being able to select from a variety of preferences (weak evaluator). Only in making such efforts at strong evaluation, Taylor argues, can one claim to be embracing the possibility of *authenticity* in one's identity. In this sense, then, failing to act as persons in sport by failing to engage with the moral context of sport implies failing to take account of our authentic selves (Fairchild, 1989).

On this definition, we also see the Lockean underpinnings to Taylor's claim, distinguished by identifying the mechanism of moral agency and identity through strong evaluations.[8] Importantly, however, Taylor's aims are not Locke's utilitarian aims. Taylor does not seek the ascription of rights, as did Locke in his philosophical framework of personhood. Rather, Taylor advocates contrastive self-evaluation as a means to authentic identity, which is the basis of moral agency.

Taylor goes on to explain the importance of authenticity in his *The Ethics of Authenticity* (1991), which also responds to the *psychological-connectedness* thesis described above. His approach to understanding moral agency states that the capability of making strong evaluations relies upon a temporally connected psyche. As Taylor (1991: 105–106) argues:

> We are embodied agents, living in dialogical conditions, inhabiting time in a specifically human way, that is, making sense of our lives as a story that connects the past from which we have come to our future projects. That means (b) that if we are properly to treat a human being, we have to respect this embodied, dialogical, temporal nature.

Taylor's claim does not invoke the earlier conflicts between Parfit, Williams and others, nor does it entail their limitations. Moral agency is not discernible by deciding whether individuals who have ceased to exist in some way, and who have been subsequently resurrected, are still the same people. Rather, it is directed at those for whom we can readily accept that there has been no psychological or physical disruption. Even for such people, Taylor's argument is limited to concluding what constitutes authenticity. The reason why this is what matters about personhood is because it is authenticity that reveals an ability (or not) to engage with life-plans, to make sense of one's life, and to see clearly what kind of life one is trying to lead. In this sense, a continuity of identity is better understood as a life *narrative*, which places less importance upon the psychological or physical connectedness problems.

This way of describing authenticity seems comparable to how autonomy might be described in ethics, though Platt (1998) suggests that autonomy is too abstract a term, since it omits to consider the way in which choices are made within a complex web of relationships that constitute our everyday lives. Platt (1998) goes even further, questioning whether any decisions can really be said to be autonomous. Platt responds to Beauchamp's (1997) definition of autonomy by claiming that it is full of vague terms, such as *interference from others* and *adequate understanding*. Thus understood, what is valuable about being human is not simply being human or being an autonomous, rational agent. Indeed, it is possible to be an autonomous, rational agent, but still miss what is valuable about being human, which is the exercising of our authenticity, where this entails consistency of moral agency and an awareness of when one is departing from this consistency.

This articulation of personhood strengthens the moral basis of autonomy as an expression of human dignity (or humanness). If it is possible to understand the value of autonomy as the capacity for exhibiting some sense of authenticity in one's moral convictions, then this can provide a means for understanding what is ethically legitimate. Thus we can claim to be persons when exhibiting the capacity to make strong evaluations. Related concepts of *liberty* and *rationality* are implicit of the claims. For example, Fleming (1987: 18) argues that 'desires always presuppose consciousness'.[9] Moreover, identifying authenticity as the important characteristic of autonomy avoids the social or speciesist connotations of rationality.[10]

Yet it would be misleading to suggest that authenticity is alone in its candidacy for being a valued characteristic of humanness. For example, Bayertz (1996) raises the concept of *perfectibility* as integral to moral agency,[11] deriving in part from Christian theology and Jean-Jacques Rousseau's notion of the *perfectibility of man*. The idea stipulates that the faculty of improvement is what distinguishes humans from other entities. Alternatively, the concept of *bodily integrity* may also be relevant, particularly in relation to autonomy in medicine. However, while these terms may be integral to our moral decision making – it has already been noted that the aspiration of improving one's lot is sensible – they do not assist in drawing conclusions about what constitutes moral agency.

In sum, concluding what is ethical about genetic modification in sport relies upon understanding what is valuable about being human. To make more sense of this, the way in which humanness is given value in various legal traditions can assist. Ideas concerning human dignity are used as a basis for protecting what is important to humans. Further investigation into this concept has revealed that dignity is understood significantly as a concern for *autonomy*, which is also a guiding principle in medical ethics and scientific research. In turn, it has been argued that the importance of autonomy is best understood as the capacity for being persons, demonstrated by being capable of making strong evaluations.

In this respect, Kant's (1785) assertion for what constitutes humanness is useful but insufficient as the basis for determining ethical legitimacy. First, it invokes unnecessarily the concept of an obligation, when it is better understood as a logical consequence of being moral agents. Instead, the current argument avoids needing to explain its basis in relation to some potentially speciesist critique, particularly since the assertion does not necessitate that *only* moral agents have value. Moreover, an approach to ethics based upon Kant's notion of moral agency lacks sustainability, since it gives rise – and has given rise – to an overriding consequential approach to moral problems, most evident in medical and scientific ethics. Being a moral agent does not necessarily commit one to concluding that the avoidance of harm to others is the overriding concern about what is ethical, as is the case for a majority of ethical discussions concerning the use of new medical technologies. Rather, it requires recognising moral authenticity as the salient characteristic of being human, both within sport and outside of it. This suggests that other sporting values, such as the drive for excellence or perfection, are not constitutive of sporting value, unless they imply something meaningful about how authenticity is carried out in competition. In other words, the use of genetic modification in sport does not matter unless its use implies some deformation of the athlete's personal authenticity.

Authenticity in practice: from bioethics to sports ethics

An illustration is useful to explain how this approach to understanding ethics is important for the current discussion. Such concern for authenticity has been made explicit in bioethics, most recently in studies of mental health. Carl Elliott (1998a) has been particularly concerned with the development of *cosmetic pharmacology*, which he describes as being the use of pharmaceuticals to treat symptoms of mental illness, rather than the causes of such conditions. Elliott argues that this method of treating some conditions, and even of defining them as medical conditions, is alarming, since it provides a means for supporting an inauthentic life, where genuine reasons for sadness are conceptualised in medical terms and then treated as illnesses. As Elliott (1998a: 178) notes:

> So I want to concentrate on just this one particular sort of worry about cosmetic Prozac, the worry that Percy had, which comes down to something like this: suppose we could relieve all these patients of their sense of spiritual emptiness or alienation, these people who feel disoriented and lost in the world. Would that be a good thing, or is it sometimes better to feel bad than to feel good?

Elliott draws upon the recent concerns about psychotropic drugs, such as Prozac, explored in Peter Kramer's (1994) *Listening to Prozac* and Laurie Slater's (1998) *Prozac Diary*, among others. Kramer describes how the use of Prozac would appear to make some people feel *better than well*. Kramer recognises that this way of interpreting the effects of such drugs involves a feeling that something has always been missing in the individuals' lives and it is as if the drug restores some kind of chemical balance or normality. In so doing, Peter Kramer's patients identify their authentic selves as being *facilitated* by these drugs. Elliott is concerned that the legitimisation of such substances as a support for human happiness mis-describes the source of the unhappiness that gives rise to the need for such substances. Elliott does not claim that there are not legitimate uses of this substance for people who suffer from clinical depression, but he is concerned with 'what it does for those who aren't patients who are shy and withdrawn, or who have poor self-esteem, or who are rather compulsive' (1998b: html).

Various links may be made between Elliott's concerns and the earlier ideas on personhood. Elliott is worried that some forms of enhancement technology encourage people to seek inauthentic means to address personal or social problems. Thus the use of Prozac and the subsequent feelings of happiness or authenticity, for Elliott, can sometimes actually undermine the capacity to be authentic. It reduces an individual to a mere 'weak evaluator' (Taylor, 1985), or, as Flanagan (1990) describes, a 'simple wanton who blows whichever way the winds of his own motivational economy blow'.[12]

As applied to sport, the importance of these concerns becomes clearer where Taylor explains his critiques of modernity that give rise to a reluctance to engage with strong evaluations, which he describes as the *three malaises*: the concern for individualism, instrumental rationality, and overly restrictive political structures. As Taylor (1991: 10) describes it:

> The first fear is about what we might call a loss of meaning, the fading of moral horizons. The second concerns the eclipse of ends, in face of rampant instrumental reason. And the third is about a loss of freedom.

From this brief overview, it seems reasonable to claim that sports are considerably beset by each of the three malaises. Modern, Western sports appear highly individualistic, valued largely for quantitative (instrumental) gains in performance, and highly restricted by the political context of sport. To negotiate the three malaises – and thus to help us understand how it may be possible to maintain some degree of authenticity in sporting performances – Taylor introduces the concept *horizons of meaning.*

The way in which the athlete negotiates rational egoism with a concern for social values is, Taylor asserts, by considering horizons of meaning as part of the process of understanding one's authenticity. Recognising that individualism is not sufficient, Taylor argues how the individual can live in society, which requires compromising the self-centredness of pursuing authenticity. Consequently, personal identity cannot be separated from the way in which identity is constructed, which is through dialogue with significant others and our relationships with them.[13] On this basis, it is possible to avoid the criticism that the authenticity approach omits the fundamentally socially situated context of sport. Moreover, the argument avoids the dialectic of liberty and paternalism, and opts for one that is inspired by liberty, but which gives value to the paternalising constraints of socially situated values. Moreover, it attempts to convey how 'sport is one specific way in which we make and remake ourselves as individuals and collective agents' (Morgan, 1994: 63).

Taylor's response to the difficult question about how this functions at an individual level employs the concept of an *artist* or, more specifically, a *creator* as the manner in which one should engage with authenticity. Taylor's analogy to art is that engaging with authenticity requires discovering what is unique to one's self. It involves the creation of something new, original, as a 'revolt against convention' (1991: 65). In full, authenticity:

> (A) involves (i) creation and construction as well as discovery, (ii) originality, and frequently (iii) opposition to the rules of society and even potentially to what we recognize as morality. But it is also true, as we saw, that it (B) requires (i) openness to horizons of significance (for otherwise the creation loses the background that can save it from insignificance) and (ii) a self-definition in dialogue. That these demands may be in tension has to be allowed. But what must be wrong is a simple privileging of one over the other, of (A), say, at the expense of (B), or vice versa.
>
> (Taylor, 1991: 66)

It seems reasonable to imagine the athlete as an artist in Taylor's analysis, where the athlete is described as a creator of performances. Through engaging with sport, an athlete creates something new in the dialectical struggle with opponents or self. In so doing, the performance creates new facts, whether through breaking records, winning events or simply participating in a competition. Nevertheless, it may still be asked how this approach to ethics can function in the reality of elite sport (which, itself, Taylor might consider to be a malaise of modernity).

In the specific case of genetically modifying athletes, the question phrased from a conventional medical ethics perspective would involve asking whether athletes are entitled to such autonomy to enhance, or – in cases of prenatal modifications – whether prospective parents should be allowed the autonomy to manipulate or select the genes of their children. In contrast, the modified explanation of humanness offered here argues that answering this question relies upon knowing what kinds of ethical questions athletes confront in their sport and whether they seek ways for thinking through these problems. More generally, it requires moral agents to enquire into what kinds of people are worthwhile to bring into the world and what kinds of people genetically enhanced athletes would be. This approach rejects the idea that harm is necessary or sufficient to determine that a particular choice is ethically unacceptable. Rather, it asserts that, even if no harm to others accrues, some choices may still be ethically suspicious, because we are interested in moral agency, informed by a concern for others.

The broader implications of this conclusion are that it challenges the assumption that people are necessarily moral agents by virtue of being human.

To explain: it might be concluded that my argument is of little use to the problem about genetically modified athletes. I began by claiming that to understand whether or not genetic modification is ethical, it is first necessary to understand what is valuable about being human. To this, I have argued that being a moral agent (or strong evaluator) is what determines our answer. Supposedly, then, our concern is only whether or not athletes are, in fact, moral agents. Yet such a conclusion may not be particularly useful in the sporting context where the pragmatic implications of knowing whether persons are moral agents are insurmountable. For example, this approach does not sit well with the process of testing athletes to see if they are doping. Moreover, it might entail concluding that athletes who are genetically modified are actually acting morally.

My broader suggestion is that, on many more occasions than might be assumed, individuals *do not* act morally or ethically. This does not mean to say that people act immorally, but suggests that moral deliberation at all does not tend to encroach upon our daily activities. As such, many people go through their lives only rarely being confronted with moral dilemmas – with what makes us human. A similar argument may be made in respect of athletes in relation to performance modification. Athletes have become disenfranchised from their moral character by the emphasis on commercial gains and the overriding value attached to quantitative performance achievements, the dangers of which are also recognised by Juengst (1998: 40):

> If the extrinsic value of being causally responsible for certain accomplishments is high enough (like professional sports salaries), the intrinsic value of the admirable practices that a particular institution was designed to foster may even start to be called into question.

So what should the moral agent in sport think about genetic modification? Taylor tells us that, because the search for authenticity is embedded within a social dialogical context, it is possible to observe some trends of concern, or what he would describe as being relatively clear horizons of meaning. Building upon Lockean-inspired social contractarianism and popular sovereignty, the concern emerges for universal rights and the 'ordinary life' (1991: 45). Taylor goes on to employ such terms as *dignity* as being the manifestation of these *horizons of meaning*, which, despite being conceptually problematic, have emerged as a basic and common good. Yet it still remains difficult to assert what are the *horizons of meaning* that might inform the athlete's choice. Indeed, a similar problem arises for prospective parents when choosing what might be worthwhile genetic modifications for their children. In sport, one might be tempted to describe sources of meaning through such terms as fair play, honour, and even technologisation. Indeed, this latter term is important, since it does not neglect the possibility that Taylor's approach might require the embracing of new technology, as technology becomes an increasing aspect of the meaning of modern-day sport.

To inform this conclusion, Butryn (2002) outlines this perspective in the sporting context, arguing that Taylor's authenticity allows the freedom for athletes to select *cyborgisation* on account of striving for their own life-goals, their inner authenticity. For example, Butryn uses Simon's (1984) example of drugs that can make an athlete more relaxed for performance, which is a consequence of using beta-blockers. Butryn asserts that an athlete might claim to want such drugs to be able to perform at his or her *authentic* level of functioning. This argument conveys a similar idea to the way in which Elliott (1999) and Kramer (1994) describe the use of SSRIs, such as Prozac, for which people claim they feel *normal* when they are using such drugs. In the sporting case, Butryn argues that this is acceptable providing that athletes can situate their pursuit of authenticity in the values of their specific practice for which it should have meaning. What remains to be explained is whether such contexts do give value to the use of such performance modification or, more succinctly, to better understand the horizons of meaning that athletes must recognise to know whether their choice to enhance has value. This does not mean that it is ethically acceptable to choose such enhancements, but that it must be a choice valued by more than the particular athlete and, importantly, not out of an interest to gain an advantage over other competitors.

In relation to performance modification, two horizons of meaning are particularly important: the distinction between therapeutic and enhancing technology, and the theorising of fair play. As such, the remaining task of this ethical view is to investigate these two parameters of sports ethics, so as to understand what limits might be placed on the genetic modification of athletes.

7 Virus, disease, illness, health, well-being . . . and enhancement

On the basis of this modified model of humanness, the ethical approach to genetically modified athletes must depart from recognising the possibility for athletes to be moral agents. If such a capacity is deserved, then we must ask what kinds of dialogue such ethical engagement might entail. It requires athletes to question the value of genetic modification in sport, taking into account the possible harms and benefits. In short, the principle involves athletes acting as moral agents, asking whether genetic modification in sport is ethically unsound for sport and why this might be so.

Potentially, this asserts a rather naïve perspective about the world of sport. Even if athletes play some part in making their own ethical conclusions, sport is governed largely by non-athletes or past athletes who hold political positions in sport. In addition, the matter is further complicated by the possibility that there might be a number of different perspectives in the athletic community. There might be some athletes who are more interested in using technology to improve human performance and others who perceive athletic performance as strictly an unaided human performance. The latter may even argue that present levels of technological acceptance in sport overly neglect the importance of the human. Given that sports are practices that rely on agreed-upon and shared rules (Arnold, 1997; Feezell, 1988) in order to operate, this may cause some problems.

However, the ethical approach from autonomy does not need to imply such a chaotic system. Instead, it might merely call for the creation of new kinds of sports, which distinguish contests by the level of technological acceptance. Thus it might entail creating sports where genetic modification is embraced and maintaining other versions of sport where it is not. Such a suggestion may be sufficient in specific cases of technological change where there is an obvious use of different technology. For example, if athletes wanted to use different kinds of tennis racket, it would be possible to arrange different competitions where different kinds of racket are used. However, for methods of doping this might be more problematic, since the modification is potentially invisible (it is not necessarily possible to see whether or not genetic modification has taken place). As such, the creation of distinct competitions would not avoid the problem of athletes trying to gain an advantage over other competitors by using enhancements in contests where such enhancements are prohibited. Nevertheless, Juengst makes a similar suggestion to create different contests when discussing the ethical status of enhancements in sport. He suggests:

> Either the institutions must redesign the game (e.g. education or sports) to find new ways to evaluate excellence that are not affected by available enhancements, or they must prohibit the use of the enhancing shortcuts. Which route an institution should take depends on the possibility and practicality of taking either, because ethically they are equivalent.
>
> (Juengst, 1998: 40)

In making this claim, Juengst suggests that there are no ethically preferable games and that, in one sense, the rules underpinning a game are relatively arbitrary. Thus there is no ethical preference between different swimming competitions, where one version allows athletes to wear flippers on their feet and the other does not. These are merely different kinds of activities. It is in this sense that Juengst describes the choice as ethically *equivalent*, though this omits to consider the non-sporting implications of such choices, such as the impact on competitors, the possible disadvantages that one choice might give rise to for some competitors. The change in javelin styles in the 1980s is one such example where the governing body was faced with the difficult decision of having to change the kinds of javelin being thrown, on account of the practical limitations of throwing fields. In these circumstances, the change in javelin type did have an influence on what it means to be a good javelin thrower and in that sense did disadvantage some athletes (Glad, 1986).

Yet one can argue that this kind of decision making frequently (and necessarily) already takes place for sports. The emergence of new events or new sports has often taken place alongside the development of a new kind of technology. In addition, sports have often sought to integrate new technologies, thus redesigning the games in some small but significant manner (Tenner, 1996). The task then is for athletes to determine the legitimacy of different kinds of performance modifications. Some basic observations can be made in this regard.

First, it is possible to conclude that sporting values can be maintained by accepting some but not necessarily all kinds of performance modification. However, it is not yet clear whether the acceptance of any kind of performance modification is necessarily unethical for sport. It makes sense that the use of a motorbike in a foot race compromises the validity of comparing the ability of a user with a non-user. Yet it would not compromise the equality of a competition if all athletes were using a motorbike. Rather, it merely changes the kinds of activity and the kinds of skills being assessed. There is a further clarification that must be made for this conclusion to withstand critique, since it prioritises a particular way of framing the ethical issue arising from such changes. Such change may not be detrimental to the fairness of a contest, in the sense that each competitor will be attempting the same task. However, it is possible that such changes would undermine the meaning of a contest. For example, if the 100m sprint in athletics were to permit the use of motorcycles, then it might be concluded that a race of 100m is no longer a valuable contest – it might not tell us anything about the relative skills of athletes.

In this sense, then, the choice to modify a sport is not ethically equivalent, unless there exists a test between competitors that reveals some athletically relevant difference between them. Even if one can recognise that some constitutive rules are historically arbitrary and that equally good games could be had if the rules were slightly different, it is not the case that *any* kinds of rules would work. For example, the game of soccer could still have value if there were twelve instead of eleven players. However, if no other parameters of the game were altered, a game of soccer involving 100 players would no longer make sense. While a way of legitimising this change would be to alter other aspects of the contest to make it a meaningful game, soccer would still be transformed into a different kind of game and would no longer make sense as it is currently understood. Although this would preserve the competitive logic of the contest, these kinds of changes might be seen as unethical, since they undermine the value that is given to the game by members of its practice community.

It is possible for athletes to recognise that they (and sports policy makers) are not always consistent in their choice to use performance-enhancing technology and for this still not to matter. Sometimes technology is integrated into competition in some innovative and interesting way, such as through the development of the klapskate in speed skating.[1] At other times, similar kinds of performance-enhancing technology are prohibited because it is seen as unethical or undesirable for the sport in question, as was the case with the spaghetti-strung tennis racket, which appeared to provide an unreasonably high level of top spin that an athlete could exert on the ball (Gelberg, 1996a). This varied way of evaluating performance enhancers arises, in part, because athletes are uncomfortably juxtaposed to enhancement where it is valuable, but only when it is achieved through specific means. Delimiting the legitimacy of means is the central problem. Credit is given to innovative approaches of performance modification, though not usually when it is to the exploitation of other athletes. Consequently, part of the question facing the community is whether to, and by how much they should, restrict the personal freedom to use various performance modifiers.

Therapy vs. enhancement

Within anti-doping, one of the central factors of legitimacy has been the distinction between therapy and enhancement. As was outlined above, WADA has now eliminated therapeutic substances from its banned list, concerned only for those methods that are performance enhancing. For many athletes, this distinction constitutes the ethical threshold for performance modification. However, the distinction is not straightforward to make, which is part of the reason for recognising that morally autonomous agents in sport can also be inconsistent with their choices to use performance-enhancing technology – and that this does not make them morally insensitive agents.

Hoberman (1988) argues that delimiting a meaningful distinction between therapy and enhancement in anti-doping policy has become (and perhaps has always been) irreconcilable, to a point where the IOC should, for example, consider redefining testosterone as a natural product in order to legalise it. Hoberman sees that part of the problem with doping is the strong social ambiguity about the appraisal of drugs, and inconsistencies abound, reflected by the varying social statuses of alcohol and nicotine. Houlihan (1999) asserts a similar view, though he adds that the reason why the drugs in sports debate has remained so stagnant is that sport operates in a logic that does not correspond with the broader social values with which drug use in sport is often associated. Thus if it were not for the perceived social deviancy of drug use in broader society, there would be less resistance or concern about the use of doping in sport.

The problem is not simply that there is trouble distinguishing between therapy and enhancement, where the former are ethical and the latter unethical, though in some cases it is specifically this problem. It is also a problem of delimiting *which kinds of therapy* and *which kinds of enhancement* are acceptable, since even within each of these categories there is room for concluding varying degrees of acceptability. One particularly problematic example arises in respect of genetically engineering people to be more resistant to a disease. For example, a genetic vaccine could be used to treat such cases as flu, herpes or malaria. In this case it is unclear whether this is to be perceived as enhancing or therapeutic, since there will be no current condition that is being treated (Glover, 1984).

A further problem is that sporting enhancements do not take place solely within competitive circumstances. Rather, performance modification in sport must be seen as part of a continual process of development from youth and throughout adulthood. Most athletes begin their elite career very early, while they are still physically developing, and it is within this context that the concepts of therapy and enhancement must more broadly be understood. Certainly it is possible to isolate the adult, elite athlete and argue what is acceptable, though again this is problematic as even an adult athlete is engaged in a continual process of biological development through intensive training.

An important start to identifying the distinction is to recognise that what is ethical for athletes – particularly in relation to performance modification technology – is heavily underpinned by distinctions between therapy and enhancement made in medicine. Thus what is considered to be medically ethical outside of sport has some influence upon what is ethical within sport. Sports physicians and medics must continue to conduct themselves ethically, where this means maintaining what is ethical from a medical perspective.[2] Juengst (1998) has concerns about applying the medical ethical model to contexts where it is not appropriate. Speaking specifically in the context of performance enhancement in sport, Juengst is concerned that the medical model is gradually appearing in contexts for which it was not designed. Juengst describes this as a *medicalisation* of ethics, though in sport the validity of this concern is in question precisely because the kinds of alteration under discussion tend to fall within the responsibility of medical ethics. Juengst is reluctant to apply the medical therapy/enhancement distinction to the sporting case, since this undermines the internal logic of sports. For the very reason that athletes are not patients, they should not be beholden to the same kinds of ethical distinction that exist within healthcare and medicine. Given that the process of administering performance-modifying technologies in sport relies upon the medical industry, it is unrealistic to propose a view of sport that does not recognise its relationship to medicine. Nevertheless, Juengst's concern is for the way in which the doping issue has been appropriated by the medical profession, which has imbued it with inappropriate requirements and values.

Within sport, there is a strong sense that therapeutic methods of performance alteration are ethically acceptable, while enhancements are not. Athletes are permitted to compete in sports using drugs that confer performance enhancement, when (and only when) they are prescribed by medical doctors. Where such diagnoses are not made – i.e. where an athlete does not have a genuine (and recognised) medical condition – they may not compete legally while using medication.

One of the most recent cases where this kind of controversy arose was at the Salt Lake Olympic Winter Games in 2002. Bronze medal winner for slalom skiing, Alain Baxter, tested positive for methamphetamine, a stimulant with unconfirmed effects, though the substance is alleged to affect the central nervous system, increasing heart and blood pressure and affecting sensory judgement. Baxter claims that he inadvertently ingested this substance, which goes by the product name Dianobol, through a nasal decongestant – specifically, a Vicks inhaler – which, in the USA has different ingredients from the same product found in the UK. In the UK, the product does not contain this banned substance and Baxter claims that he did not know this and bought the US product while in Salt Lake City, expecting its ingredients to be identical. His story is not untypical of a number of similar pleas of innocence from athletes in the past five years. However, for the IOC's anti-doping policy, this matters not in the least, since its rule of *strict liability* deems that athletes are responsible for what is found in their bodies, regardless of how it got there.

In this case, while some importance is given to the potentially harmful effects of the substance, the major concern is for its performance-enhancing properties. Had Baxter received a doctor's certificate recognising that he has a condition which warranted the use of such a decongestant, then there would have been no problem, because this would be a therapeutic use of the substance. Yet one more recent case brings into question whether the rules are always upheld in this very rigorous manner, as the strict liability measure suggests. At the Commonwealth Games in 2002, the 100m sprint Gold medal-winning athlete, Kim Collins, was found to have Salbutamol in his body, a drug used to treat asthma. As it transpired, Collins had received a doctor's certificate for the substance found in his body, though it was not disclosed to the officials at the correct time. As such, Collins was, technically, engaged in illegal doping. The position taken by the Commonwealth Games Federation (CGF) on this matter is rather interesting. Instead of adhering to the rules, the Federation proceeded to make an ethical judgement based upon the specific circumstances. As such, the CGF allowed the athlete to retain his medal, which was the first ever Commonwealth medal for his country, the Caribbean island of St Kitts and Nevis.[3] The position contrasts greatly with the decision taken by the IOC in relation to Baxter's case and many others like it.

This seeming anomaly might speak more to the different kinds of agencies that are behind the decisions – the IOC versus the CGF – than to much else. However, the important point is that there are *even* inconsistencies about the therapeutic use of doping methods, which bring into question the basis for assuming that it is tolerable for athletes to use drugs (medication) when they are ill. Sport is not the only context where this distinction becomes difficult to apply. A central part of what follows will elucidate the medical ethical underpinning of this distinction, by drawing upon other cases in medicine where the distinction between therapy and enhancement causes problems. In so doing, it is expected that the sporting debate will become far richer in helping to clarify the inconsistencies and the specific points of disagreement that might be raised in relation to policy on these matters.

The language of health

The title of this chapter intends to highlight the idea that the distinction between therapy and enhancement is far more complex than these two terms would suggest. It also involves the need to understand concepts such as virus, health, disease and illness. The title also suggests that there may be some continuum of terms which have different kinds of meaning that correspond with differing kinds of ethical reaction when applied to sport specifically and medicine in general.[4] Part of the problem raised by making ethical distinctions between therapy and enhancement is that it relies upon this complex discourse invoking various concepts, such as disease, pathology, illness, viruses, normalcy, naturalness, species-typical functioning, flourishing, health, artificiality and enhancement. These, and other, terms are often used in a rather muddled fashion when talking about the proper use of medicine (or the proper role of performance in sport).[5] Recent research has produced a vast number of papers in medical ethical journals with titles that reflect the inconsistencies of these concepts and the problems they raise for the medical justification of treatments. While the concept of enhancement is of most interest to the current discussion, it must be understood in the context of the distinctions between it and other health-related terms found within the medical discourse of which, I argue, it is a part.

In addition, the various terms demonstrate some trend from being predominantly biological to being highly imbued with social meaning, which, in turn, give rise to questioning the medical justification to alter such characteristics. Questioning this aspect of the therapy/enhancement distinction is an important and relevant part of the discussion about genetic modification from a bioethical and a sports ethical perspective. If one accepts that the realisation of genetically predisposed conditions depends largely on the interaction of genes with the environment, then there might be even less reason to accept many forms of diagnosis as medical rather than social.[6]

As some indication of how this discussion becomes further confused, sports policy makers have also tended to use such terms as *natural* and *artificial* in the ethical rhetoric surrounding drug use, as a basis for discussing the legitimacy of performance modifiers (Houlihan, 1999). These terms continue to be used in a rather *ad hoc* manner and are often given as an intuitive response to the ethical status of new technologies,[7] even though they do not really contribute to anti-doping regulations or have much credibility in critical sports ethics (Arnold, 1997). For many years, distinctions of legality have been premised upon what is natural or artificial to the human, which is still not entirely eliminated from anti-doping policy. Yet basing the ethical distinction on these terms is problematic for philosophers, since it appears to require asserting some definition of human nature which is essentially contested. Asking what is natural requires being able to distinguish it from what is artificial. This is particularly difficult in sport, since the very practice of sport might be described as artificial or technological. As Blake (1996: 140) notes, 'the body of the athlete is no longer (if it ever was) a self-contained biological unit'. Everywhere in sport it is possible to identify artifice, and it often plays a vital role in constituting the performance, either through training mechanisms or in competition. In addition to this problem, establishing what is natural does not necessarily imply anything meaningful about what is ethical. Consequently, it is of limited use as a basis for rejecting innovations or discerning moral differences. Yet arguments founded on a statement about what is biologically natural continue to be made in relation to medical interventions.

Even within medicine, the positions about the meaning of disease, health or enhancement are also contested. As Caplan (1992: html) states:

> another reason for the relative absence of discussions of the definition of health and disease is that when there is a lack of consensus about the appropriate classification of particular traits, states or behaviors as constituting instances of either disease or health the disagreements sometimes become so heated that there is little incentive to join what may appear to more closely resemble a fray rather than a discussion. There is still disagreement about the scope or application of the concepts of health, disease or normality to gambling, sexual promiscuity, pre-menstrual syndrome, hyperactivity or homosexuality. The battles over the classification of these behaviors and traits have been heated and fierce (Caplan and Engelhardt, 1981; Bayer, 1981; Engelhardt and Caplan, 1987). Uncertainty about whether or not to attempt to treat short stature in children, low blood sugar and hypertension have also produced heated controversies as to their disease or health classification and, consequently, the appropriateness or inappropriateness of therapeutic intervention. Controversy about the scope and domain of the concepts of health and disease sometimes is so divisive that it may seem prudent to some to simply avoid asking questions about

the application of concepts such as health and disease to new knowledge in the area of human heredity.

In this context, it is possible to discern quite oppositional opinions about the distinction between therapy and enhancement; one that may be termed *biological determinism*, and another that may be called *social constructivism*.[8] However, this distinction has been labelled in a variety of ways, such as *non-normative* or *naturalist* vs. *normative*. The first argues that there is an observable biological basis for concluding why certain medical interventions are strictly within the proper interest of medicine, which is to repair and make well people who suffer from some form of dysfunction.

This *biological-determinist* position asserts that the line between therapy and enhancement is not difficult to draw at all, since it is possible to identify biological markers for what constitutes disease and dysfunction. Notably, Christopher Boorse (1975, 1977) pursues this biological hard-line, proposing his Biostatistical Theory (BST), which argues that health is merely the absence of disease and that it is possible to determine what is species-typical functioning as constitutive of a healthy organism. On this view it is possible to observe a value-free definition of what constitutes health, based upon species-typical functioning. For example, monogenic (single-cell) diseases such as sickle-cell anaemia (SCA), cystic fibrosis (CF) or Huntington's disease can be described without any recourse to environmental influence. As Glannon (2001: 19–20) explains, SCA is a disease caused by:

> a mutation in the allele coding for hemoglobin, the oxygen-carrying protein in red blood cells. Two abnormal copies of the allele (one from each parent) cause the individual's red blood cells to become deformed, leading to blockage of blood vessels throughout the body. This results in acute pain and disability early in life and often an early death.

This kind of explanation is all that can be said about what makes something a disease, according to the biological-determinist perspective.

Conversely, the *social constructivist* argues that concepts such as disease, health and enhancement derive from socially prescribed values and that the scientific basis for many claims to what constitutes disease is poorly founded. Moreover, it critiques the biological-determinist approach, arguing that it entails treating similar conditions differently and has less concern for conditions that place individuals in a disadvantageous position (Daniels, 1992).

Struggling to negotiate this distinction, Caplan (1992) poses the question: '*What is disease?*', after having identified that science also struggles to distinguish between such terms as health, disease and normality. One case that illustrates how this problem can arise in relation to medical disease is Turner's syndrome, which, as Post explains, 'in girls, results in shortness, infertility, and laterally displaced nipples' (1991: 230). In such a case, the disease is not life-threatening, nor does it shorten life span, though it is medically recognised as a disease, and consequently is necessary to correct or treat. This example brings into focus the idea that medical diagnoses are value laden, since the correction of this syndrome would be largely for social rather than health reasons.

To this, Caplan adds that there are two points of contention when discussing the meaning of disease. The first has to do with 'the role played by the determination of normality in the identification of disease'; the second concerns 'the role played by values in the definition of disease' (html). With respect to the former, Caplan notes that many physicians consider *difference* to indicate disease and so fail to recognise that variation is inherent within species, and that it is merely extremes of difference (at the end of the scale where they are least functional) which have come to be recognised as disease.

This normative labelling of biological conditions is problematic for Caplan, since it transgresses into the moral labelling of biological states. This is concerning, since it tends to be used in a way that devalues disease-ridden individuals, when the most that may be said of such people is that, sometimes, the value associated with a condition might or might not correspond with the interests of the individual. As an example, Caplan considers that shortsightedness has the disadvantageous connotations of disease only if one wishes to spend a day out hunting rather than, say, in a library reading. Barilan and Weintraub concur, adding that 'the decline of many diseases such as tuberculosis is clearly linked to improved standards of living and not to the introduction of effective medical treatments' (2001: 321). Such a perspective stresses the importance of social values and change for determining what constitutes disease.

A further example of how the medical diagnosis of something as a disease can be socially constructed is found in the nineteenth-century appraisal of *masturbation*. Engelhardt's (1974/1999) analysis of how masturbation came to be diagnosed as an illness is extensive, arguing that the perception developed out of a suspicion that sexual activity was somehow debilitating. Engelhardt notes, that this is not only a nineteenth-century problem of bad medicine. In the twentieth century we have also seen scientific work endeavouring to find solutions for women who have the *disease* of frigidity or the inability to have an orgasm. One of Engelhardt's main concerns about this discourse is that 'Medicine turns to what has been judged to be naturally ugly or deviant, and then develops etiological accounts in order to explain and treat in a coherent fashion a manifold of displeasing signs and symptoms' (1974/1999: 11). Similar claims have been made (in the recent past) in relation to homosexuality and criminality. These various normative arguments give due reason for recognising that the labelling of a condition as a disease can sometimes be influenced greatly by social and moral values. This is not to say that there is no biological basis from which to identify dysfunctionalities or that sickness is somehow merely a sociological circumstance. Rather, these examples serve to identify that medicine is not solely a biological discourse and that there is a social context to medicine that is also imbued with moral language.

Engelhardt also makes this argument in the same place as considering what is problematic about recognising masturbation as disease. He argues that, 'although vice and virtue are not equivalent to disease and health, they bear a direct relation to these concepts. Insofar as a vice is taken to be a deviation from an ideal of human perfection, or "well-being", it can be translated into disease language' (ibid.).

Negotiating the distinction

These categorical distinctions have been unfortunate, and far too often over-stated. It is unlikely that a social constructivist would consider that there is *no* biological basis for many medical conditions, or that there is nothing physically or mentally debilitating about them. Equally, a biologist could recognise that the everyday experience of disease could be made better (or even negligible) for many people by society being made more accommodating. Thus being confined to a wheelchair need not be a disability if the world is built to accommodate such ways of functioning. These are not complicated or contentious claims.

Similarly, despite all the best intentions to rectify the problem, a normativist could not deny that suitable accommodations are made for all kinds of debilitating condition. For this reason, some importance must be given to medical decisions that might be taken to try and relieve suffering. Yet a hard-line biologist would recognise that it is possible to lessen the severity of suffering for people with some conditions through social intervention, rather than relying upon medically corrective treatments.

This reveals a further distinction and new term that might either confuse the discussion even more or reveal some central distinction. Potentially, the social-constructivist argument could amount to nothing more than a problem with such terms as *dysfunction* or *disability*, which tend more to focus on the social inconvenience of disease (Glannon, 2001), rather than describe some definition of what constitutes disease. Thus the social constructivist might accept that somebody with a biological disease might or might not be disabled. This is of particular concern for Cherry (2000: 519) who adds that:

> To describe a patient as 'having a disease' is to advance not merely a claim about factual data, or even simply a value judgment, but to fashion social expectations. To characterize an individual as ill represents a claim that he has a difficulty or dysfunction that ought to be solved and that this problem can be explained in medical terms.

On this view, the social constructivist might accept that a biological definition of disease is possible, providing it is acknowledged by the biologist that the *disease*[9] experienced by the person can be minimised to a point where it eliminates the descriptors of dysfunction and disability. From here, the discussion may be seen as becoming merely etymological, where disease might require replacing with such terms as abnormality, irregularity or improper functioning. However, it is only the latter of these that does not have any socially pejorative connotation. Yet this is insufficient as a conclusion, since it amounts only to finding a term that does not have some socially negative meaning to describe something that is biological. Therefore, we might replace abnormal, irregular or improper with (perhaps ideally) a term that is invented. This is partially what has taken place in the move from using such terms as cripple, invalid or handicapped. This replacement implies shifting the use of language to undefined terms, when in the end this new language will again come to be value laden (Ayabe and Tan, 1995). The goal of such changes in language is not merely to continually shift the way in which we describe people with disabilities, but to avoid using such terms where they correspond with some negative or derogatory evaluation.

Perhaps a mediating term for the biologists and social constructivists could be *illness*, which Scott (1984) considers must be understood entirely as a matter of physical malfunctioning. On a similar view, Silvers (1998) argues that the role of medicine is therapeutic, since it aims to reduce disadvantage suffered on the basis of biological differences. Yet, even here there might be problems. Boyd notes that the origin of the word *ill* derives from *evil* and tends to have had meanings associated with '"wickedness, depravity, immorality" or "unpleasant-ness, disagreeableness, [or] hurtfulness"' (2000: 9). Moreover, McKnight (1998) develops Fulford's (1989) view on illness, arguing that illness is value laden.

Thus we have once again a situation where the terms are unable to distinguish between the social connotation and the biological component of the condition. However, Boyd (2000) also outlines that the modern medical definition of illness tends to refer to a feeling of being unhealthy, thus placing the emphasis upon the *perception* of the person said to be ill, rather than on objective biological characteristics.

This is particularly useful given the earlier moral agency argument, since it reinforces the role of the individual to make the judgement. However, it does not entirely satisfy the biological determinist, who would surely claim that a biological abnormality is disease, regardless of whether the person feels ill. We know this not to be true, since there are various instances of abnormality or disease where we do not readily identify the sufferers as being diseased or ill. For example, one of the most obvious conditions is that of pregnancy, which, medic-ally, may be understood as being a state of illness, though it is accompanied by a process recognised to be natural and thus the symptoms are understood as side effects of this condition, rather than as being symptoms of illness (Chadwick, 1987).

Instead, Boyd introduces the concept of *sickness* as the social manifestation of illness, thus placing the emphasis on how an individual is perceived by others. This term has a useful connotation, since the presence or absence of sickness is often a way of masking or revealing disease. A number of chronic diseases, such as arthritis, are not necessarily observable in persons. As such, they might not be perceived as being sick, though they might feel in ill health. Boyd (2000: 9) concludes:

> Disease then, is the pathological process, deviation from a biological norm. Illness is the patient's experience of ill health, sometimes when no disease can be found. Sickness is the role negotiated with society.

This attempt at distinguishing the meaning of different terms relating to disease demonstrates the relatedness of the concept *health*. Here, the disputes become further heated, since there are a number of ways in which one can understand health.

At this point, it is useful to restate that the inquiry seeks to find some distinction between therapy and enhancement in order to conclude what kinds of application of medical technologies are acceptable in sport. So far, it has been questioned whether the therapy/enhancement distinction is sufficient and argued that it is necessary to pursue further the difference between these terms and those in between. It is particularly appropriate to reclarify this now, as health is often seen as the mid-point term, where being *better than well* (Kramer, 1994) or enhanced goes beyond it, and being *sick* is to be less than healthy.

Similar to disease, illness and sickness, health is also a term that can be articulated with different connotations from each of the seemingly oppositional perspectives of biological determinism and social constructivism. Moreover, health is the key term upon which disputes between these two perspectives have emerged. In many cases, in endeavouring to derive the proper role of medicine, and therefore its limits, health has arisen as the major point of contention. Again, this restates the initial problem of deciding how to justify some modifications to biology and how to reject others. Yet this is only a partial explanation for why health has become central to a social discourse on medicine. It is also a reflection of the way in which the medical profession has evolved, from being relatively positivistic and impersonal, to being more concerned with well-being and individual needs.

The World Health Organisation (WHO) defines health as a 'state of complete physical, mental and social well-being, and not merely the absence of disease or infirmity' (WHO, 1948: html), though Boyd (2000) believes this is far too ambitious. Boyd's argument is particularly interesting for current purposes, since his challenge to the definition does not have to do with it being biological or social. Rather, his concern is for the broader conditions that do not fit within the narrow use of terms found within the WHO definition. As Boyd (2000: 12) states:

> Nor is the fact that a condition is unwanted enough to describe it as ill health: it may be the normal infirmity of old age for example and again a condition's abnormality is not enough either – a disability or deformity may be abnormal, but the person who has it may not be unhealthy; and much the same may apply to someone who has had an injury. . . . And things are even more complicated when assessing mental ill health. Abnormal states of mind may reflect minority, immoral or illegal desires which are not sick desires.

Yet this reveals that Boyd's disagreement is with the mixed use of terms implied by using the concept of health indiscriminately. As he says, the WHO is probably 'aiming in the right direction' (ibid.). Nordenfelt (1998) makes a similar claim, again noting that the WHO definition is too ambitious, since it proposes that complete well-being can be an achievable state. One perspective that is implied by these statements is that a person-centred approach to understanding the experience of disease or ill health is important in order to ensure that medical needs are met. This perspective is concerned broadly for *well-being* as an open-ended concept rather than one that is described by fulfilling a prescribed number of conditions. Although the term has not often been used in relation to distinguishing between therapy and enhancement, it fits with the normative approach to this distinction. Indeed, it corresponds with the WHO definition by recognising that health is not determined solely by the physiological manifestation of disease or illness, but more to do with the equally fuzzy concept of well-being. Such an approach is particularly appealing from the perspective of understanding and defining mental health, where the biological/social distinction is even more difficult to discern. Yet well-being is an equally problematic concept to isolate as a basis for distinguishing what is the legitimate role of medicine, since it can require asserting some objective conceptualisation of the 'good life' (Downie *et al.*, 1996).

From well-being to enhancement

The conceptual distinction between promoting well-being and enhancement is not great, though the prospect of the latter raises even greater worries for the biological determinist, who now finds renewed friendships with the social constructivist, who also has problems with accepting enhancement technology as a valued application of medical technology. For many, enhancing humans implies a frivolous desire, contrasted with the necessity of medical treatment. Given this way of perceiving enhancements and the risk implied by medical intervention, it is not surprising that they are of little interest to funding priorities in healthcare systems. Consequently, it is also not surprising that medical enhancements for sport would be given little value by medical practitioners and ethicists. However, while society might give value to enhancement, this does not make it a priority for the funding of research for such purposes. While one might have an intuitive Huxlean wariness about enhancements, Cole-Turner notes that the problem is not that we (in the West) are against enhancements; it is that we are 'enhancement enthusiasts' (1998: 153). Yet the concern is that this interest in optimising health has transgressed into an obsession with body sculpting and working out, so-called *cosmetic* modifications. We seek breast reduction, penis enlargement, colonic irrigation, life extension and drugs to clear our minds as if this is what enhancing our lives means.

At an etymological level, there is something paradoxical about questioning the moral status of enhancement technologies. By definition, enhancements are beneficial and desirable; otherwise they would not be enhancing. However, it is not wise to conclude the moral distinction on this simple point, since the crucial matter is only shifted towards wanting to understand better what would count as an enhancement. This clarifies what is problematic about the ethical discourse concerning health, disease and enhancement. For each of these terms, the biological determinist and social constructivist can make a case which explains either of their perspectives to their own advantage. Thus the biological determinist would argue that enhancements (whatever they might be) refer to *aesthetic modifications* (Daniels, 1992), which have nothing to do with health, suffering or disease in the biological sense of each of these terms. On this view, the biological determinist would surely conclude that genetic modifications for sport, or any modifications that involve the use of medical technology or processes, have no value or importance. From this perspective, such modifications should not be made to the athlete, since an aesthetic choice of wanting to be good at sport is not a good enough reason for medical intervention.

Conversely, the social constructivist might argue that enhancements for sport are not necessarily different from other kinds of bodily modifications, which are supposedly justified on the basis of a concern for health. As such, it is not sufficient for medicine to devalue such alterations on the basis of their not being medically justifiable. The stronger assertion is that medical justification is not a valid point of departure in this case. Rather, the discussions should be more attuned to the needs of the individual seeking the enhancement in their unique social context. Consequently, the social constructivist would remove this therapy/enhancement distinction, considering its formulation to be nonsensical.

The social-constructivist argument highlights the importance of the individual's choice in relation to the modification, thus seeking to eliminate the bias arising from the value-laden connotations of therapies/enhancements. This problem becomes particularly acute in relation to a number of cases and is made very clear by cases of mental illness. In such instances, the ability to assert a biological-determinist perspective on what counts as sickness becomes even more tenuous. The case of selective serotonin reuptake inhibitors (SSRIs) raises the question as to whether medicine has overstepped its role and begun to treat social problems rather than biological conditions.[10] For example, Ritalin is prescribed to treat a condition called Attention Deficit-Hyperactivity Disorder (ADHD) and is used to improve concentration. However, as Elliott (1998b: html) notes:

> there is some evidence that it also improves attention and focus in children who don't have ADHD. Whether that is the case or not, it is certainly true that the annual U.S. production of Ritalin increased by 500 per cent from 1990 to 1995, and an estimated 2.6 million people are now taking Ritalin in the U.S., the majority of whom are children between the ages of 5 and 12.

Alternatively, when badly prescribed, Prozac is said to provide a *fix* to problems, such as low self-esteem, disenchantment with relationships or lack of enthusiasm for work. Such psychotropic drugs are said to be a way of overcoming such problems by allowing one to feel happier and more accomplished and could allow, for example, shy people to become more extrovert and talkative; all supposedly positive benefits (enhancements). Yet Prozac is an anti-depressant and is supposed to be prescribed for patients with clinical depression. While the prescription of these and other drugs for the clinically depressed is not, in itself, particularly worrying, there is a concern for whether the number of diagnoses of clinical depression are more than they should be. There is also a concern for how some patients have reacted to these drugs, particularly those who do not have clinical depression. Even though it would appear that they are well, making such a claim may not be medically sound.

The importance of these observations and the reason for being cautious about the social-constructivist argument is recognised by Elliott (1998a, 1999, 2001), who considers it to be dangerous to approach illness from the perspective of social construction, though not because it is a poorly formed explanation for such conditions. Indeed, Elliott is proactive in recognising that many maladies are, in fact, socially constructed. However, his concern remains that it has encouraged the overcoming of such problems with pharmaceutical solutions that embody the biological-determinist model through what he calls *cosmetic psychopharmacology*. Elliott is concerned that these social maladies are being treated with the biological model of disease.[11]

In response to these drugs, what is most interesting about Elliott's argument is that he considers that they reflect a tendency to overwrite entrenched personal life struggles with the *wrong* kind of solution.[12] Instead of taking drugs, Elliott argues, such people should be concerned with solving their problem on an intrapersonal level, recognising that there might be some aspects of their life that are not positive and that require changing in order to be happy. To try and solve such problems using drugs, Elliott claims, undermines personal autonomy and, more importantly, the capacity for being authentic. This is why Elliott (1999) argues that the real ethical concerns in relation to enhancement technologies have to do with the concern for personal *identity*, for ensuring that individuals are leading *their own* authentic life, rather than one that is built upon the use of drugs.

What are we to do with these various health-related concepts, which appear to debunk the distinctions made between therapy and enhancement? So far, it has been suggested that delimiting the acceptable means of performance modification for athletes is a difficult business. For sport policy makers and, presumably, for many athletes, the distinction between therapy and enhancement, which underpins the ethical distinction between the two, has been argued as a simplification of a complex health-related discourse. If the health-related 'language' is to be used as some basis for determining what is ethically acceptable in sport, it must develop a more comprehensive methodology for establishing what kinds of 'health' are desirable in sport. The term 'enhancement' has been shown to be etymologically complex and often used in sport, where it is not appropriate. Moreover, there would seem to be other kinds of healthisms that are readily accepted in sport, despite their being informed by the same kinds of ideologies that underpin the concerns about enhancement. In short, anti-doping policy appears to assert (and value) a biological-deterministic view of therapy and enhancement, when the basis for its concerns has to do with social constructions of these terms, particularly enhancement. Just because enhancement appears to fall outside the proper domain of medicine and what is healthy, it is seen as unethical. Yet one can justify the pursuit of enhancement on the same rationale as one pursues good health.

I have endeavoured to demonstrate that the relationship between these concepts is not as linear as one might assume. However, it is possible to distinguish different kinds of alteration which bear varying (and thus distinct) proximities to health, both through enhancing and reducing it. However, there are a number of in-between cases which bring into question how we understand dysfunction or disease, which can greatly influence how we respond to enhancement technology. These cases require further elaboration, since they can inform our understanding of the *ethical* distinction between therapy and enhancement in sport.[13] In this context, the final part of this chapter will provide a critique of this normative discourse on health and suggest a way forward that can also be useful to guide the discussion about the legitimacy of making such distinctions in sport. I will do this by way of an example, which aims to provide a bridge between medical ethics and sport ethics and which can aid the conclusions about genetic modification for sport.

Human growth hormone: a problem for all concerned

Although the problem of distinguishing between therapy and enhancement may be similar for medicine and sport, there are few examples that have been widely discussed in both contexts. However, human growth hormone (hGH) is one such example, where medical ethicists have sought to question its legitimacy (Diekema, 1990), and where sports authorities remain opposed to its use, though for rather complex reasons (Murray, 1986b). This polypeptide hormone is produced naturally in the body, released from the pituitary gland and is responsible for controlling natural growth throughout the body. It is also used to break down fat and convert it into energy. Within sport, hGH has been high on the anti-doping agenda for over a decade and the interest has been to try and find ways of detecting misuse of the artificial product hGH. Growth hormone has managed to evade the anti-doping tests, as there is currently no way of testing for its use. Although there has been no demonstrated improvement in athletic performance from the use of rhGH, or evidence of widespread use, it is considered to result in leaner body mass, shorter recovery times between training, gains in strength and general performance enhancement (Hintz, 2002).

In medicine, the use of growth hormone is disputed as a legitimate and therapeutic method to boost hGH secretion, when a deficiency in the naturally produced hGH is present. Using hGH in such cases does not lend importance to the socially laden understanding of *health*, failing to recognise that such a condition might not be something that is in need of correction. One of the usual hypothetical cases to raise this contradiction involves imagining that there are two children, one of whom has a hormone deficiency that leads to it being approximately 150cm in height. The other child has a genetically predetermined height of 150cm and, as such, there is no deficiency in the hormone system. These are the circumstances posited by Allen and Fost (1990), and later by Daniels (1992), when trying to resolve what role medicine should have in the treatment of this condition. The question raised by this example is whether medicine has a role to correct the height deficiency in one, neither or both children. Daniels (1992) argues that the role of medicine is not to uphold justice or fair treatment, but to ensure that health-debilitating conditions are treated. Consequently, for Daniels, it does not matter that there is a child who will be short by genetic predisposition. Daniels makes a distinction between therapeutic and enhancement (or aesthetic) choices on this basis, concluding that it is entirely legitimate to treat similar conditions differently, as might be said for height.

By implication, this example illustrates how decisions about some medical conditions are informed by social values. I purposely avoid the terminology of *shortness* and *tallness* in order to not fall victim to a normative discourse, which pervades the medical articulation of such conditions. I will return to this point later. To elaborate on this case and respond to Daniels' argument, the following hypothetical case elaborates on the socially informed choice within medicine in relation to growth hormone.

Imagine that there is a child who does not appear to be very short at all, but, in fact, is rather tall for his or her age. In such circumstances, even if the child is growing at a lower rate than the parents, there will be no reason for a physician to conclude (or even worry) that the child has an hGH deficiency, and the concern for this will not be present. After all, the child is likely to grow up to be over 180cm. However, biologically, the child does have an hGH deficiency, since, if the genes were functioning well, he or she should have been 195cm. On the basis of there being only a biological reason for prescribing artificial hGH in order to correct a deficiency, the child should receive treatment to correct this deficiency. Indeed, Daniels' argument requires that such correction be provided. Yet it is highly improbable that a physician would make such a prescription and the reason for this choice not to intervene is that the concern about height is largely a concern about the disabling consequences of being short, rather than the biological dysfunction that shortness may imply. Indeed, it seems unlikely that such deficiency would even be noticed, given the normative model of medical knowledge.

Of course, the physician may also claim that the child need not have rhGH since it involves unnecessary risks of side effects, when the child is not really at risk of harm by being under the average height. However, again, in making this claim, the physician would be asserting the argument that the medical bases for prescribing rhGH are in fact social, not medical. The reason why children are prescribed with boosts to their hGH has to do predominantly with a concern for not being disadvantaged in a society which, at best, is suited to *average* height people or, at worst, is prejudicial towards short people. As such, the *proper role* of medicine in this case breaks down.

Given this conclusion, the more complicated matter is to decide which social circumstances justify the use of drugs such as hGH to supplement the biological limitations of specific individuals in their life circumstances. The ethical legitimacy of therapy or enhancement requires taking into account what is valuable for any individual and appreciating the importance of the treatment in their particular case. In the current context of hGH, this means determining whether the lifestyle choice to become an elite athlete warrants the prescription of such drugs while developing as a child and, subsequently, whether they are legitimate on the basis of wanting to perform at elite levels.

Human growth hormone is also an interesting case to consider because it can be used in various ways for sport. As such, we might evaluate its use more from the perspective of the developing child, who may have some aspiration for a career where being tall can be useful, such as sport. Alternatively, it is possible to address its use from the perspective of adult athletes seeking to develop their athletic capabilities even further in order to do better in competition. Each of these applications also stresses the varying role of medical ethics, which may require different modes of reasoning for each application. For example, in respect of prescribing hGH for children, one must engage with the limits of parental autonomy, strong arguments about paternalism, and concern about physiological growth. Conversely for the adult athlete, arguments from paternalism lack such strength and the concern for autonomy would be predominantly for the athlete.

If a child is required to be of a certain height to have a reasonable expectation of becoming an elite athlete, then the use of hGH when young could assist the child to maximise his or her choices (deciding whether to become an elite athlete or to choose something else). Without such enhancements, the child may not be in a position to choose elite sport should he or she so wish. This way of presenting the problem implies much more than an *aesthetic choice*, particularly since many young people train very hard to be good at sport and invest a lot of their time and ambitions into becoming excellent. Such commitment is not something to be discouraged. To ingratiate a child's aspirations, particularly when he or she shows some propensity for realising these dreams through hard work and investment, seems desirable, as it provides the child with the best opportunity to make a choice independently later in life. Potentially, without hGH, this may not be possible for some prospective athletes, unless the authenticity model is followed.

Human growth hormone is not the only example of how this problem of acceptability arises in sport, though it does provide an interesting context for relating bioethical concerns to sporting ones and how the arguments about biological determinism and social constructivism arise. It is useful to explain how this is helpful in relation to the therapy/enhancement problem, so that it is possible to understand how sport can progress with this debate about what makes one kind of technology acceptable and another not.

A revised framework

What are the consequences of these varied perspectives for sport in general, and specifically for the genetic modification of athletes? The arguments make it difficult to reject the social-constructivist conclusions, since the biological expression of the distinction is largely useless if we care for an individual's well-being. Therefore, even if certain forms of dysfunction can be linked to improper genetic operation, the number of social illnesses or diseases far outweighs the number of biological ones. Yet this does not mean that all kinds of enhancement should be tolerated in sport, since this is not an argument for a blanket acceptance of therapy or enhancement. Moreover, the biological-determinist view has the unfortunate consequence of undermining individual authenticity – the self-realisation in the context of horizons of meaning – by treating social maladies with biological solutions.

Nevertheless, the social-constructivist perspective is more capable of acknowledging how biological definitions reduce the human experience of disease. Even if one can identify some diseases as having predominantly biological causes (Smith, 2001), it is reductionistic to conclude that the origins of disease are solely (or predominantly) scientific (Neese, 2001). As Neese (2001: 37) argues:

> the disease concept must have emerged when people tried to communicate to each other that something was wrong with their bodies. . . . People with no idea about microbes, genes, or even anatomy, must have used the concept of disease to refer quite generally to any undesirable bodily condition, and perhaps to mental conditions as well. . . . The very origins of the disease concept involve a value judgment – suffering and disability are undesirable.

Neese's position does not neglect the realism of medical problems, nor does it reject that there is some biological foundation to suffering. Rather, Neese argues that 'the origins of the concept of disease are not in pathology, but in suffering'. Consequently, Neese gives salience to the experience of disease for an individual, thus expanding the kinds of conditions that should be considered to be a disease, even if they are not recognised as pathological.

Neese goes even further, challenging whether there is a concise articulation of many conditions. He raises the example offered by Haig (1993) that diabetes in pregnancy might be a disease for the mother, but is seen to be beneficial for the foetus. Neese concludes that the key concept of contention is *normality*, arguing that in varying contexts a disease can have varying levels of positive or negative connotation – though even here there are problems of definition. For example, if abnormality is the negative evaluation of disease where normality is assumed to be health, then there must be occasions where a disease can be statistically normal in a culture, though still be debilitating. In sum, Neese presents a case for an evolutionary definition of disease which abstracts from the individual, but which also recognises the salience of individual evaluations of conditions. Along similar lines, Ledley argues that the concept of normality does not make sense even from the biological perspective, since all genetic differences are superficial. Thus Ledley considers that even those who 'suffer from genetic disease do not necessarily have more mutant genes than those who are apparently normal' (1994: 163). Ledley continues, 'there are over 30,000,000 other variations which occur within the human genome, most of which cannot be conveniently categorized as normal or abnormal' (ibid.). Indeed, Ledley recognises that:

> even mutations which cause recognisable diseases such as sickle cell anaemia, phenylketonuria, or cystic fibrosis can confer an evolutionary advantage on their carriers in other climates and social conditions. The sickle cell gene may provide protection against malaria, phenylketonuria may not be a disease in societies which have limited protein intake, and the common cystic fibrosis mutation encodes a protein which may function at low temperatures. In contrast, certain genetic variations which are considered benign or even beneficial today could be recognised as pathogenic under different environmental or cultural conditions in the future.
>
> (ibid.)

Consequently (Neese, 2001: 38) that the values 'humans use to decide what is disease are socially influenced', even if they are built on preferences shaped by natural selection. Thus Neese offers a further way in which to negotiate the biological-determinist and social-constructivist distinction.

There seem further reasons to reject solely biological-determinist approaches to health, particularly in relation to what kinds of alterations should be allowed in sport. Indeed, the basis of biological norms as a means for delimiting what is acceptable enhancement in sport has met much criticism in the use of gender testing, which remains part of international sport to this day, albeit now in special circumstances, as was explained earlier. Introduced in the 1960s by the International Olympic Committee as a means to catching female athletes who were using steroids, the tests were highly controversial and deemed to be as scientifically flawed as the racial tests emerging at a similar time outside of sport (Simpson *et al.*, 2000).[14]

In relation to this overview of health-related terms, some more specific conclusions and suggestions are possible which can assist in developing a more useful way of approaching the problem of delimiting the ethical limits of performance enhancement in sport. The importance of this framework for sport will conclude this chapter, along with a statement about how this discussion has informed our understanding of the ethical significance of genetic modification in sport. My main points may be summarised as follows:

1 Understanding health and its related terms as *states* is fundamentally flawed and has led to an inability to discern moral distinctions between therapy and enhancement.

2 The medical discourse concerning health has been too narrow in its use and explanation of various health-related terms. A clearer explanation of these various terms and how they fit within the biological and social framework has been necessary to evolve the discussion beyond metaphysical questions.

3   The biological-determinist and social-constructivist perspectives are not mutually exclusive, though the social-constructivist position is most useful, since it derives from a concern for the *well-being* of the individual, thus engaging with human values to elucidate the ethical distinction between the value of therapy and enhancement.

4   This distinction should be premised upon well-being as understood as moral agency (or a concern for *identity preservation*), which can be informed by the theory of an *ethics of authenticity*.

Health as process, not state

First, I argue that it is misleading to conceptualise ideas such as health, disease and enhancement as conditions of *state*.[15] Yet it is assumed in many philosophical discussions about the importance of distinguishing between therapy and enhancement in medicine that it is possible to isolate *states* of health. In contrast, a more appropriate metaphor would be to describe health and its related terms as *processes*. This perspective is supported by Nordenfelt's (1998) articulation of *health promotion* as well as Rudnick's conception of normality as a 'regulative idea' (2000: 579) or a process.[16] The former recognises that the medical use of health and related terms must first be understood as defined by technology. Even biological-determinist views of disease are expressed through technological means and are identified through technologies (Hofmann, 2001a, 2001b, 2002). Biological symptoms or medical conditions are not stable or fixed; they are processes of change occurring within a body, whether this is imagined on the molecular level or through the experience of these symptoms. Silvers (1998) reinforces this perspective, arguing that many treatments can never be fully described out of their social context, even though it is possible to describe symptoms in a way that is unequivocally debilitating. Similarly, Rudnick's position describes the normative language of health as not 'a possible end-state' (2000: 579), but rather as a 'regulative idea'. Failing to recognise this notion of process, Rudnick suggests, commits the mistake of assuming that ends of medical intervention occur when the pathological is transformed into the normal. In Rudnick's sense, this is mistaken since normalcy is not a possible end-state to which medical intervention is working.

Understanding health-related terms in this way makes it possible to avoid essentialist approaches to condemning enhancement and tolerating therapy, since the identification of a healthy individual takes into account the specific values and 'authenticity' of that individual. It avoids many of the assumptions arising in Barilan and Weintraub's (2001) articulation of the conventional assumptions about health and enhancement – that the former are good and the latter bad. This latter point is crucial in order to avoid rejecting modifications, which can give value to human experiences, such as genetic enhancements. The position does not neglect the role of biological symptoms in the (self-) diagnosis of an individual's health. Rather, it simply does not rely only upon a medical definition of these symptoms and feelings.

Narrow medical discourse on health

It has also been problematic that the terms relating to therapy and enhancement have not been explained in reference to the concepts of disease and disability. Many controversies have arisen from this weakness in the literature seeking to make valid distinctions between the two, though a full engagement with a broad range of these related concepts has not really taken place. This is particularly important given the social-constructivist approach to understanding health, where it is difficult to omit the value-laden aspect of many of these terms.

Biological determinism vs. social constructivism?

Related to these arguments is the conclusion that the biological-determinist and social-constructivist approaches to the distinction need not be mutually exclusive. If the interest is for the well-being of an individual, then there is no benefit in either perspective taking its hard-line approach. Yet, in addition to this, the biological determinist must be the most gracious of the two, since the social constructivist is exclusively (and excessively) concerned with the well-being of the individual (though not in the *complete* sense of the term prescribed in the WHO definition).[17] However, accepting the social-constructivist approach requires a commitment to a concern for the moral well-being of the individual and an appreciation of his or her moral agency and ascription of values to various ways of being, which can include enhancement.

The distinction between therapy and enhancement: moral agency and identity preservation

These conclusions are consistent with van Hooft's (1998) understanding of the proper role of medicine as a concern for relieving *malady*.[18] Using this notion, van Hooft negotiates the dualism arising from the distinction between suffering and pain as a basis for determining when medicine should intervene. Van Hooft claims that a concern for malady is primarily a concern for suffering, even though it is not independent of biological characteristics. Moreover, this conclusion should guide the ethical distinction between therapy and enhancement. This position also responds to the difficulty raised by the example of mental illness, by recognising that suffering is not necessarily reflected by bodily symptoms or disease. Rather, it is a consequence of a person's perception of his or her health. Van Hooft avoids falling into strong normativism or a commitment to accepting enhancement as a medically justifiable intervention. Instead, van Hooft's argument implies that the therapy/enhancement distinction has little meaning aside from whether the said intervention is one that will relieve suffering. If it is, then this is a justification for its use, and within medicine this *tends* to be for conditions that are accompanied by biological characteristics.

An illustration of how this argument works in practice may be found in relation to the prospect of genetic screening and the ethics of eliminating *questionable* diseases, such as deafness. Deaf culture has been of considerable interest to bioethicists concerned with establishing the proper role of medicine (Crouch, 1999; Elliott, 1999; Spriggs, 2002). It is a case where the so-called disability is not perceived as such by many of its members. Rather, many deaf people reject the label of disability, arguing that the emphasis from public health policy should be not only on curing deafness, but must also address the social stigma associated with deafness (Chadwick and Levitt, 1998). In such a case, van Hooft's argument would suggest that there is no required role for medicine to play in alleviating deafness, since we need not describe deafness as suffering. Even the legitimacy of allowing deaf children to be born, when it might be possible to alter the child to allow hearing, cannot be taken for granted as acceptable or desirable. To claim the counter, I suggest, would be comparable to asserting that people who have humanly perfect hearing would also have reasonable grounds to claim that they should have enhanced hearing if it were possible.

The typical argument of pro-correction is that the deaf child is unnecessarily cut off from important aspects of human experience which are available through hearing. In this sense, for cochlear implants to be part of the proper role of medicine is legitimated, since the modification provides benefits without any (or too much) prior suffering. As such, van Hooft would argue that deaf children experience unnecessary suffering through withholding treatment that could have enhanced their lives.

It may be necessary to draw a distinction between the right to treatment and requesting treatment. Similar kinds of debate arise in relation to other issues in medical ethics, such as euthanasia. In this case it may be considered morally and ethically problematic to withhold care and allow somebody to die. However, of key importance for physicians is whether there exists some responsibility – either to end a life or to maintain it. The discussion about correcting deafness is of a similar kind. While one may willingly accept that the withholding of treatment for medical conditions, where such treatment is available, would be ethically suspect, the difficulty with the deafness example is that the benefit of this treatment is disputed. It is not clear whether or why it is better to have the facility of hearing. As Chadwick and Levitt (1998) note, it is not clear whether deafness leads to suffering or even to a lack of ability to succeed in life. In addition, there are contexts where having hearing might place a child in a position of greater suffering than being deaf, such as where a hearing child is born to deaf parents. In this case, the child may be excluded from the very important relationships with parents and it might be more desirable for the child to lack the facility of hearing.

More broadly, Levy (2002: 284) recognises that 'Deaf activists argue that deafness is not a disability, but instead the constitutive condition of access to a rich culture'. Nevertheless, Levy also notes that the kinds of social circumstances that have given rise to this valued culture by deaf activists is also a product of disadvantage and social stigma. For this reason, Levy is critical (but compassionate) towards this desire to avoid genetically avoiding deafness, at the same time arguing that it is a mistake to choose deafness for our children when we ourselves are deaf. Yet Levy's position relies upon a comparison over what is a 'richer' kind of life, suggesting that a life where one can hear allows one access to experiences that are not available to deaf people. For this reason, Levy's position fails to take account of the richness argued for by deaf activists and relies upon making a judgement about what is a preferable way of life. Objectively, it would seem necessary to conclude that a life with hearing is preferable, though this prioritises a particular version of what constitutes an open future, which is contested by deaf activists.[19]

While modifying deafness to allow somebody to hear might not be construed as an enhancement (even if it does enhance the hearing of the person), the example problematises the notion of therapy, such that *therapeutic* modifications are not necessarily the easily justified alterations from an ethical perspective. As such, the task is not really to try to distinguish between the ethical status of therapy and enhancement (where the latter are more unethical). Rather, the problem is to determine which kinds of enhancement *and* which kinds of therapy are morally legitimate. It cannot be assumed that the moral exemplar of good medicine is to provide therapeutic modifications. Nor can it be assumed that enhancement reflects a cavalier concern for humanity or recklessness with respect to our genetically modified future. Such a conclusion allows for recognising that there are some kinds of genetic modification that are both therapeutic and unacceptable as well as concluding that there are some methods of enhancement that are entirely acceptable. Brock (1998) concurs, arguing that it is impossible to draw an *ethical* distinction between therapy and enhancement. Instead, the ethical conclusions should be guided by seeking to enable a life that is open to various options. Consequently, where an enhancement or a therapy makes such a contribution, it may be deemed acceptable. This approach can be ambiguous when applied to sport, since sports modifications might be rejected on account of them being necessary only for some kinds of life-plans. On such a view, what matters is maximising choice for a number of possible life-plans, not maximising one specific choice, such as desiring to be an elite athlete.

In conclusion, this ethical approach to performance modification in sport does not prohibit the use of enhancing technologies from the perspective of whether such alterations ought to be medically permissible. A conventional approach to medical ethics does not offer a sound basis for determining what should be permitted within sport. This also provides a general critique of medical ethics and its approach to enhancements beyond sport, which tends not to have sympathy for what it may describe as cosmetic modifications rather than genuine and meaningful needs. In principle, the conclusion does not prohibit the use of any kind of genetic modification in sport. Yet neither does it allow enhancement to be selected without serious consideration or justification. However, further details are necessary before it is possible to make specific conclusions about such modifications. It has yet to be considered how the *horizon* of fair play informs an athlete's ethical view of sport and his or her own performance, or how we ought to perceive such identities (recognising that it is not only athletes but also potential individuals whom we are discussing in this matter).

8 Unfair advantages and other harms

The concept of *fair play*, understood more broadly as the moral concept of *justice*, is frequently the first resource when seeking to articulate what is valuable about sport. Long before fair play was theorised in academic journals, the spirit of the concept was present in documentation about early forms of competition, where maintaining the rules and being noble in defeat were an indication of an athlete's good, moral character (McIntosh, 1979). This has led many researchers to misrepresent the sporting context as something that leads necessarily to the cultivation of moral virtues and desirable behaviours. One has only to examine the world of professional sport to recognise athletes whose behaviour weakens the idea that sport builds some sense of morally admirable character. Nevertheless, it is appealing to believe that sport continues to be a context whereby it is valued largely for being *capable* of embodying ideals of fairness and equality. There is an expectation (or aspiration) for sport to be fair, even if the athletes participating in competitions fail frequently to achieve such high demands. The ethical principle of *fairness* has gained unquestionable status in sport, though it is worth explaining why fairness matters in sport. It seems reasonable to claim that fairness is an important guiding principle for athletes' theorising about what constitutes an ethical or unethical performance enhancement.

Conceptualising fair play

The most recent and comprehensive analysis of fair play in sport is provided by Sigmund Loland (2002b). His text, *Fair Play in Sport: A Moral Norm System*, situates the discussion about fair play within modern, competitive sport, asking whether fairness is at all possible in contemporary sport. Loland is aware that sport has become increasingly dislocated from its idealised origins, where there was once a sense of sport being more honourable when less money was involved and where it yielded less political influence. Of course, Loland is also aware that such nostalgia is largely fictional, decontextualised, and that it is unlikely that sport has ever been less competitive or political.

Within sport, Loland suggests that '"formal fair play" prescribes keeping to the rules or . . . keeping to the socially shared interpretation of the rules in terms of the ethos of the sport in which we are engaged' (2002b: 41). Moreover, drawing upon Rawls (1971), Loland elaborates by stating that the sporting competition is a voluntary, cooperative endeavour, whereby competitors accept restrictions upon individual liberty so that competition is made possible. Thus athletes are required to maintain the agreed-upon rules, or else they cease to play the game. This is because rule-breakers have revoked the voluntary, tacit agreement to play under the same conditions as other competitors, which makes the game possible.[1] Such a view is also found in Feezell's (1988) argument for why cheaters cannot play the game. As understood, if one is cheating, then one is not playing the game at all, which makes it impossible to win or lose in any meaningful sense. Feezell is careful to indicate that *cheating* is not simply or even necessarily breaking the rules, but has more to do with failing to adhere to the expectations of the competitive ethos within the sport, requiring a judgement of practical wisdom, informed by experience and the knowledge of the tradition (1988: 66).

To understand why maintaining fairness in sport is valuable, one must turn again to the Kantian concept of 'respect for persons', which underpins the modern articulation of rights and individual liberties (as was indicated in Chapter 5). Fair action is considered valuable in itself, because it maximises the capacity for autonomous action. In the context of what has already been discussed here, one can align such ideas with the interest to promote moral agency, or act in a manner that permits individuals to think freely about what matters in their own life. Thus the value of maintaining fair play is explained by the value of having a concern for respecting others, which is, in turn, grounded in the desire to be treated by others in a comparable way. Yet it is possible to describe the interest to respect others as a concern for preventing harm (and not only harm to oneself), thus avoiding the challenge of explaining the kinds of obligation athletes accept when entering into competition. This idea is introduced in Chapter 1, where I resynthesise Schneider and Butcher's (2000) philosophical overview of doping, deriving the following categories of harm:

- Harm as being unfairly disadvantaged.
- Harm as risk of damage to health.
- Harm as unfairness.
- Harm as undermining the nature of sport.
- Harm to other members of the sporting community.
- Harm to society.

On this view it need not follow that athletes are *obliged* to maintain respect for others, on the basis of some essentially contested agreement between competitors (Eassom, 1998). This process of describing a concern for fairness as a concern to prevent harm must be understood as integral to the discourse in previous chapters for constructing what constitutes moral agency. It involves problematising the distinction between therapy and enhancement and the concept of humanness. A concern for fairness is only one method of reasoning which an athlete can use to evaluate the ethical status of a performance enhancement. Therefore, the harms that I outline above are not presented as a basis for determining what is ethical about sport. Rather, my claim is that there are a number of similar, consequential arguments which I will broadly theorise as being *harms-based* arguments, of which fair play is one. In short, the concern for fairness is a concern for harm.

The kinds of harm I discuss are, deliberately, very broad. Where it has been typical to discuss the harm of performance enhancement in sport solely as a medical concern for health, I have argued that a broader notion is necessary.[2] As such, harm might entail the restriction of liberties or choices; it might involve monetary loss or the inability to sustain a preferable lifestyle. It might also entail the enjoyment of pleasure or pain. Yet harm necessarily implies that the reason why unfair action is ethically unacceptable is because it restricts others. It is possible to identify Mill's (1843/1995: 1218) *harm principle* arising in this ethical view, which states that:

> As soon as any part of a person's conduct affects prejudicially the interests of others, society has jurisdiction over it, and the question whether the general welfare will or will not be promoted by interfering with it, becomes open to discussion. But there is no room for entertaining any such question when a person's conduct affects the interests of no persons besides himself, or needs not affect them unless they like (all the persons concerned being of full age, and the ordinary amount of understanding). In all such cases there should be perfect freedom, legal and social, to do the action and stand the consequences.

However, the mechanism for negotiating harms need not be solely utilitarian or even consequential. The kinds of harm to which I allude do not really lend themselves to the kinds of quantifiable comparison that could make possible determining which course of action is the least harmful. Instead, conceptualising the concerns of fairness as one of many harms provides a means for evaluating which kinds of harm matter most from the perspective of various interested parties, noting also that the negotiation of these perspectives is not static or infallible.

In Chapter 1, I argue that these various harms are sufficiently contested in sport, which prevents a robust rejection of drug taking and other forms of doping from sport. This does not imply that potential and actual harms within sport resulting from performance enhancement are of no matter. Rather, it is more a criticism of the inadequacy of these arguments to articulate sufficiently what is ethically problematic about enhancing performance using such means. The kinds of harm arising from such methods are not harms (aside from the persuasive medical argument, which still might not entail prohibition of many kinds of performance enhancement) of any persuasive nature.

The concern for these harms in respect of genetic modification looks very different. It is not that the arguments are more persuasive (that the harms are more plentiful) and that all forms of genetic modification should, therefore, be banned. Indeed, the conclusion is more to the contrary. It suggests that some forms of genetic modification might actually be ethically desirable within sport, since they provide a way of reducing harm in sport. Yet to make such conclusions requires detailed description of the varying methods of using genetic technology to enhance performance and should not be considered solely in a generic sense, even if one might identify generic ethical issues related to a number of different applications of genetic modification to sport.

In this context, two tasks must precede the ethical conclusions about the use of genetic modification in sport. In Chapter 1, I outline many of the sporting arguments for why doping and other methods of performance enhancement might be considered unethical. The priority for this chapter will be to explain the other, non-sporting, potential harms arising from the prospect of genetic modification. Once this overall appreciation for the potential harms of genetic modification in sport is clearer, it will be possible to respond to these and outline some tentative conclusions concerning both the bioethical and sporting arguments about whether genetic modifications are ethically desirable for sport.

The new harms of genetic modification

Social engineering

In Chapter 7, it was explained how the difficulty of discerning a clear distinction between therapeutic and non-therapeutic uses of medical technologies gives rise to a concern about social engineering. If the distinction between these terms is unclear – as I suggest – then there is the potential to find biological solutions to sociological problems.[3] The case of genetic sex selection is a particularly good illustration of this problem. The process of sex selection would entail using gene testing at the embryonic stage of development – while it is still legally acceptable to have an abortion in many countries – to determine whether one's prospective child is of the preferred sex. At a later stage, further applications of this technology might include testing for skin colour, eye colour or body size. The resulting harm of this is its eugenic nature, which, for some, suggests that some kinds of people are more valuable than others. Macer (1990: html) goes so far as to say that non-therapeutic selection should be illegal since there is already a shortage of resources. In addition, Macer argues that:

> Modern society is moving towards viewing reproduction as a commodity, producing a luxury item, a newborn child free of defect. It may make people less tolerant of the variety of human beings. In the case of sex selection it represents prejudicial attitudes, which are inappropriate in a world where we are trying to get rid of such prejudice.

Importantly, this example demonstrates that it is not only genetic *modification* that creates concerns about social engineering. However, genetic screening makes the debate much more acute, since it acts in a way that has the appearance of being far less challenging, because it is possible to discard potential lives at an earlier stage.

The criticism of sex selection is that social discrimination would take place by prioritising a given sex over the other. There is a further concern that such applications of genetics will lead to a situation whereby such choices are treated with much less seriousness than they ought to be and might lead to a *frivolous* use of technology to pick and choose which lives are worth bringing into the world (Benn, 2001). The strength of these criticisms hinges upon what constitutes a *good reason* for wanting to make any such selection, if one exists. If the choice is based on a perceived difference in the importance of one sex over another, then there would be reason for concern. However, the position is weaker when it is premised on a non-sexist rationale. For example, a couple may have already had four births of one sex and seek to have an alternate sex for their fifth child. It is easier to sympathise with this desire and it would not raise any serious moral concern about the devaluing of certain kinds of life. Speaking about this matter in the United Kingdom, McMillan (2002) doubts that any request to use such technology would be premised upon socially discriminating reasons and, as such, there are few reasons to prohibit such choice.

Yet it is also possible to sympathise with the idea that it is desirable, even necessary, for people in some cultures to have a son in the family. This example is often used as a basis for demonstrating the point that the use of such technology is, negatively, socially laden. It is often quoted that the alarm concerning sex selection arises in places such as India or China, whereby the prestige and value of the family relies upon its having a son. From an external perspective, it is easy to be critical of this choice and to describe the decision to abort female foetuses as unsustainable on account of it reflecting an entrenched social inequality between genders, which is only perpetuated by permitting sex selection. However, in such cases there is a genuine and sincere basis for making the selection, rather than simply being a flippant choice. Consequently, it is necessary to be cautious with the moral evaluation, as it is not clear that such choices should not be allowed. Indeed, one might wish to suggest that the serious moral issue is not the selection of sex, but promoting a climate whereby such value is not attributed to one sex in particular.

The significant harm arising from this choice and other non-therapeutic modifications is that it could provoke a horrific abuse of the treatment of life. There are concerns that particular kinds of people might be deemed to lack value simply on account of seemingly trivial characteristics. As Elliott (1998b: html) explains:

> One possible worry about some enhancement technologies is what the Georgetown University philosopher Maggie Little calls the problem of 'cultural complicity.' The demand for certain technologies is created by cultural forces that many of us would see as harmful. They are harmful because they make some people feel inadequate, or unhappy with the way they are. One example would be the desire of some Asian girls and young women to have surgery in order to make their eyes look more like those of Westerners. Another more obvious example is the pressure that many

American women feel to conform to a certain body type, and which leaves many women and girls feeling that they are too fat, or that their breasts are too small, and so on. At the extreme end of the spectrum these cultural pressures help to produce psychiatric illnesses like anorexia nervosa.

Ensuring that prospective parents have a *good* reason for wanting a child of a particular sex might be incredibly difficult, as the process by which it would be possible to make such a conclusion is unclear. For example, it is not obvious how one might establish whether people have good reasons for trying to engineer a life to be more capable in sport. However, these pragmatic difficulties are not a justifiable reason for prohibiting these choices in such important matters. At most, they constitute an argument for providing a system of counselling to ensure that not just *any* reason is considered a good reason for selecting a particular kind of life over another, though such a system might be easily manipulated.

Similar claims about social engineering may be made in relation to other applications of genetic modification. To engineer specific kinds of genes, or to remove specific kinds of dysfunction, is inherently eugenic. The interest is to create better lives, which presupposes what constitutes a better life. Moreover, these *better lives* are not to be understood simply as genetically superior, but by what such superiority implies. For example, let us suppose that it is possible to engineer a life to have a greater capacity to endure long-distance running. By engineering such characteristics, one is claiming that it is socially advantageous to be capable of enduring for longer. Even for seemingly desirable modifications, such as the correction of genes that lead to very difficult or painful lives, the choice to use such technology is a choice of preference for one way of being human over another. As is the case for sex selection, demanding justification for such modifications would also be difficult to apply, where the experience of disability may be characterised as predominantly social. As such, this is not an argument against the elimination of genes that clearly lead to a life of suffering, such as is the case for cystic fibrosis. However, a more difficult example where the justification of this choice becomes more problematic might include something like Down's syndrome. Again, Little's (1998) concerns about *cultural complicity* are important to take into account here.[4]

In sum, there is a potential to promote harm by allowing genetic manipulation or screening for social (or non-therapeutic) purposes. Regardless of where one draws the line on therapy and non-therapy, harms will arise. Thus the parents seeking to have a boy as their next child, rather than a girl, would be harmed, since their reproductive freedom will have been limited, if such selection were prohibited. From a consequential perspective, this harm might be more desirable than the many kinds of harm that arise from legitimising such choices. However, it is also alarming that the legitimate use of gene therapy might lead to a greater tolerance of gene enhancement, which itself might be an additional harm.[5] Indeed, restricting the use of such technology may also be argued as eugenic. By *not* allowing individuals to make their own choices about their children, one also institutionalises what kinds of people should exist. In this case, the eugenic premise is that *only people who are not genetically modified should exist.* Consequently, if the criticism is that genetic modification is inherently eugenic, then it must be asked why that particular form of eugenics is less desirable compared with the alternative, which forbids such people from existing. I suggest that the eugenic character of genetic modification is not ethically or morally more problematic than the eugenic character of asserting that non-modified people are preferable. Moreover, inhibiting such choice would commit the additional harm of preventing such choice.

Knowledge and access issues

A related concern about screening is the prospect of testing individuals for specific genetic conditions. Currently, genetic testing is available for a number of single-gene disorders, some of which are possible to treat, such as sickle-cell anaemia, Huntington's disease and cystic fibrosis. Genetic testing is also used extensively in newborn screening, which looks for metabolic errors such as phenylketonuria (PKU), caused by the lack of an enzyme and which results in an abnormally high level of the amino acid phenylalanine. If such a condition is untreated, it can lead to progressive mental retardation. Consequently, the benefits of such technology are, intuitively, easy to recognise and explain. Other exciting developments in this area of research involve the possibility of predictive gene testing, which can allow the detection of susceptibilities before a condition becomes apparent. However, the technology remains limited in being able to identify meaningful conclusions about polygenic disorders, due mainly to a lack of knowledge about the way in which many genes interact (Nuffield Council on Bioethics, 1993). The identification of sport genes has still a long way to go before it gains any kind of acceptance as a legitimate application of medical technology, though it is a question that is being taken seriously (Perusse et al., 2003).

It is important to clarify the distinction between genetic testing and genetic screening, which is explained by Glannon (2001: 43–44):

> Genetic testing must be distinguished from genetic screening. The first refers to testing individuals who are known to be at increased risk of having a genetic disorder with a familial mode of inheritance. The second refers to testing members of a particular population for a disorder for which there may be no family history or other evidence of its presence.

Even the value of medical applications of genetic screening and testing are contentious. Knowledge of one's genetic future – which is implied by learning the results of screening and testing – is considered by some to present potential harms to individuals. These harms are additional to the possible harm arising from any disorder that an individual may have. For a number of reasons, questions have been raised about whether it is healthy for a patient to be aware of his or her genetic future. An additional criticism of genetic screening and testing is the idea that such knowledge has no value. For many kinds of genetic disorder there is no possible therapeutic cure and so, arguably, it offers no benefit to the individual by conducting such tests (Ayabe and Tan, 1995). In addition, for some kinds of disease, genes are not the only determinant of contracting an illness. In such cases, knowledge of the possible condition may be to the detriment of the patient's health and may actually increase the tendency to contract the illness, somewhat of a self-fulfilling prophecy. However, one might also recognise that knowledge of a condition, even if it cannot be treated, can be useful to explain how better to minimise the suffering of the individual by eliminating other possible conditions.

Similar arguments are raised in regard to the patient's family, whose health may also be affected by such knowledge (Häyry and Lehto, 1998; Häyry and Takala, 2001; Macer, 1990). Ethical questions arise over whether family members or reproductive partners have a right to such information (Parker, 2001; Vehmas, 2001). The limits of such rights are captured in an illuminating case found in Macer (1990), who describes a situation in Illinois, USA, which tried to force married couples to undergo mandatory premarital testing for HIV. As Macer explains, the premise was that 'the spouse should know if the partner has HIV, and the public health motivation was to slow the spread of HIV' (ibid. html). This example can be analogous to the sporting context, where athletes might be required to disclose their genetic information for the sole purpose of ensuring fair competition. However, Macer continues, it is ethically unacceptable to enforce such screening (ibid.), since it is overly legislative of individual freedoms.[6]

Ethical issues also arise in terms of who else, besides family, should be given (or is entitled to) access to genetic information. Recently, this concern has gained importance in relation to whether insurance companies have a right to knowledge about the genetic constitution of their clients. Before genetic screening was possible, companies could not claim a right to such knowledge. Consequently, the possibility of using such technology has given rise to a further ethical issue. In such circumstances, the individual will be condemned to knowing his or her genetic future and may even be the subject of prejudice on account of a negative prognosis. A further reason for doubting the value of such testing is that it would be prejudicial to those for whom a genetic disorder can be identified. Where the technology does not detect other kinds of disorder, those who might be susceptible to the unknown conditions are favoured – their genetic dysfunction goes unnoticed.

Of course, insurance companies are already entitled to know the state of health of their clients, and the possibility of accessing genetic information is, in one sense, merely an extension of this right. Moreover, it is possible to understand the basis of such entitlement, given that insurance is understood as a contract between two parties. Thus if one party (the client) has knowledge about a dangerous medical condition (such as a genetic disorder) and the other party (the insurer) is not privy to such information, then the client is able to capitalise on that knowledge by requesting a more extensive insurance policy.

Burley (1999) suggests that 'society at large should share the costs of the bad genetic luck that its individual members suffer' and that therefore there should be some requirement for insurance companies to offer a reasonable degree of protection, despite knowledge of the predisposition. While this might be seen to disadvantage other clients of the insurance company, it is mistaken for such clients to consider that they are different from the genetically disadvantaged. Instead, they might merely describe themselves as technologically (rather than genetically) fortunate that a test has not been found for their genetic risk.

Research has also examined the possibility that employers would have an interest in accessing the genetic prognoses of their employers, in a similar way to how other kinds of medical information are required (Henderson, 2000; Rothstein and Knoppers, 1996; Shapiro, 1991). In this respect, the harms can vary. For example, it would be particularly useful to know that if one is a haemophiliac, then a butcher's job is not the most ideal career choice. However, this is one very simple example, where others do not make such a clear link between a given profession and the importance of a particular genetic disposition. In addition, it is less clear whether information would be used predominantly in the interests of the employee or the employer. In either case, it is possible to sympathise with the concerns, though arguably it is the individual who would suffer more from others knowing their genetic prognosis. The key question is whether individuals are entitled to conceal this information. The insurance case suggests that they are not, though in sport this has yet to be clarified.

Engineering future values

Embracing genetic modification could also be harmful for prescribing what is to be valued by future generations. As Mackie (cited in Glover, 1984: 149) recognises, 'if the Victorians had used genetic engineering, they would have made us more pious and patriotic'. This quote typifies the concern many people have about the prospect of using germ-line genetic engineering. For example, let us suppose that it is athletic capability that we seek to promote through genetic modifications. By making such a choice and by outlining what characteristics of athletic performance are worthy of manipulating – perhaps speed, strength or flexibility – one asserts what is valuable about sporting performance and prioritises such values over others. In this case, the emphasis is placed upon winning, being successful and securing an advantage over others. Being prepared to alter oneself to fit within such a framework of value is harmful to society because it instils a prescribed way of evaluating sport specifically and life in general.

To further illustrate this concern, it is useful to examine Munthe's (2000) analysis of the ethical issues arising from using genetic technology for sport. Munthe assumes that genetics would be used to boost muscle mass, prolong endurance capacity or enhance flexibility. As such, it is performance enhancement – in the quantitative sense – that is most interesting in relation to genetic technologies. Munthe does not consider that genetics might be used, for example, to make athletes play more fairly or to be interested less in winning and more interested in acquiring altruistic tendencies and learning the value of, for example, team spirit. Of course, it will be argued that biological traits are the most likely to be altered by genetic modification. Furthermore, the concept of engineering behavioural characteristics would provoke far greater concerns about the eugenics nature of genetic modification.

Nevertheless, of the many ways in which genetics might be used, it is not inconceivable that genes will be identified as determining various kinds of physical and psychological traits. Consequently, it is possible that social characteristics could have some demonstrable genetic origin, at least in some cases (Rosas, 2002; Wilson, 2002). It would surely be considered spurious that it would be possible to engineer more altruistic behaviours. Yet this scientific criticism should not overshadow the implication of my claim, which is that the kinds of modification individuals choose to manipulate – even if they are biological characteristics – impose a deeply contested moral view about preferable ways of being. Munthe's discourse reflects a particular ideal of sport, which is also reflective of taken-for-granted values in sport: those of performance and physical, quantifiable achievement. Yet it is the very content of this sporting ideal that is in need of question, since these values in themselves do not reveal anything meaningful about individual authenticity. The pursuit for performance alone does not tell us anything about the way in which those performances are imbued with meaning by the horizons of significance an athlete identifies within their sport. This is not to say that they do not have value, but that they omit an important element which relates to the athlete's own sense of personhood.

This imposition is ethically problematic precisely because it prescribes what has value. To engineer or enhance certain characteristics of an athlete is to assert these characteristics as being the most valuable in sport. This prioritising of quantifiable measures of performance results in an emphasis upon specific kinds of characteristics to the neglect of others.

Interrupting evolution and 'playing God'

A related harm resulting from germ-line cell manipulation is the potential to interfere with a perceived *natural* course of evolution. This perspective is neither straightforward to explain nor widely accepted as an ethical issue. It argues that the modification of genes within the human species will be detrimental to (1) future humans or specific species, and (2) the entire ecosystem.

A number of arguments can be given for why this is harmful. For example, in relation to both of these issues is the fear that modifications will promote a reduction in *genetic diversity*, which would threaten the survivability of species. The genetic engineering of animals and plant life constitutes a general concern for the evolutionary well-being of the ecosystem (Putnam, 1999; Reiss and Straughan, 1996). By itself, the ethical concerns might be less significant if it were only humans who are altered. However, this is not the case, and so substantial fears arise about manipulating humans in ways that lack an acceptable level of scientific certainty. Such concerns have been emphasised in recent debates about cloning humans, though they are perhaps less far-reaching than the widespread use of cloning technology in agriculture.

There are a number of reasons why the reduction of genetic diversity is considered harmful. First, it may be seen as reckless to engineer germ-line cells, since we do not yet have enough knowledge about evolution and the consequences of genetic manipulation to understand fully the harm (or benefit) that might arise from such alterations. This harm is particularly strong in the case of germ-line cell engineering, which some argue would alter the process of evolution in a meaningful sense by engineering the genes of future generations. In addition, there is the potential for negatively affecting the human gene pool and a general equilibrium in nature. As Glover (1999) argues, germ-line gene therapy may be seen as not just curing a disorder in one person, but also as changing the gene pool.

However, there is a further level of concern about genetic diversity, which is not quite as obvious. It is not simply that the aspiration to design better species might lead to a reduction in genetic diversity. Rather, it is also possible that such designs might embody alarming ideological motivations, which steer the design of human characteristics towards a non-medical model of health (if such characteristics would be healthy at all). To clarify, there are two different claims about the reduction in genetic diversity. The first argues that the reduction in diversity arises from the motivation to make life healthier, thus giving rise to an ideal human phenotype. A further reduction in diversity might arise out of social imperatives to design a *desirable* human being. This is alarming because it may give rise to what Post describes as a 'tyranny of the normal' (1991: 225), whereby a process of normalisation (comparable in effect to institutionalised eugenics) is effected upon humans. The possibility for selecting *better* genes might provoke a culture of genetic cleansing, where the alarming implications of *institutional* genetic cleansing make way for the equally alarming circumstances of *individualised* genetic cleansing. In such social conditions, fashion and popular trends give rise to a normalisation of genetic characteristics. Post (ibid.) suggests that it is:

> imperative to consider the possibility that our cultural definitions of normalcy might shift so that enhancement genetic engineering becomes increasingly attractive. . . . Our desire not to bring suffering into the world must be tempered by a recognition that suffering is a part of life.

Appleyard (1999) discusses this problem at length, highlighting the comparison between *individualised* eugenics and *institutionalised* eugenics, the latter of which is most remembered by aspirations of political leaders in the Nazi years and more recently by other dictatorial regimes. On his view, the tyranny of a liberal society, where individual autonomy is prioritised and where people can choose how their children are brought into this world, can also have a comparably pessimistic ending. Appleyard suggests that this would have a normalising effect upon people's choices about their children and that this is as destructive as institutionalised eugenics. Thus when acting in the interests of their children-to-be, parents would seek to determine those characteristics that will make the child more predisposed to social acceptance and endeavour to remove those characteristics that might lead to social exclusion or, less dramatically, to the possibility of ridicule, being teased or simply feeling abnormal. As Appleyard (1999: 86) says, 'people in general are powerfully driven to gain a competitive advantage for their children or, at least, to ensure that they are not at a competitive disadvantage.' In this sense, ethical issues arise from understanding that the legitimisation of genetic modification would lead people to engineer their children to be alike. In so doing – by eliminating difference – future generations are not burdened by the social injustice of being *different*, but by the greater burden of being the *same*.

Appleyard's argument comes as a response to advocates of modern genetics who argue that it is entirely different from institutionalised eugenics (Glover, 1999; Ledley, 1994) and that, by comparison, modern genetics is ethically acceptable. Appleyard's retort is that, while the method may be substantially different, the effect would be similar and this is cause for concern. The possibility that difference could be removed from society is contrary to democratic, multicultural ideals, which continually seek to embrace and nurture difference and where tolerance and morality is predicated on having to make a conscious decision to accept and embrace difference. It requires, as it were, the capacity for being an autonomous, moral agent. While difference may not be inherently valuable, it makes for a much more interesting existence, and the prospect of similarity in physical and mental characteristics is alarming since it reduces the value of being human by eliminating chance.

The ideas of Post (1991) and Appleyard (1999) are also a useful basis for responding to those authors who dismiss the biological rationale for upholding the reduction in genetic diversity argument. Neither Macer (1990) nor Harris (1999) are convinced that technology will lead to a reduction in genetic diversity in itself. Moreover, Harris is not convinced that genetic diversity is such a concern in this case. As an example, he notes that the birth of Dolly the sheep gave rise to the *myth* that she specifically, and genetics generally, poses some 'threat to humanity, the human gene-pool, genetic diversity, the ecosystem, the world as we know it, and the survival of the human species' (1999: 61). Macer (1990: html) agrees, arguing that the main concern is that it:

> is doubtful as to whether this sort of selection would really have much effect biologically. The major effect is on reduced social variability. If we want to maintain or should we say develop a society where people's autonomy is respected then we should not allow the acceptance of genetic restrictions on non-disease characteristics. This means that society could for the benefit of society, and protecting its members from developing narrow views whether they be sexist or intelligence seeking, restrict the freedom of individuals to use techniques to affect the children. We already limit the environmental freedom of parents, we also need to limit their genetic freedom to choose.

In sum, the widespread acceptance of enhancement technology would provoke a homogenisation of the human species, where parents might select their children to ensure their normality and acceptance into society. Parents will seek to enhance those qualities that are culturally desirable and, consequently, genetic engineering becomes a mechanism of eugenics, even though it is left to the free will of individuals. The alarming scenario is suggested whereby all humans might look, think and behave alike, thus perpetuating the disturbing situation where human autonomy is undermined and people cease to be evaluated as unique individuals. Within sport, this argument is relevant for projecting a future for sport that is determined by present-day values.

Aside from these scientific and social reasons for rejecting cloning or germ-line cell modification, there are also religious reasons for rejecting such alterations and limiting the use of genetic technology. Conceivably, this approach to genetics requires an entire section of its own, though it may find some common ground with the concern for interrupting evolution, since each has little regard for the naturalistic fallacy of asserting that the good is defined solely by what is natural (Reiss and Straughan, 1996). I do not intend to enquire into the complex variety of religious doctrines, which might or might not be interpreted as embodying some ethical position about the value of genetic technology. However, it is reasonable to recognise that religious arguments may have a significant bearing upon the application of genetic modification to sport, which also has a very strong religious (and/or spiritual) component. Indeed, if one accepts the religious position as comparable to the *naturalness* argument about why genetic modification is unethical, then it is even more apparent that many sports fans would seek to assert that genetic modification does not embody sporting values.

Genetic essentialism

A further concern about genetic modification is that it will lead to an invest-ment of interests based solely upon genetic information, when genetics should be understood as only one element of what influences human achievements. This has already been argued in relation to the emerging discourse about the roles of genes. In particular, Abby Lippman (1992) argues that there has been a *geneticisation* of society, where variations between individuals have been reduced to genetic differences. This perspective is also sometimes described as *genetic essentialism*, and is considered by Nelkin and Lindee (1995) to be alarming because of the power such assumptions might have to determine individual choices and priorities. Hedgecoe extends these concerns, arguing that an *extreme medicalisation thesis* can lead to a 'cultural iatrogenesis' (1998: 237) where medi-cine has destroyed the potential of people to deal with human weakness and vulnerability autonomously.

Neither the human being nor the elite athlete is constituted entirely by genetics. As such, to place so much importance upon genes would misconstrue the relationship between nature and nurture, to the expense of the latter (Elliott,

1999; Macer, 1990). In turn, this is harmful, since it reduces the rich contexts of sporting performance to practices that place value *only* in results and performance rather than, for example, strength of character. This is alarming from a social and ethical perspective, since it purports to reduce human practices to levels of quantifiable measures and impoverished social experiences.

In relation to *knowledge and access harms*, Ayabe and Tan (1995) explain how genetic information can lead to essentialist views, which in turn lead to genetic discrimination. Indeed, Keyley (1996) illustrates these concerns by way of an example of the legal system in the USA. Recently, custodial cases in family law have been redefined by genetic essentialism. As Keyley describes, 'Under the rubric of "genetic essentialism", the family is being redefined as a "molecular, genetic unit" and social/psychological aspects of family identity and functioning are being ignored' (1996: 717). In cases where the custody of a child must be decided, it is preferable to place the child with the genetic familiar rather than the 'genetic stranger' (ibid.), as it is generally believed that there is some greater benefit from being with persons to whom one is biologically related.

Within sport, the implications of *genetic essentialism* are alarming for the very reasons that they are given *against* the importance of performance enhancement. As such, the championing of quantifiable measures in elite sport is at the expense of other kinds of value associated with sport. The discourse of genes implies an essentialist view of sporting performance, which marginalises other factors that contribute to an athlete's performance capacity.

Life harms

One of the broader claims against genetic modification is the harm it inflicts upon the value of life. From such a view, the idea of *playing God* is a mask for a culturally entrenched concern about the way in which life is treated by *unnecessary* technology. Genetically modifying life creates a mechanism for viewing life as a means to an end, for treating life as an artefact (or technology), rather than something that has inherent value. Consequently, by altering a potential life for reasons other than health – as might be the case for germ-line cell modifications – one is objectifying it by imposing a template for how that life should be. However, as Harris (1998: 244) explains:

> if genetic connections are established for things like musical ability, athleticism, and intelligence, there will be immense pressure to specialise in the education of children earmarked for success or failure in such areas.

This argument has been raised recently in relation to cloning. The alarming possibility that parents may wish to clone themselves or others so that they can have a particular kind of child has been condemned for being fanciful and exploitative. The idea that one can engineer people at all raises concerns for the motivations of parents and how such parents might treat a child once it is born. In the case of pre-selection this is particularly alarming, though it also has relevance for other kinds of genetic modification. Again, this is comparable to sex selection and it is the motivations of the engineer (or parent) that are ethically alarming, as opposed to the technology itself.

In response to such harms, the pre-embryonic threshold may serve as some guide to acceptable engineering. Thus if the life is pre-embryonic, then it cannot be harmed in the sense that one might understand a life to be harmed if it is altered after this fourteen-day period of cell divisions. Supposing that this *primitive streak* (Warnock, 1985, 1987) stage is accurate and, providing that modifications take place before this time, then the life is not harmed. This should not imply that pre-embryonic life can be treated without any regard. Indeed, there is some basis for ascribing minimal rights to such lives to recognise that they are not just expendable.[7]

In addition, the concern for *life harms* is less persuasive if one accepts that modifying potential lives does not necessitate treating them as ends in themselves. It does not follow that any parents choosing to engineer their child will treat that life as a means to an end. As Harris (1999: 70) argues:

> There is no evidence for . . . the supposition that if people choose to use a cloned genome in order to create *their own children*, that these children will not be loved for themselves, let alone not treated in a civilized way.

A further concern from the life harms perspective is of a more practical nature. It has been argued that genetic modification is far too experimental and wasteful of life to be ethically sound. For this reason, such applications of genetics are unequivocally unethical. In response, all advances in medicine and technology require some degree of experimentation – it is simply a case for finding at what point a technology is deemed to be overly experimental. As Macer (1990: html) says:

> The answer to the question how much experimentation is ethical, could be none, or some depending on the age and the experiment in question, or it could be any up to a certain age. One moral assumption that can be made is that it is completely unacceptable to make use of a child or an adult as the subject of a research procedure which may cause harm or death. . . . The argument whether an early embryo is of the same status as a fully developed foetus is a slippery slope argument.

Certainly, one cannot reject the idea that the current approach to experimental medicine may require closer examination to an extent that it might be necessary to prohibit the development of such medical therapies. It is tempting to argue that experimentation with genetic modification is justified on account of our already experimental approach to technology. However, such an approach does not imply that all kinds of experimental technology have value; there are other criteria that are attached to research than solely its possibility to lead to important discoveries. For example, it matters whether there is some expectation that it is possible for the research to be fruitful.[8] Nevertheless, there is substantial sympathy for a great deal of experimental work in medicine, particularly within genetics, and many scientists regard it as having tremendous value.

However, from this harm emerges a concern for the sanctity of life and its protection from exploitation through commercialisation. In the past two years, this has been of great concern due to the emergence of companies that wish to buy and sell human eggs and sperm (Miah, 2003b). Such companies appear to be gaining a stronghold for prospective parents who might wish to buy their way into parenting – in a comparable manner to the way in which one purchases private healthcare (Resnik, 2001). It is conceivable that a similar template for genetic modification may emerge in the highly commercial domain of sport, should such modifications be allowed.

A genetic super-class

Some fears of genetic modification are also grounded in a belief that it would lead to a restructuring of social divisions by genetic capability; between the modified and the unmodified. Such ideas are informed by a belief that the social provision of healthcare – at least in the United Kingdom – is already heading towards a system whereby private care is the only way to ensure that one receives a satisfactory level of service. The likelihood that genetic modifications will be expensive, at least at the beginning, is sufficient to sustain these concerns. Within sport, this has far-reaching implications for the possibilities of maintaining some level of fairness in competition. Consequently, the harm arising from this prospect is one of fairness and the possibility for equal opportunity. Being born without modifications would – it is presumed – lead to being socially disadvantaged in some measurable way. Moreover, it might be expected that *performance* inequalities may also lead to further elitism beyond sport.

Summary to new harms

This chapter began by arguing that challenges to fair play in sport constitute particular kinds of harm. On this basis, an athlete's concern for preserving fair play has to do with ensuring that sport, athletes and other members of the sporting community do not come to any harm. In this context, I outline a number of possible harms arising from genetic technology specifically, as these are additional to the kinds of harm related to performance modification and sport. This overview of new harms is not exhaustive of the various harms that arise in relation to genetic modification in general. For example, I have neglected to study the possible modification of animals or the consequencies of environmental manipulation, both of which have implications for sport. Indeed, a significant amount of discussion has arisen recently in relation to the use of genetically engineering race-horses, something presaged by John Hoberman in his *Mortal Engines* (1992). Instead, I have focused upon the possible harms arising from *human* genetic manipulation and the broad, possible uses of genetic information.

Collectively, they provide a strong case for being concerned about the use of genetics in sport, though it is not yet clear whether this case is sufficiently persuasive to permit concluding that sport would be more enriched by prohibiting genetic modification. Chapter 9 will focus on the specific applications of genetic modification to athletes, detailing the extent to which these new harms do arise in the sporting case. Subsequently, I will address the sports-specific harms in the context of genetic modification.

Part IV

Genetically modified athletes

9 Enhancing, altering or manipulating people?

Previous chapters have argued that there are a number of sporting and non-sporting ethical issues arising from the use of genetic modification in sport. Initially, it was suggested that these ethical issues might be framed by concepts employed within medical ethics, such as autonomy and human dignity. This way of theorising the ethical implications of genetics in sport is strengthened when recognising that genetic technology is heavily reliant upon what is considered to be the proper role of medicine. These concepts have been questioned and challenged by suggesting that a concern for autonomy and dignity is more accurately a concern for personhood and identity. Still, relying upon the importance of *autonomy*, as is also the case in medical ethics and bioethics, it is necessary for ethical discussions to acknowledge the moral agency of athletes as a salient characteristic of what matters in sport. Indeed, this should be the point of departure for an ethical view of sport. This permits athletes to question their relationship to technology in their sporting practices and legitimately select genetic modification and other enhancements as a process of self-realisation.

There are also a number of considerations an athlete must encounter when reasoning about the value of such a choice. In particular, such a decision requires coming to terms with the distinction between therapy and enhancement, though this has been argued as being far more complex than has previously been recognised in sport and medical ethics. For this reason, it is possible that revealing this distinction to be far more sophisticated and complex lends strength to the athlete's choice to genetically enhance. In addition, athletes must evaluate the various and potential harms arising from the use of genetic technology.

It is important now to outline the specific ethical issues relating to the various kinds of application of genetics to sport, so that we may derive some tentative conclusions about their ethical status. Already, Chapter 2 has outlined a number of arguments against doping in sport. In addition, Chapter 3 has discussed the scientific possibilities of genetic technology applied to sport, detailing the various categories of application devised by Munthe (2000) and Tamburrini (2002). Chapter 8 then detailed many of the ethical fears about genetic modification more broadly understood as potential harms arising from genetic modification. It is now necessary to outline whether these concerns are valid where genetic technology is used to alter sporting performance.

Already, I have suggested that genetic modification may actually enhance the value of sporting performances. This general statement must now be made more specific in the context of the imminent applications of genetics. As has been argued throughout, I will include the use of genetic information within this final analysis, even though it is not a form of manipulation. A useful way to assess specific cases of genetic modification in sport can be in a similar format to the structure of Chapter 3, which outlines the various categories of genetic modification. However, some minor clarifications are necessary in response to the conceptualisations offered by Munthe (2000) and Tamburrini (2002).

As was explained in Chapter 1 and briefly in Chapter 3, different kinds of performance modifiers in sport give rise to similar kinds of ethical question, many of which have been outlined already. For example, a concern about the fairness of using beta-blockers is comparable to the concern about the fairness of using carbon-composite tennis rackets. Similarly, one might explain the ethical issues regarding genetic modification in a way that others have argued for the ethical status of more familiar methods of performance enhancement, such as doping. However, Chapter 8 demonstrates that genetic modification implies a new array of ethical issues, which are not as apparent for other methods of performance enhancement in sport. It is not that genetic modification does not also raise the more conventional doping concerns, but that there are additional ethical issues which suggest that genetic modification cannot be considered solely in the same terms as other methods of performance *enhancement* or, more broadly, performance *modification*.

A similar claim may be made about the different categories of genetic modification. It is possible to identify a number of ethical implications of genetic modification for sport, which may also arise in relation to other performance modifiers such as drug use. For example, there may be a similar concern for the preservation of equal competition arising from drug use, as well as from genetic modification. Second, it is possible to identify a number of different technologies of genetic modification which give rise to similar ethical issues. For example, the concern about social engineering is important, both in relation to the use of genetic pre-selection and germ-line cell modification. These overlapping parameters of genetics and sport make it difficult to provide a succinct response to the ethical issues without repeating the same kinds of argument, though this is to be expected. Nevertheless, it is possible to provide an overview of the various kinds of genetic manipulation, explaining how each might fit within sport.

Also in response to Munthe (2000) and Tamburrini (2002), an attempt will be made to identify *categories of ethical issues* alongside *types of genetic technology*. In each of their categorisations, the ethical issues are framed by the different kinds of genetic technology. Instead, I will develop a framework of ethical issues that relate to genetic technology in sport. This can provide a useful way of understanding the broad ethical issues arising from genetics, regardless of the specific application. I will suggest that there are important differences between the applications in terms of their immediate, ethical importance. For example, I will suggest that genetic selection and the broader use of genetic information in sport presents ethical issues that have thus far been unexplored in sport. Finally, I will provide further scientific details about the different categories and emphasise the importance of understanding the science, to allow a critical perspective on the ethical issues arising from this new technology.

In sum, this chapter will focus on those unique, new ethical concerns arising from genetics, rather than the conventional doping arguments. Chapter 10 will then give responses to specific sporting arguments, which are commonly found in discussions about doping and performance enhancement.

Generic bioethical concerns about genetic modification in sport

The safety argument

For many scientists, concerns about the safety of individuals who may be genetically modified remain crucial. It is widely regarded that genetic modification is still in its infancy and very little is known about genetic diseases. Even less is known about how genes may be used to promote enhancement in sporting performance. However, potentially any of the applications of genetic technology could promote safety and reduce harm in sport. For example, the engineering of somatic or germ-line cells could make the person more resilient to disease or injury. Permitting athletes to engineer *resistance* genes could make the athlete healthier and, subsequently, more capable of performing and training well for sport. In addition, if genetic information could reveal that a child might have a predisposition to a specific kind of medical condition or injury, then it could be used to inform that child about the potential risks associated with competing in a given sport and prevent them from incurring an injury. This kind of application has been documented significantly in relation to the way in which insurance companies might exploit genetic information. It seems quite consensual that genetic information could provide knowledge about predispositions for genetically related conditions. By extension, such information might also indicate whether one is advised to avoid specific kinds of physical activity. For example, genetic information may reveal that one has a predisposition for a muscular or bone disease of some sort that would make it quite dangerous to perform specific kinds of activity. The Australian Law Reforms Commission (2003) reports on this possibility in sport.

Regardless of these effects, the analysis does not deal sufficiently with the ethical issues arising from safety and harm. While there is a basis for arguing that genetic modification can be conducive to health, the issue of harm has a further complication. Whereas increasing safety entails creating an environment where an individual is at less risk of physical or mental debilitation, the concept of harm can be seen more broadly, as is argued in Chapter 8 (harm as non-physical injury).

In addition, harm is not a sufficient basis on which to reject genetic modification, except in the context of a discussion about what kinds of *harm* are acceptable in sport. After all, sports policy does not seek to make sports completely safe, since it is easy to recognise that some sports are possible only by accepting a certain level of risk. Consequently, in the case of genetic modification, the argument from harm must ask whether genetic modification is more harmful than other legitimate methods of performance enhancement and whether the harm that is created by the technology is an integral or acceptable part of the sport. It could be argued that the risks to health taken by genetically modified athletes is no greater than the risks taken by participating in some sports at all. For example, boxing and equestrian events entail significant risks, regardless of whether the athletes take drugs. In these activities, the potential for severe injuries is remarkably high and the harm from using drugs to run fast might be seen as relatively negligible by comparison. Equally, the risks from genetic modification might be substantially less than these other forms of performance enhancement (Dixon, 2001).

In sum, the concern for safety may be a persuasive case to prohibit the use of genetic manipulation in sport, but it is not a sufficient position, since it must allow for the possibility that safer technology may lessen the potential for harm. The deeper question to be answered is whether genetic modification is still ethically acceptable in conditions where the technology is sufficiently safe. To conclude only with the safety argument does not allow us to answer this further question.

Genetic modification, sport and social justice

A further, pervasive bioethical concern about genetic modification in sport, particularly genetic modification for enhancement, is its potential to be socially divisive or a precursor to a genetic super-class. In sport, this worry is legitimate for each of the various forms of manipulation. For genetic pre-selection and screening, certain kinds of individuals are chosen over others or, more accurately, certain kinds of genes are selected over others. The same argument applies for somatic cell and germ-line cell modification, the consequence of which is that specific kinds of people are in a genetically advantageous position by having a more enhanced genetic disposition. Even if this does not necessarily translate into any realised social advantage – it is not sufficient to be genetically gifted to be successful – the claim is that such enhanced individuals would have an advantage over non-modified people.

An initial reaction to this argument critiques the idea that genetic engineering selects specific kinds of individuals over others. However, this neglects the salient features of personhood – the sense in which an individual can claim to be in touch with his or her moral authenticity – and, for this reason, it need not be too much of a concern. For example, the idea that genetic modification eliminates dysfunction and that this may be a reason for concluding that it implies that individuals with such disorders have less value is not really applicable. Choosing to make such alterations does not alter the value given to those specific individuals who are making such claims. Engineering genes is not the same as engineering identities.

Nevertheless, by permitting such alterations for sport, it is possible that the technology will exclude a significant number of people, since the technology is unlikely to be available or affordable for everybody. These circumstances disadvantage persons both within sport and outside of it and are likely to be a significant priority for sports authorities when deciding whether this technology is ethically sound for sport. However, the different applications give rise to differing forms of social injustice. For example, the use of somatic cell modification would disadvantage other competitors within sport, though it may not really confer any further social advantage beyond sport. Conversely, germ-line cell modification would confer an advantage to the future generations of the enhanced athletes, assuming that the kind of modification an athlete receives is the kind that would be a socially advantageous characteristic of being human. Currently, this is not particularly clear, as there are only so many professions where greater endurance or strength are valuable and they do not tend to be those that are of high social status. Indeed, sporting modifications may prove to be completely innocuous in the discussion about fairness and justice, outside of the sporting context. Nevertheless, it is an ethical argument that spans the different kinds of modification and it is a reason for being cautious about the legitimisation of genetic modification.

Genetic essentialism in sport

The final generic bioethical concern I will consider here arises from the tendency for legitimising genetic technology to give rise to genetic essentialism, the view that differences between the performances of different individuals are solely the product of genetic differences. Again, for each of the various kinds of application under discussion, genetic essentialism is ethically alarming. In sport, the value given to the use of genetic pre-selection and screening presupposes a way of evaluating persons only by their genes. Thus, even if there were merit in the use of genetic screening as a basis for determining who might be the next generation of elite athletes, investment in this technology would be to the neglect of other characteristics, which may also be useful in deciding which are the next elite athletes. The reason why this is alarming is precisely because genes alone do not determine how good an athlete will be in competition. Genetic essentialism is of concern here because it could create a situation whereby promising athletes might be deterred from *struggling* simply because they are told that their genetic predisposition is not optimal.

As was noted earlier, the President of the International Olympic Committee, Dr Jacques Rogge, does not see anything too problematic with this use of genetics. Indeed, it may not be particularly different from a child being told that he or she will never be an elite athlete after being watched by talent scouts. However, Rogge is mistaken in assuming that there is nothing wrong with this latter process either. It is possible that the entire approach and philosophy of *selection* in sport requires critiquing, if one aspires to devising worthwhile sporting values. Potentially, this argument may lead to a contentious critique of competition more broadly, though it is not necessary to go this far at the present stage. All that is required is to recognise that the selection of athletes based solely on their genes invokes a way of evaluating others that negates the value of human agency and this is both unfortunate and unnecessary. Moreover, it asserts a way of evaluating potential athletes solely on their performative capacities, rather than their potential willingness to overcome the challenges necessary to become an elite athlete (assuming, of course, it is not also possible to find a gene for motivation).

The same kind of genetic essentialism applies as a concern for the other methods of modification (somatic, germ-line, pharmacogenomics). If genes become interpreted as determining how successful one can be in various aspects of life, then the use of such technology should be avoided, since the conclusion is mistaken. This is particularly alarming in a world where home genetic testing is already available and highly under-regulated. If there are not suitable measures to try and evolve an interpretation of genetics as an integral part of understanding what determines social success, then there may be further reasons to prohibit the use of genetic technology for sport. Avoiding this problem is possible providing that no special status is given to genetic selection in the process of talent development. If this problem is not addressed, then sport performances would be further dehumanised, where dehumanisation is defined by the absence of autonomy, personhood and authenticity.

In addition to these *generic bioethical concerns*, there are a number of case-specific implications of genetic modification for sport which require greater explanation and response. For example, the *life harms* described in Chapter 8 are relevant mainly for germ-line cell modification and so will be discussed in that section, whereas *knowledge and access issues* will be explained in relation to the use of genetic information in sport. The next section of this chapter will speak to specific kinds of genetic modification (responding to the ethical arguments arising from bioethics) when such technologies are applied to the sporting context.

Pharmacogenomics and pharmacogenetics

If one wanted to conceptualise genetic modification in a similar manner to drug use, then the science of pharmacogenomics is perhaps the most analogous. Pharmacogenomics (also known as pharmacogenetics) seeks the application of genomics – the study of the genome – to new pharmaceutical products, so that it might be possible to create more effective and safer drugs. The distinction between pharmacogenomics and pharmacogenetics is now considered arbitrary and they are used interchangeably. However, pharmacogenomics refers to the general study of all of the many different genes that determine drug behaviour, whereas pharmacogenetics refers to the study of individual differences (variations) in drug metabolism and response (McCarthy, 2000; Moldrup, 2002; Sneddon, 2000).

Yet, despite their similarities, pharmacogenomics may provide *less* strength to the credibility of anti-doping campaigns. Pharmacogenomics may make drug use in sport far less controversial or ethically problematic, since new drugs would, expectedly, be made much safer and promote health much more effectively (Buchanan *et al.*, 2002). If this were the case, then it would weaken the *medical* case against drug use and genetic modification substantially. Moreover, it nullifies the argument made by anti-doping activists who claim that pro-enhancement ethicists ignore the deleterious side effects of pharmaceuticals. Indeed, the anti-doping concern for health *encourages* the development of pharmacogenomics. From a philosophical perspective this is a particularly interesting prospect, since it will allow the sharpening of the debate about the legitimacy of performance enhancement and, potentially, move it beyond the limitations of the safety issue, which is often seen as a sufficient basis for prohibiting the use of such substances.

There is an additional concern about pharmacogenomics, which was addressed in Chapter 7. The chapter argues how health-related concepts are culturally constructed, rather than being grounded in biological objectivity. For this reason, pharmaceutical solutions to medical conditions may sometimes be used to address social problems. The application of pharmacogenomics to sport would be comparable, since it would encourage athletes to seek enhancements to their performance through drug technology, should they be made legal. Indeed, the very fact that such drugs might be developed for sport could also be argued as symptomatic of a drug-dependent society. Again, it is important to note that this is a conclusion based upon a bioethical argument, rather than one that is concerned about the ethics of sport.

There are some more familiar problems with the development of pharmacogenomics, which are nearly identical to issues concerning the use of drugs. For example, if products arising from pharmacogenomics were illegal, then the same kind of unfairness argument could be raised and is currently being made about the use of banned substances in elite sport. It is my suggestion that this issue is not particularly worth pursuing here, since genetic technology does not really produce any new ethical issue. In addition, such a concern relies upon the new products also being banned from competition. While it may be argued that this is very likely, a more intriguing line of questioning could be pursued if they are not. It is a more straightforward problem to conclude whether the use of a substance is unethical if it is banned, than if it is legal.

Somatic cell modification

Somatic cell modification involves altering the non-hereditary cells of the body, which may be contrasted with the hereditary germ-line cells of an organism. Unlike pharmacogenomics, somatic cell modification necessitates an alteration to the genetic composition of an athlete. In contrast, pharmacogenomics might simply imply using knowledge about genomics to develop more effective pharmaceutical products, which might be used by an athlete to enhance performance (though not on a genetic level). This is the first way in which the use of genetic technology would entail altering the individual's specific and unique genetic composition. In genetic science, somatic cell modifications are more advanced when compared with germ-line cell modifications and, as such, the modification of somatic cells is also first in the sense of being the most imminent application of genetic modification. Altering the germ-line cells of individuals is considerably more complicated and experimental than manipulating the somatic cells. However, even for somatic cell research, success has been limited and much remains unclear about what may be expected from their modification.

In sport, a modification to the somatic cells of an organism could take the form of altering the specific genetic composition of an athlete's muscular capacity. Chapter 3 outlines the possible applications of somatic cell research using insulin-like growth factor-1 (IGF-1). Research suggests that this protein might be introduced to an organism using a viral vector, to treat muscle-wasting diseases, such as muscular dystrophy. By implication, the research suggests that this application may also have some use for athletes seeking to boost their muscle mass. It still remains uncertain as to whether this is going to be possible and, if so, safe. However, if the research continues to be successful, then this might be an imminent use for athletes seeking to genetically enhance their performance.

One of the arguments for not allowing this kind of technology in sport has to do with its accessibility, broadly defined in scientific and financial terms. Thus if somatic cell modification is expensive and relies upon an extensive access to scientific facilities, then it is unethical because it is unfair that only the rich and scientifically developed parts of the world will have access to such facilities. Of course, the same kind of argument may also be used in relation to other kinds of technology in sport, about which there is little ethical debate. For this reason, there is no obvious reason why the kinds of expense related to genetic technology would be any special reason to prohibit the use of the technology. Perhaps the only basis for what makes genetics special is the global context within which policies on genetics must be made. Thus while one might argue that, say, altitude chambers are also only likely to be affordable to countries which are wealthy, the additional difference between altitude chambers and genetic technology is that the latter comes with a cultural baggage that is important to recognise. Altitude chambers have little or no value or meaning outside of sport and specialised medical practice. In contrast, genetic science could have far-reaching implications for societies, which gives it a special status.

The deeper question is whether it would still be desirable to use genetic technology, if everybody had access to the technology. From here, it is possible to pursue the question of fairness further and to introduce an unexplored interpretation of the fairness argument. In sport, there is almost certainly going to be further division within the elite athletic community as a result of legalising this technology. At most, we might expect genetically modified athletes to be slightly better performers than non-genetically modified athletes. This has two divisive consequences: between athletes within competition and between athletes outside of competition. Thus permitting somatic cell modification may mean that non-modified competition loses its value, as spectators may be more interested in witnessing the enhanced athletes in contest. As such, the non-modified will lose their privileged position in elite sport, though perhaps only in the same way that the less genetically gifted also lose such opportunities for celebrity. This would certainly be undesirable for the non-modified athlete, but it does not mean that there exists a responsibility to ensure that non-modified athletes continue to be valued in society.

The second form of disadvantage refers to how non-modified athletes might lose social status *only* because they are not genetically enhanced or, perhaps more broadly, how genetic modification would devalue the profession of being an elite athlete. Such a disadvantage might also be measured financially in terms of sponsorship and so on, which could prevent non-modified elite athletes from being competitive and professional. Again, this consequence of permitting genetic modification is unfortunate for those athletes who may no longer be able to maintain a career as an elite athlete, but does not necessitate its prohibition. After all, we would not prevent the manufacture of a more sophisticated innovation, such as a faster microprocessor, just because it prevents older technology from being competitive. However, the related concerns for *social engineering* and the *engineering of future values* are important to consider here. The ethical issue is not simply about replacing one technology with another, but altering what makes being human valuable. The claim raised earlier about the engineering of *values* is clearly implicated by somatic cell modification, even though such alterations are not passed down to the next generation genetically. The ideological connotations of engineering *betterness* are also alarming, though do not warrant prohibition, since they are not insurmountable.

Germ-line cell modification

Engineering the hereditary germ-line cells carries a greater level of responsibility for many people, since it has implications beyond the individual harm to the person modified. Various arguments have been discussed about this application, including playing God, life harms, engineering future values and interrupting evolution. Applied to sport, germ-line modification falls prey to each of these ethical concerns. Consequently, if any of them is considered to have strength, then it would be a persuasive case for why germ-line genetic modification has no place in sport (and also why it has no place in society at all). Currently, there is fierce opposition to engineering the germ-line cells of human beings for similar reasons to many of those I have given above. There does not appear to be anything new from the sporting context for what makes this technology ethically problematic, except further uncertainty about the probability of such engineering to yield meaningful results for athletes.

It is necessary to elaborate on one as yet unexplored argument that is provoked by altering these building blocks of life. It is an argument often found in relation to cloning, and it is concerned with the way in which the modification of germ-line cells to create elite athletes could further encourage the tendency to *objectify life*. This would entail encouraging prospective parents to engineer specific characteristics, such as those for sport, on the basis of some view about what kind of life is worth living for their child. In relation to cloning specifically, this may involve being disinclined to encourage a child to pursue an interest, on the basis of having concluded that the individual, from which the child had been cloned, was never any good at that activity.

The reason why this is not considered particularly important in the present analysis is because this argument, albeit important, is not unique to sport. The concern about objectifying life is the same whether it is athletes, musicians, mathematicians, or anything that is the aim of the modification. It encourages prospective parents to have a limited vision of what kind of life would be valuable for their child, which overstates the role of parenting significantly. As Brock (1998: 62) argues:

> If one has been extensively shaped by another person, one might lose one's sense of self-creation and individuality, both of which depend on the belief that one has significant capacity to control and determine over time the kind of person one becomes by the choices and commitments one makes.

Nevertheless, sporting modifications may be more defensible, since they may be seen as being conducive to the promotion of health. If it were possible to engineer future generations to be healthier and, perhaps therefore, more capable in elite athletic performance, then this would be a desirable choice. A sporting genetic modification understood in this way provides even greater support for the critique of this position, which states that providing such enhancements would be comparable to other kinds of advantage we seek to provide for our children, such as piano or singing lessons, or simply a good education. On this basis there seems little reason to prevent individuals from engineering sport-like characteristics, though the basis for doing so requires prospective parents to want their children to become elite athletes specifically.

Genetic pre-selection, screening and testing

Chapter 8 explains how genetic screening and testing give rise to ethical issues concerning *knowledge and access*. The Australian Law Reforms Commission (2003) highlights how genetic information might be misused by sporting authorities and considers it to be an issue that requires further ethical and legal investigation. The ALRC is particularly concerned with preventing genetic discrimination and protecting individual privacy. For the former, it recognises how, if athletes are required to reveal their genetic information, they might be prohibited from competition on the basis of having a condition that might place the athlete in a vulnerable position when competing. The example the ALRC uses is boxing, where an athlete might be prevented from competing on account of some genetic precondition, which suggests that the athlete is more susceptible to serious injury (British Medical Association, 2002; McCrory, 2001). This is considered problematic because the ALRC recognises that genetic preconditions do not necessitate that an illness will be realised. This is because genetic predispositions are only one factor in the development of a gene-related pathology. The ALRC's concerns about privacy have to do with what might be claimed by an individual about his or her right to keep genetic information private from the sporting authorities. Each of these issues will be addressed in turn, though they are related. For example, if athletes were given a strong entitlement to privacy of genetic information and if this premise is adopted more broadly within sport, then it is less likely that individuals would be subject to genetic discrimination, since it would not be possible to evaluate individuals on the basis of their genotype, or individual genetic map. However, each of these issues does have some varying consequences for sport, which require separation.

Concerns about discrimination are comparable to those raised against the use of genetic information as a basis for determining life insurance premiums (Ayabe and Tan, 1995; Burley, 1999; Gorner, 2000; Keyley, 1996; Knoppers, 1999; Sandberg, 1995).

In addition, some points of departure may be found in employment rights cases where Hendriks (1997: 557) argues that 'the unrestricted use of genetic information poses a number of threats to the exercise and enjoyment of human rights'. The likely use of genetic information by employers as a tool to reduce economic risk and to select genetically desirable employees invites discrimination, since it reduces individuals to genetic predispositions. As if this discrimination were not alarming enough, such genetic essentialism may also lead to a situation where individuals seek genetic enhancement to remain socially competitive. This consequence may even encourage prospective parents to seek the latest genetic enhancement to provide a good start in life for their child. In such circumstances, it is also possible to see how this might lead to social stratification between the genetically rich and genetically poor. In general, open access to genetic information may lead to undesirable circumstances.

In sport, the way in which these kinds of circumstance might come about could be on the basis of some anti-doping rationale. Thus it might be claimed by anti-doping authorities that they should have access to the genetic information of athletes, so that they can determine whether an athlete is cheating, assuming that genetic modification is (1) possible and (2) prohibited. From the anti-doping authority's perspective, the concern would be that genetically enhanced individuals enjoy an advantage over other athletes who are not genetically modified. As such, the initial question is whether athletes have the right to protection of their genetic information in sport. If sport can be conceived as an agreement between various parties, then it might also be inferred that the athlete waives such rights by virtue of participating voluntarily. However, if such information remains private, then governing bodies have no legal basis upon which to react to engineered athletes within competition. This is problematic for sports, since not being able to distinguish the genetically modified from the non-modified would result in competitions between unevenly matched opponents, where the unevenness is a relevant aspect of the contest. A suitable comparison where it is similarly meaningless to create a contest would be between different weight divisions in boxing. Where there exist different genetic divisions in sports, these are also meaningless competitions. Of course, this is also a case for accounting for inherited genetic variance, not only engineered variance.

To help think through whether athletes would have to disclose their genetic profile, one can draw parallels with the privacy of the athlete and the desire to ensure that athletes are not using doping methods. For example, for the sake of equitable competition (Ledley, 1994), athletes could be asked to disclose genetic information for the same reasons that they are required to undergo doping tests (Rose, 1988). However, in so doing, it must be recognised that the public domain of competitive sport would most likely become public knowledge and might impact upon the individual's rights outside of sports competition. The ALRC provides a good example of this when considering genetic disorders that might put an athlete in a position of high risk, if competing in a specific kind of sport.

Similar questions arise about genetic information as have arisen in the case of other kinds of performance enhancement. This debate hinges upon whether an athlete is obliged to provide such information or whether the athlete's rights override this authority. Our conclusion about this depends largely on the kind of information being sought. If sporting authorities are interested in learning about whether athletes have a genetic condition that places them at greater risk in competition – as is argued for the boxing example – then our reaction is quite different from the ethical implications of requesting genetic information to discover whether or not an athlete is genetically modified. For the latter, our concerns for the athlete would be minimised if we knew that this information could not be used in any way that might be prejudicial to the athlete outside of sport. However, it is necessary to know more about the precise kind of information that would be discovered from such testing. It is possible that the kinds of tests seeking to establish whether an athlete had been enhanced would also show if an athlete is genetically disadvantaged. In contrast, information that reveals whether an athlete were likely to be at a greater risk in his or her chosen sport would seem to have a directly negative connotation for related parties, such as insurance companies.

The disclosure of genetic information to governing bodies must be done cautiously so as to ensure that genetic discrimination does not take place (as this would be in violation of Unesco's (1997) draft declaration on the human genome and human rights). However, within sport, the ability to ensure that this does not happen is uniquely problematic. If governing bodies ignore genetically enhanced competitors, then the unenhanced will suffer a competitive disadvantage and, perhaps, future generations would be coerced into enhancement for fear that they will no longer be viable competitors in sport. Admittedly, this situation is already reflective of competitive sport and of the difficulties arising from trying to apply international anti-doping policies. Arguably, the *clean* athlete is already within a coercive environment, where the need to remain competitive demands that athletes must dope.

Perhaps, then, there is some rationale for basing an approach to genetic modification on relevant aspects of the anti-doping model. This conclusion must be able to explain why, for example, genetics is more like drugs than any other kind of technology, which is not brought within an anti-doping framework. Such a perspective presumes that the two examples of performance enhancement are alike and may be treated similarly. While it is true that some applications of genetic technology are similar, there are additional ethical issues arising from genetic modification, such as the broader social context of genetics and the desire to enhance humans, knowledge and access issues relating to genetic information, the potential to prescribe what kinds of things are valued by future generations, the possible disruption to natural selection, genetic essentialism, and the prospect of a genetic super-class. For non-genetic doping, these ethical and moral concerns are not so important, since the modifications to athletes are consequential largely from the perspective of competitive fairness. For these reasons, treating genetic and non-genetic doping as similar would be comparable to treating doping in the same way as addressing the performance enhancement achieved by equipment such as Speedo's FastSkin swim-suit (Fitzsimons, 2000). Genetic enhancement and doping are quite different forms of performance enhancement that cannot be treated alike, although much can be learned about how governing bodies might seek to justify the prohibition of genetic enhancement by examining anti-doping policy.

If governing bodies must respond to the existence of genetically enhanced competitors, it would be necessary for athletes to disclose their genetic information. Furthermore, upon receiving such knowledge, sports authorities would need to preserve fair competition or else ban genetically modified athletes from competition, which would also be discriminatory. As such, either sporting authorities legalise genetic modification, or they endeavour to create different kinds of competition. The latter of these proposals would still necessitate testing to avoid the genetically modified athlete trying to enter non-modified competitions.

However, genetic discrimination is only one manner in which genetic information might be used to the disadvantage of some athletes. Other possible misuses of genetic information in sport might include genetic screening to identify prospective elite athletes. This technological process of *genetic scouting* makes some very controversial scientific assumptions about genetics, which are not consensually endorsed. Currently, such research is criticised because there is little or no basis for concluding that performance in elite sport is significantly determined by genetic conditions. One of the foremost claims against talent identification is that it is driven by an elitist motivation to be internationally successful in sport. This is morally questionable for a number of reasons.

First, it makes explicit that, from a national perspective, it is winning that matters in sport. This is particularly alarming given that the allusion to become an elite athlete is not consensually regarded as a prudential choice. A career in elite sport is strewn with uncertainties and a high improbability of being successful to such an extent that one can secure a reasonable standard of living. Second, genetic selection could unjustifiably dissuade a child from getting into sport, thus robbing children of any aspirations of success before they have even tried. This is alarming since no sound conclusions have been made about the extent to which genes determine athletic success. It is also important to differentiate between sports when discussing the ethical implications of genetic information. It is likely that the usefulness of such information will vary between sports as a predictor of performance. Potentially, informing a child that he or she does not have the genes to become an elite athlete could prevent such a child from enjoying considerable success in any number of sports where this information is less relevant. This need not take place in such an obvious way and so does not mean simply adopting a particular ethical view out of a concern for how such knowledge would be misused. Rather, the argument recognises that there would be an inevitable essentialising of human performance, as genetic alteration becomes normalised in society.

In conclusion, the motivations for gaining access to the genetic information of infants and children, to help decide who is worth investing in for sport, are ethically questionable. The basis for arguing that there is a medical foundation to the use of such technology is weak. Moreover, the expressed or implied interest in securing national success in elite sport is not a justification for investing in such technology at this stage of the research. Within the scientific community, there is no agreement that genetics can be the most important factor determining success in elite competition, and it would therefore be unsound to base such research on this premise. Instead, the process of talent development should be concerned about understanding the role of parents, coaches and the rights of children in sport so as to formulate policy about what is in the interest of the children participating in sport at a young age (Tymowski, 2001). One of the significant concerns in elite sport is that the child is not sufficiently protected by current standards of care. The pressure and desire of parents and coaches for their young athletes to be successful can lead to a lack of consideration about the general well-being of a child. For this reason, further work must take place to negotiate a greater level of protection for the child in sport before permitting the use of genetic information for talent identification.

Summary

These various responses to the bioethical concern about genetic modification in sport do not condone prohibition absolutely. The safety argument against genetic modification is a particularly strong argument against the current use of genetic modification. However, it is not a sufficient basis from which to explain what is unethical about genetics in sport, nor does it provide an adequate explanation for what counts as a legitimate, therapeutic use of the technology. The idea that genetic modification also challenges the realisation of social justice or creates greater social division in society also relies upon contingent economical factors related to the technology, which is itself underpinned by the way in which this is made legal in society. The kinds of disadvantage a non-modified human might face in a world where there exist genetically modified athletes is minimal, particularly given the critique of genetic essentialism. However, if such technology is considered to be legitimate, attempts must be made to minimise the potential for misunderstanding the role of genes in performance, thus avoiding the consequences of believing in genetic essentialism.

The bioethical concerns about pharmacogenomics applied to sport are not substantial, assuming that the science will give rise to safer drugs. However, encouraging the use of drugs carries the additional concern of promoting a drug-dependent society, which has implications beyond what is ethically desirable in sport. Somatic cell modification seems likely to be a technology that is very expensive in its early years. For this reason, it may be seen as unethical in sport since not all competitors will have access to the technology. However, if such difficulties are overcome, then the use of this technology might require constructing two different kinds of competition to accommodate the various philosophies of athletes and how they perceive their relationship to performance and technology. For those athletes who see their performances as transcending human barriers, the use of genetic modification might be desirable. For athletes who do not give such value to the quantifiable aspects of their performance, it would be desirable to construct sports that marginalise the use of technology. This might result in a lower social status attached to being a non-modified athlete, though this is difficult to discern. Nor is it a reason to prohibit the use of such technology by autonomous, moral agents. Germ-line cell modification carries the additional burden of altering future generations. It is also a much more complex science than is somatic cell alteration. For these reasons it is difficult to encourage the use of this technology, since doing so would encourage a climate of sport where anything goes and where ethics in sport has nothing to do with the means of achieving performance. Moreover, engineering germ-line cells might encourage an objectification of human life that implies disrespect for individuals. For similar reasons, genetic pre-selection is alarming since it encourages the construction of lives based upon contested, ideological assumptions about what is valuable. In itself, it is not problematic that people have such beliefs, though pre-selection entails making such decisions for future generations, thus undermining their possibility for discerning what matters.

These choices to enhance, alter or manipulate must also be understood in the context of broader bioethical debates, which do not give prime importance to sporting values. Chapter 10 will deal with some reactions to genetic modification from the sporting perspective, though these arguments must also fit with bioethical responsibilities, which may prevent humans from altering themselves and their children in a way that would force sports to redefine their approach to the value of *genetic enhancement*.

10 Sport needs genetic modification

In addition to the bioethical reactions to gene doping are arguments that rely upon some ethical view of sport and what is legitimate within specific sporting practices. It remains to be seen how the genetic modification case responds to a number of the sporting arguments against doping raised in Chapter 1. Yet many of these arguments are not relevant to the genetics case, for two reasons.

First, the suggested approach of an ethics of authenticity rejects the paternal/liberal distinction as the appropriate manner in which to frame the ethical issue about performance enhancement. The ethical dilemma is not simply about which kinds of performance enhancement should be legalised and which should be banned. At most, any such decision should not rely solely upon an ethical view of sport. Rather, there are more entrenched philosophical and anthropological ideas related to the notion of personhood that are necessary to consider when questioning the value of human enhancement and genetic modification. Coming to terms with whether genetic modification in sport is ethical relies upon the way in which the human is characterised in sport. This is not an arbitrary choice about the limits to which we identify technologisation as being integral to being human. Rather, it can be derived from the way in which concepts such as humanness, human dignity and autonomy are described in legal documentation on human rights. On this view, the choice to genetically enhance is legitimate, since the salient aspects of being human involve a concern for protecting personhood. This argument is applicable to sport, partly because the ethics of sport and the ethics of medicine also build upon similar conceptions of what is human. Ethical issues concerning the use of medicine in sport are underpinned by ethical codes of scientific research and principles of medical ethics.

Second, establishing whether genetic modification is ethical in sport is not straightforwardly about the *good* of sport, because genetic modification is a technology that has deep intra-personal implications for the individual beyond sport. In this sense, when considering the ethics of gene doping in sport, sporting authorities need to reconceptualise the athlete as a human being who has rights regardless of his or her genetic characteristics. This commitment demands that sporting authorities do not dismiss the need (or interest) to provide a forum whereby future humans may choose to be genetically enhanced and where this is seen as a valuable and relevant characteristic of being a sports person.

This chapter will review the sporting arguments made against doping. It must be understood in the context of Chapter 1, which formulated a framework for conceptualising different kinds of arguments about doping in sport. However, the application of this framework to the genetics issue in sport varies in that some arguments are addressed by the broader bioethical arguments. For example, in Chapter 1 it was noted that a significant argument about doping arises out of a concern for probable 'harms to society'. These broader concerns in relation to genetic modification are considered in Chapter 9 dealing with the bioethical arguments. In contrast, this chapter will speak to the specific sporting arguments concerning genetic modification.

Genetic modification and undermining naturalness

The argument concerned with *harms as undermining the nature of sport* asserts that some forms of performance enhancement in sport are unethical because they negate an essential or inherent characteristic of sport that gives it value. In Chapter 1, this was also referred to as the prelusory goal of sport (Suits, 1973). Yet there are at least two important ways in which the term 'natural' may be used with this argument. First, it might describe the essence of sport as something predominantly human. In respect of our particular problem about enhancement, this latter view might resemble the following: *sport is valuable because it is a test of natural human capabilities, not the capabilities of technology to augment humans.* Second, naturalness might describe some essential aspect of sport, the absence of which would negate the value of competition. The point of contention for each of these positions (in relation to performance enhancement) is the extent to which technology is recognised as being integral to humanness.

Naturalness of humans

To assist with this discussion, it is useful to consider a similar question that has been asked in bioethics, particularly in relation to reproductive technologies, such as *in vitro* fertilisation. In this case, the parallel critique of technology states that assisted reproductive technology contradicts some essential or natural part of being human. This adopts a particular view of the natural, where this is loosely meant to imply some scientifically measurable distinction between nature and artifice. This type of argument does not constitute a reason for prohibiting the use of genetic modification in sport because its definition of the natural is contested. Indeed, I suggest that the natural is, at best, a meaningless concept though, at worst, potentially divisive, since it would seem to lead to the conclusion that some kinds of human are more valuable than others. There also seems to be an obvious sense in which this kind of conclusion would be mistaken. For while this view might conclude that *in vitro* fertilisation is an *unnatural* method of procreation, the resulting entity is most definitely something that is of the natural world – a human (or animal) life. At least, its moral status is not compromised by virtue of its having been created by *unnatural* methods.

A similar response may be given in relation to genetically modified athletes. While modifications to individual genomes might be characterised as artficial, this does not negate the moral value of the modified individual. There is a further sense in which this naturalness argument is also misleading, which can be elucidated by considering the prospect of germ-line cell modifications. This is a particularly useful case, given that tampering with embryos is often considered a highly emotive and controversial subject. Recent discussions of this kind include the utility of superfluous embryos and ownership of embryos. I suggest that the way in which the naturalness argument is used in relation to sport (and more widely) arises out of a context that is predominantly non-scientific. Our feelings about what is and what is not natural are tied to examples in culture that we find either anti-natural or not. Turney (1998) makes a similar case, arguing how our appreciation of the monstrous (perhaps also the unnatural) arises through such examples as Mary Shelley's Frankenstein, where the unnatural is portrayed as grotesque (and even evil). For this reason, it does not seem obviously apparent as to why the modified embryo would similarly be described in such terms. Indeed, if we were to provide the further example of modifying embryos before they are recognisably human, then the sense in which these lives appear grotesque becomes nonsensical. As such, genetic interventions at these embryonic stages do not tamper with the natural at all, since the natural has not yet been constructed at this stage in an embryo's life.

It makes no sense to talk about human cells with value-laden language such as the 'natural'. Given that such changes or interventions would occur so early in life, it is more accurate to describe these interventions as constitutive of the natural for the modified individual. Moreover, given the earlier argument about what constitutes personhood, the genetically modified athlete has the potential to be as human as a non-genetically modified athlete, since the biological characterisics of a human being alone do not determine whether one is a person.

In contrast, for pharmacogenomics and somatic cell modification, which entail manipulations on the adult (or at least, fully developed) human being, the naturalness argument is probably at its strongest. The argument considers that enhancing human biology is unnatural and, as such, should not be done. Consequently, because pharmacogenomic and somatic cell alteration would take place so late in the life of a human being's biological maturation, it is true that it entails tampering with the human body in a way that alters its initial condition. In this sense, it is unnatural inasmuch as it consists of using scientific technologies to bring about biological changes. Nevertheless, a similar case can be made about other factors that affect the performance of an athlete, such as diet, vitamins, sleep patterns and so on. Moreover, being able to identify an 'original constitution' is particularly difficult when discussing the development of a human life.

For our present purposes, the cases of pharmacogenomics and somatic cell manipulation are no more or less unnatural than drug use. For this reason, similar responses used in relation to drug use in sport can apply in relation to genetics. Yet a further defence of the naturalness of genetics might be that modifications of this kind – and drugs derived from genomics – could be based upon the individual's own biology. Thus, whereas previously drugs relied upon synthetic replications of biology, pharmacogenomics could provide drugs that are biologically more comparable (or identical) to the individual's own DNA. As such, it would be even more ridiculous to assert that the athlete is somehow becoming unnatural by using such products.

In the case of genetic pre-selection, there is no relevant claim to the technology being an unnatural process at all, since it does not involve tampering with the human being. Consequently, the unnaturalness argument does not negate the value of genetic modification in sport. Potentially, modifying humans in this way can permit athletes to be more natural, since they could use their own DNA to enhance their performance. Alternatively, if modifications take place early in life, they should be understood as playing some part in constituting the natural and, as such, cannot be seen as unethical for reasons of naturalness. One may also wish to argue that there are already ways in which athletic performances are unnatural in the sense that they are constituted partly by technological means. On this view, the distinction between artifice and nature in sport is not possible to make and is, indeed, a questionable basis upon which to discern a moral or ethical distinction.

Naturalness of sport

A similar argument, which deserves its own response, is the idea that genetic modification might compromise the *internal goods of sports*. A method of performance modification that compromised the internal goods of any given sport would have to interfere with the attainment of those goods that are achievable only through participating in that particular practice (Morgan, 1994). For example, an internal good of tennis might be the experience of a rally or the performance of a serve. Any technology that reduces the quality of that unique experience, or which makes it easier, would compromise the internal goods of tennis. This position may be used to explain why the speed of the first serve in men's professional tennis is considered to be increasingly problematic. In this case, the dominance of the serve can be seen to undermine valued aspects of the game (Coe, 2000; Miah, 2000).

Yet it is important to clarify what counts as an internal good and how genetic modification might affect it. On this subject MacIntyre (1985) is unclear, though he includes such things as money, fame, power and privilege as *external* goods, since they serve to enhance an individual's status, which has little utility for the practice community at large. Furthermore, these kinds of goods are external in the sense that they do not describe special or unique aspects of a given practice. It is possible to earn money, fame and power in all sorts of professions, which says nothing about the unique character of any sport. In contrast, MacIntyre (1985: 187) describes a practice as:

> any coherent and complex form of socially established cooperative human activity through which goods internal to that form of activity are realised in the course of trying to achieve those standards of excellence which are appropriate to, and partially definitive of, that form of activity with the result that human powers to achieve excel, and human conceptions of the ends and goods involved, are systematically extended.

MacIntyre goes on to explain that internal goods can be achieved through competition to excel. Moreover, this contrasts with external goods, which are always an individual's property and possessions. While this distinction might allow us to identify some goods as strictly external or internal, it is unclear how some important goods might be characterised. Brown (1990) argues that the good of *winning* must be a borderline case because there are different kinds of winning that have different kinds of value. Winning, *per se*, is not a good that may be claimed as exclusive to a particular practice because its importance derives from the specific setting within which it is achieved. For this reason, technologies that enhance one's capacity to win may be described as internal to the practice.

This does not seem to be an argument than can be applied to genetic modification, since genetic capacities do nothing to reduce the capacity to experience internal goods of sports. A genetically enhanced tennis player would still be able to perform the various skills that a non-enhanced tennis player could enjoy. (Indeed, genetically enhancing reaction time might actually avoid the problem of the dominant serve in tennis.) However, it is necessary to make a distinction in relation to the importance of internal goods in sport. While it may appear that genetic technology does not prevent the attainment of internal goods, it is not yet clear whether it promotes their attainment. Arguably, genetic enhancement could permit a greater acquisition of internal goods, since it would enhance the quality of the experience. Athletes would be more competent and achieve more consistent levels of excellence.

In contrast, it is possible to identify examples of enhancing technology that do compromise the internal goods of a sport by allowing an athlete to appear more *skilful* without needing to train. This kind of example is reflected in Gardner's (1989) analysis of the U-groove golf-clubs, which allowed a novice golfer to appear more skilful by providing more control over the stroke. Similarly, Gelberg's (1996b) critique of the asymmetric Polara golf ball could also be argued as a technology that undermined the internal goods of golf, by allowing a golfer to improve the accuracy of the stroke. Since genetic modification does not de-skill sport, and thus does not prevent an athlete from experiencing the internal goods of a sport, there seems no reason to reject such technology from sport on this basis.

Genetic modification and unfairness

When analysing the reasons for rejecting drug use in sport, it was also questioned whether it is reasonable to claim that an implicit *contract* exists between athletes, which delimits the acceptable means of performance enhancement. If it is unclear whether some agreement exists between competitors regarding the acceptability of doping in sport, it is even less clear in relation to genetic modification. While athletes might intuitively reject gene doping in sport for similar reasons that they might give for rejecting doping in general, a further question must be asked about the acceptability of being genetically disadvantaged without modification. Undoubtedly, many athletes may identify their genetic gift as a salient aspect of what gives sport value. Thus the purpose of competition is partly about revealing who is the most genetically gifted. Yet this perspective seems to favour the genetically advantaged. Moreover, it does not seem to make sense to suggest that genetic variation is a valued part of competition. Indeed, many sports recognise genetic variation as an irrelevant inequality in sport and seek to minimise this disparity between competitors by separating different competitors into different divisions. A straightforward example here would include a number of contact sports, where weight is considered to be an irrelevant inequality to contests. Thus, where athletes are radically different in their weight, they are split into different contests. There seems good reason why athletes should want to eliminate the irrelevant inequality of genetic variance in competition. Athletes are engaged in activities where a commitment to training and putting in time to practise are considered to be important aspects of becoming a winner in competition. If genetic advantage could circumvent the need to struggle with one's performance, then sport would lack value. For this reason, if genetic advantage is considered to have some influence on success in sport, it is desirable for athletes to want genetic handicaps in sport.

In the case of pharmacogenomics, it would be easy enough – and expected – that sports authorities would simply place these drugs on the banned list without giving due consideration to their potential to level any *natural* genetic inequalities. Much of the present discussion asks for a greater clarification of the bases on which such choices are made. Yet, even if genetic modification were made illegal, there are complex and controversial implications to concluding that a genetically modified athlete has broken an alleged contract, and that therefore they are cheating. On the conventional definition of cheating by doping (the *strict liability* policy), the germ-line engineered athlete would be a cheat by virtue of being born with a genotype which has been augmented in a manner that will predispose him or her to being a more competent athlete. Such a disposition will have been afforded by a parent or guardian who chose to enhance this person's genetic constitution and, having such a condition, would be outside of the rules. Yet it would not be reasonable to label such a person as a cheat, since they will not have actually altered themselves to gain some advantage in sport. This is true insofar as the term 'cheat' implies something meaningful about the character of the cheat.

It could still be argued that, regardless of their intention to cheat, if genetically modified athletes are permitted in sport, then they would be breaking rules. Yet it is important to know whether athletes are aware that they are breaking the rules when we come to describe an individual as a cheat, with the negative moral language that such a label implies. It is reasonable to avoid characterising such individuals as cheats in the same way in which individuals knowingly break rules in order to gain a competitive advantage. But still, the challenge for governing bodies of sport would be deciding what is to be done about the unwittingly modified athlete. With the intentional cheat, it is less difficult to justify the decision to ban him or her from competition. However, as was indicated earlier, it is not sufficient to genetically discriminate between humans who want to participate in sport and so some provision must be made for them to compete.

One may even try to argue that it is the guardian who is responsible for the cheating that takes place and, unfortunate though it is, the child must suffer the consequences of this in sport. This perspective makes it difficult to penalise (and condemn) cheats or ban them from competition, since it would be unfair to punish an individual for something that is not his or her fault. In the same way in which it would be unreasonable to disqualify a naturally gifted athlete from competition, it would equally be unreasonable to disqualify a genetically modified athlete from competition. If the criticism of genetically modified athletes is that they failed to disclose that they have been modified – and thus are seen to be deceiving other members of their sporting community – then there must be some provision for their being able to compete, once they disclose that they are modified. The prospect of germ-line genetic modification reinforces the arguments suggesting that doping in sport is not merely a consequence of individual cheats, but of a culture to dope. Germ-line modification makes this shared responsibility explicit and it would be unjust to ban athletes from competition if the reason for being banned is not their responsibility or the consequence of their own actions.

Neither does genetic modification create an unacceptable level of unfairness in sport, since the kinds of inequalities arising from such enhancements do little to change the fairness of competitions. Indeed, genetic modification may even promote equality rather than make it more unfair, since it could be used to eliminate genetic variation. Of course, this reveals nothing special about gene doping, since a similar argument may be made about conventional forms of doping. Also comparable to other forms of doping, genetic modification may simply change the kinds of people who are successful in sport; it will no longer be the genetically 'gifted', but the genetically 'engineered'.

A further reason why one might argue that genetic modification is unfair is that this kind of difference will have been afforded by a deliberate intention to gain an advantage. Such intentions are unacceptable for a number of reasons. First, the choice relies upon the inability of others to also secure such enhancement. In addition, the act of deception would fail to treat other competitors with any degree of respect. Indeed, I have argued that the intention to gain a competitive advantage is not a defensible basis on which to justify the use of performance enhancement. Instead, the choice to enhance must reveal something meaningful about the way in which technology is given value within sporting performances. Yet it is rather tenuous to claim that germ-line modifications intend to place a person at an advantage within sport, since such a decision may not be made with any particular sporting career in mind. Genetic modification would most likely have some general health or enhancement rationale, rather than a specific sporting benefit rationale.

The degree to which the unfairness provoked by genetic modification is unethical depends upon how one theorises what is the accepted level of fairness in sport. On one view, organised sport is already inherently unfair in many respects, since it does not differentiate between genetic differences. At most, sports such as boxing or judo distinguish between body weight. However, there are many more sports that provide no opportunity for athletes of a disproportionate genetic predisposition to compete than there are which recognise humans of different body types as equally worthy of elite sporting status. This is clearly reflected in the constitutive rules of sports such as basketball or volleyball. For example, in volleyball the net is such that one must reach a certain minimum height if one aspires to elite-level competition. Of course, the same may be said of other sports, which might, for example, require one to be short to excel. One might also surmise that, whatever one's body type or genetic predisposition, it is possible to find a sport at which one could excel. From this perspective, and taken collectively, sport is not prejudicial, but offers opportunities for all kinds of persons. However, more can be expected from sports, since it does not often work out that one finds pleasure in the particular sport most suited to one's genetic characteristics.

Little (1998) argues that, although it is morally unfortunate that not all kinds of individuals can become elite athletes in their desired sport, this implies no social responsibility to correct this wrong. In contrast, Breivik (2000: 154) considers that 'sports organisations have an obligation to make it possible for all, not only to take part in a certain sport but also to compete at a high international level.' In the context of genetic modification, the advantage gained by using such means would be unfair only if sports were the kinds of activity where the *genetic lottery* is a valued facet of the competition. Breivik (2000) argues that this is not valuable in sport and that everybody should have the same chance of winning. This is because Breivik sees value in sport as reliant upon being this kind of activity – where there are opportunities for anyone to become successful.

Thus, if somebody is born with a genetic predisposition that gives rise to a less-than-ideal body type for their chosen sport, then this person should still have the opportunity to be the best in the world at this sport – for his or her particular body type. In his critique of the role that chance plays in sport, Breivik (2000) concludes that chance does not add value to sporting performance. Moreover, allowing chance to have some bearing upon the outcome of sport competition undermines the value of the contest. This is not to say that everybody should be equally entitled to win at elite sports contests. Rather, it is to make a distinction between failing to be good enough and being genetically prevented from being good enough to be an elite athlete. Thus failing to remove (or minimise) the irrelevant inequality of genetic variance fails to maintain what is valuable in sport.

While Breivik does not extend his conclusion to discuss whether genetic modification would be a beneficial means of performance enhancement in sport, one may infer that the use of genetic modification would not collapse this important aspect of sport. As far as altering genes is concerned, there is no implied disadvantage incurred on the sport itself. To be genetically modified does not circumvent the test of a sport or the challenge of becoming an elite athlete. Equally, genetic pre-selection does not alter any constitutive element of sport to an extent that one could claim it to be unfair, since it has no bearing upon the skills that are required to become good. As such, there is no basis for rejecting genetic modification for reasons of fairness in sport.

Genetic modification and coercion

It might also be argued that genetic modification is unacceptable because it is the *result* of a *coercive* pressure to be enhanced, which is unethical because it undermines individual autonomy. On this view, the important point is not that the method of performance enhancement is harmful, although the medical argument may also be used as a reason why this argument is persuasive. Rather, it has to do with the ethical status of a choice that is made within a coercive environment. Where a decision must be taken in coercive conditions, it cannot be said that an individual makes a freely desired choice, since his or her options will have been reduced. This limitation is considered ethically problematic, since it inhibits individuals from pursuing their own life-plans or, perhaps, from maintaining their own authenticity. As Murray (1983: 29) identifies:

> if we take freedom to be one of a number of values, whose purpose is to support the efforts of persons to pursue reasonable life plans without being forced into unconscionable choices by the actions of others, then the coerciveness inherent when many athletes use performance-enhancing drugs and compel others to use the same drugs, accept a competitive handi-cap, or leave the competition can be seen as a genuine threat to one's life plan.

However, this is a rather difficult claim to substantiate in sport, since coercion can operate on very subtle levels which have nothing to do with sport. In the cases of genetic modification and the use of genetic information, a similar argument can be made to conclude that their use would result in a coercive environment. In such circumstances, all prospective athletes would be coerced into using genetic modification to remain competitive. Yet there seems nothing necessarily unreasonable about this, since elite sport is already the kind of activity where individuals participate under pressure. Sport is already a coercive environment and this is constitutive of what makes it valuable. As Tamburrini (2000a: 205) argues in relation to doping, 'if an athlete risks her health to attain victory, while others are more prudent, it is only fair that the victory goes to the former'. One might criticise Tamburrini for identifying the wrong kind of risk that is valuable in sport. Yet genetic modification would not need to be seen as a risk to health and, as such, would not be the kind of coercion that is ethically alarming.

Genetic modification and the sporting community

An ethical view of sport might also assert an *expectation* for athletes to be *natural* or unenhanced, even if it is not possible to explain this view with respect to some coherent view of what constitutes the natural. For this reason, it may be argued that allowing genetic modification in sport would result in a *disappointment* and that this carries moral weight. This worry is also tied up with ideas about the way in which athletes should be *role models*, as they are public figures who are influential in shaping young children. One can understand this kind of concern in relation to drug taking and doping in sport, which would seem inextricable from the concern about drug use more broadly. Moreover, as genetic modification in sport gradually becomes defined as a deviant practice, one might have similar concerns. Yet genetic modification does not come with the same cultural baggage that underpins drug taking. Genetic modification cannot be considered as a deviant practice. Indeed, genetically modified athletes will not be very different from non-modified humans. For this reason, it would not be acceptable to characterise the genetically modified as morally less valuable. Where genetic modification is not undertaken in a deceptive environment (i.e. where genetic modification is banned), there should be no negative ethical connotation associated with this kind of enhancement.

To genetically modify a human does not alter the moral character of that human; he or she can still maintain the kinds of character that we find admirable in athletes. Indeed, the claim to *expectation disappointment* is subsequent to the moral evaluation of the technology. If genetic modification is seen to be a relevant and important facet of elite sport, then there would be no expectation disappointment when discovering that athletes have been genetically modified. Consequently, the concern about expectations must succeed the discussion about whether or not genetic modification is beneficial for sports.[1] I have argued that genetic modification can enrich sporting performances by providing greater levels of excellence in performance, reducing the risk of unsafe drug enhancements, allowing athletes to express their authenticity through their relationship with technology, and to promote the acquisition of internal goods of sport.

Concluding whether genetic modification in sport would be a valuable method of performance enhancement in sport depends, crucially, on how the technology is evaluated in the first place. If genetic modification is seen as a positive, enriching aspect of being human, then genetically modified athletes need not be seen as a bad example at all. However, if it is characterised as merely another form of doping, it is likely that this possibility will be lost.

Re-inventing sport values

The ethical arguments against the use of doping in sport do not have the same force when applied to genetic modification. Moreover, it would be a mistake to categorise genetic enhancement as merely another form of doping, since it is a conceptually and culturally different kind of technology. These arguments suggest that there is limited strength to the persuasiveness of reasons for prohibiting genetic enhancement in sport and even, to the contrary, there are stronger arguments for their acceptance. The contested values of sport and what they say about the value of performance are central to these conclusions. If sports are valuable in part because they are practices in which people try to improve human performance, then the value of genetic modification is significant. This is relevant not only for those sports that might be described as 'pure athletic events', but is also applicable to, say, soccer, where the capacity to run faster, be more agile and stronger can also promote a greater capacity for excellence. Genetics could provide a means towards enhancing these kinds of capacities, at no expense to the qualitative appraisal of these accomplishments (unless such modifications are banned, and thus using them would be seen as cheating). However, if measurable performance is seen as a contingent characteristic of the present-day articulation of sport, then genetic modification contributes very little.[2]

Placing this back into the context of the earlier arguments, genetic modifications are legitimate in sport when the choice to use them reflects some account of what constitutes athletic authenticity. Understanding the value of any form of enhancement in sport relies upon a specific version of what it means to be human. Where athletes identify genetic modification as a technology that is consistent with their version of humanness, this provides a basis for its acceptance. The reaction to this argument may be that the only reason athletes would seek genetic modification would be to gain an advantage over other competitors. As such, to legalise such modifications would negate the value of these enhancements, since they will be available to all. Yet genetic modification is more similar to, say, the development of fibreglass poles in pole vaulting, or the Fosbury flop in high jump than other methods of doping. It would be an innovation that enhances the capacity to express sports-related skills. It removes the performance inhibitor of less-than-optimal genes. Moreover, it would provide a means to eliminate the irrelevant inequality of genetic variance. While quantitative performance is not the entire picture of sporting values, it is a significant and necessary aspect of elite sport. The expectation to witness human excellence distinguishes elite sport from recreational sport. In particular, the value of improving performances is of central importance to elite sports for which genetic modification is most likely to be immediately relevant, such as track and field events. As Loland (1998b: html) recognises:

> The fascination for records is a key element in our fascination for sports. Records are the stuff of which legends and myths are made. Johnny Weissmuller's 1924 one hundred meter freestyle swim under the minute, Wilma Rudolph's fabulous sprint records from the early 1960s, and Michael Johnson's explosive two hundred meter record run at the 1996 Atlanta Games, are all paradigmatic examples of Coubertin's ideals. The record stands as a symbolic message of human greatness and infinite possibility.

By extension, Tännsjö (1998) refers to our fascination for excellence as an admiration for strength rather than weakness – the winner is admired. Tamburrini makes this claim explicit by arguing that, '*in general terms*, the result achieved by an athlete is a central element in the attribution of excellence' (1998: 42). Also in favour of associating performance attainments with excellence in sport, Hoberman (1992) argues that the pursuit of modern sport is necessarily about experimenting with human limits. This value derives from entrenched ideas about what constitutes human identity and possibilities, and is caught up in the Enlightenment project of progress. For this reason, the argument why physical achievements are important to sport must be considered. As Loland (2000: 42) notes, 'The logic of quantifiable progress has in a common-sense manner become a normative ideal in sports.'

Munthe's (2000) argument about genetic technology in sport makes a similar claim about sporting values, giving little importance to the more qualitative values in sport such as fair play or the demonstration of sportspersonship. For Munthe, these values are inevitably contested and vague. Perhaps Munthe's position tends ultimately to claim that there is something fundamentally wrong with contemporary, elite sporting values and so his articulation of how genetic modification might fit within this may be interpreted as an ironic assertion. Regardless, the values Munthe asserts as being the most important values in sport – rightly or wrongly – are these performance characteristics and a desire for spectacle. Yet the position begs the question as to what is meant by enhancement in performance. What would actually constitute an *enhanced* performance?

As was noted in Chapter 8 (in the section on engineering future values), one of the criticisms I have of Munthe's position is revealed by what is *not* considered as a possible use of genetic modification. Munthe proposes that genetic modification would be used to enhance such attributes as strength, speed and other performance qualities. Munthe does not envisage using such technology to, say, make athletes play more fairly or to be less interested in winning and more interested in acquiring altruistic or cooperative behaviours. The immediate and obvious response to this would be that such ambitions are not achievable by genetic modification, and so to propose these as possible applications of genetic modification would be preposterous. Moreover, one might have even more serious concern about engineering actual *behaviours* rather than biological characteristics. However, Munthe does not offer these reasons for why he does not consider other possible applications of genetic modification. What I find alarming about his characterisation of how genetic modification might be used in sport is the taken-for-granted values in sport it implies: those of performance and physical, quantifiable, achievement. It is the very content of these values that needs to be questioned when discussing whether such technology should be used in the first place. Yet, when evaluating the ethical value of genetic modification, it need not only be seen as a method of enhancing performance in some manner that is comparable to doping. As Lamsam *et al.* (1997) describe, it is possible that gene therapy may also be used for reparative purposes in sport.

For Munthe, genetics can provide more physically competent athletes and this appears to be his benchmark for sporting excellence or, at least, his justifications for rejecting possible arguments against genetic enhancement begin from this basis. In contrast, I propose that such excellences are meaningful only if they reveal something fundamental about what it means to be human. The enhancement of performance does not constitute a step towards better versions of sports. Rather, it is the way in which the enhancement is achieved and, more importantly, what *kind* of enhancement is attained that it is necessary to understand in order to conclude its value.

The point of departure for this conceptualisation was given in Chapter 5, where it was argued that an ethical view of sport must begin by articulating what it means to be human. Sports are interesting because they constitute the performance of human beings: individuals engaged in a difficult practice, within which an excellent performance is reflective of years of training and commitment. Sports performances consist of an extraordinary integration of skill and talent, which is devalued if athletes can be given such abilities by performance-enhancing technologies. This position identifies the dehumanisation and de-skilling of sport as persuasive arguments against the use of any technology that contributes to this. Yet genetic modification is not this kind of technology. Genetic modification does not undermine the important aspects of being human in sport, since it does not jeopardise individual autonomy in competition. Following Kretchmar (1992) and Schneider and Butcher (1994), this argument does not contend that sporting excellence is defined only (if at all) by performance-related characteristics, but merely that it does not jeopardise other characteristics of sporting excellence.

Prioritising individualism in a social practice

One of the most immediate criticisms arising from my approach might be that this ethical view on sport overly prioritises individualism, which is a mistake since sports are primarily social practices. On this basis, to suggest that athletes must arrive at a personal conclusion about how to legitimate use of technology in their performance cannot make sense because sports rely upon people giving more value to shared and agreed-upon conventions, than to self-improving authenticity. This perspective, again, derives from a conceptualisation of sport as some kind of contract or agreement, where individuals sacrifice personal freedom in order to participate in a common practice. Yet my argument does not recommend that genetic modification should be managed in sport by allowing each athlete to individually select whether they believe a particular method of performance enhancement is in tune with their *individual narrative*. Such a proposal would be naïve and useless in sports, which rely upon shared rules, since it would lead to circumstances where athletes seek all available methods of performance enhancement to optimise their possibility to gain an advantage over others. In addition, one may presume that this decision would come, not from a sincere interest for authenticity, but from an interest to gain a competitive advantage. This description of the problem does not refute the strength of the *ethics of authenticity* argument. The individual authenticity position still holds, but only if athletes actually *do* act in the interests of their own authenticity. The example where athletes are making the decisions based on an interest to gain a competitive edge does not provide any such justification.

It may be argued that my position neglects any realism in the circumstances of elite sport. Indeed, Breivik (1987) and Eassom (1995) explore the way in which athletes are caught within some kind of prisoners' dilemma, where they are compelled to use any means of performance enhancement available to them; otherwise they face being disadvantaged in competition. For this reason, it might be argued that athletes are not likely to make their decision to genetically enhance (or not) based upon some version of what it means to be human. Instead, they will make their decision based upon whether they can improve their chances of winning by using such enhancements. In response, it is important first to note that this criticism appears relevant only for modifications to the somatic cells of the body or through using pharmacogenomics to develop new kinds of drugs. It is not a criticism of using germ-line cell modification, where the modified individual cannot yet be characterised as an athlete.

In addition, the perception of the authenticity argument as being individualistic is misrepresentative. First and foremost, the argument aims to provide a way for athletes to engage with what is meaningful and valuable about their profession. From a position of individual authenticity, the argument allows athletes to determine what should be the approved methods of performance modification. However, this process of decision making takes place in the context of presumed or perceived values, which are shared within the practice community of any given sport. Once such decisions have been made, it would then be possible to stipulate a policy for any given sport, though it is imperative that such policies are possible to reappraise. As such, the emphasis on the method is dialectic rather than individualistic. It requires interaction between the athlete's perspective with the *horizons of meaning* of the given sport.

My thesis does not reject the importance of making rules that every athlete must follow. Rather, it attempts to derive methods of reaching ethically defensible conclusions about which kinds of performance modifier reinforce sporting values and which do not. On this basis, my argument does not defer to individualism exclusively. Rather, it bases the formulation of shared rules upon what is of value to sporting practitioners. It calls for a democratisation of sport which allows different kinds of people to become elite athletes, regardless of their genetic (bad) luck.

To explain this, MacIntyre (1979: 93) is useful when arguing that 'we are what we are in virtue of our relationships', a position which also acknowledges that respecting autonomy is necessary to respect somebody as a person. Thus, on MacIntyre's (1979: 95) view:

> Autonomy is not, as Kant thought, a property of every rational agent. It is an achievement and a social achievement, as is rationality itself. It is in and

through our network of relationships that we achieve or fail to achieve rational control of our lives . . . if we are to look for autonomy and rationality, we should seek them not in individuals abstracted and isolated from their social roles and relationships, but in individuals at home in those roles and relationships.

This view may appear to give primacy to understanding persons as social beings, thus reducing the importance of the individualist authenticity ethics argued above. However, the two perspectives need not be mutually exclusive. The ethics of authenticity approach does not eliminate the importance of the situatedness of athletes within their specific practice. The *horizons of meaning* argument allow athletes to recognise the values of their practices and, in fact, to promote them.

In sum, I have argued that it makes sense only to recognise athletes as autonomous agents, capable of making their own life decisions, where such decisions do not harm other individuals or devalue the practices within which those choices take place. In the case of pre-natal genetic interventions, we would defer to the authority of parents to make such choices, while ever conscious of wanting to ensure that parents make such choices with the best interests of the child at heart.[3]

11 Conclusions and implications

Athletes' rights: legally, we have complications

On the basis of the current arguments, sporting authorities would find it difficult to justify banning genetically modified athletes from sport. Moreover, it is not even clear whether sporting authorities should have the power to make such decisions, given the broader context within which genetic modification would take place (i.e. non-sporting alterations). Equally, the ability of sporting authorities to request genetic information from athletes so that they might test for enhancement is difficult to justify, particularly where it may require a significantly invasive procedure (as might be said for a muscle biopsy to determine the modification of muscle tissue).

This difficulty is complicated further by the fact that it may not even be possible to test for genetic modifications in sport. It is not yet clear how detection of genetic modification would be possible, since:

> the protein produced is identical to the endogenous (or original) protein, the artificial DNA is only present locally when using injection with pure DNA or genetically modified cells and the sequence of artificial DNA has to be known to enable detection.
>
> (Schjerling, 2001)

Further support for the idea that prohibiting genetically modified athletes from sport is ethically and legally unsound may be found in two related areas of study: the emergence of athletes' rights and the development of international agreements in bioethics. Kidd and Donnelly (2000: 10) provide an overview of how athletes' rights have evolved, recognising that:

> Human rights legislation has also inspired increasing respect for athletes' rights, the recognition that athletes must be afforded the same protections enjoyed by all citizens, particularly with regard to freedom from discrimination, selection for representative teams, the allocation of other benefits, and discipline and punishment.

Similar arguments may be found in legal discussions about drug taking and other methods of doping, though it is surprising how little the two fields of sports ethics and sports law have interacted on this debate. One exception is Thompson's (1982/1988) overview of the conditions in which it is morally justifiable to require athletes to submit to urinalysis examinations. Thompson considers that the central conflict of this issue has to do with the interpretation of *privacy rights*. Various articles detailing issues in relation to doping test procedures recognise that there is a fundamental privacy issue at stake that must be weighed against the importance of fair play in sport (Palmer, 1992).

Within this broader, social scientific study of sport, concerns have arisen about the use of anti-doping measures for catching *cheaters* in competition. In particular, the Court of Arbitration[1] has been proactive in protecting athletes' rights. Balancing the harms of drug use with the harms of invasive doping test procedures has been of significant concern for the Court. In addition, parallel ethical issues have arisen in respect of the provision for sporting opportunities for people with disabilities. Indeed, the way in which disability is separated from able-bodied sport may serve as some guide for how genetically enhanced (or deficient) athletes might be treated. If genetically modified athletes are excluded from competition, then this could exclude a significant proportion of people, solely on the basis of their having been modified. It might even exclude persons modified for medical reasons, should their modification nevertheless leave them genetically enhanced for sport.

The exclusion of such people from sport conflicts with their rights to be free from genetic discrimination, as advocated by the United Nations Education, Scientific, and Cultural Organization (Unesco) *Universal Declaration on the Human Genome and Human Rights* (Unesco, 1997: html). In particular, the Declaration makes the following stipulations relevant to this discussion:

> Article 2: Everyone has a right to respect for their dignity and for their rights regardless of their genetic characteristics.
> . . .
> Article 6: No one shall be subjected to discrimination based on genetic characteristics that is intended to infringe or has the effect of infringing human rights, fundamental freedoms and human dignity.

These articles do not imply that sporting organisations should allow genetically modified athletes to compete against the non-modified. Rather, they provide a basis for arguing why it would be unreasonable to prohibit genetically modified athletes from competing in sport, which would entail providing a supportive context within which the modified athletes could compete, even if this is separate from the non-modified athletes.

It is also important to recognise that paternalistic legal arguments about doping have their roots in the importance of *physical* harms, a perspective that does not have such strength in the case of genetic modification (except in respect of its abuses).[2] Providing that the technology has been deemed medically safe, genetic modification would not be overly detrimental to the athlete's biological health. Consequently, other kinds of harm must be the reason for justifying paternalism. Yet, the paternalist view is premised upon seeking to protect athletes from themselves (Brown, 1990) and 'unnecessary risks' (Catlin and Murray, 1996: 237). From the sporting perspective, this approach has been particularly relevant in the context of drug taking and doping. On this matter, the perspectives of Simon (1984) and Brown (1984) are summarised by Fraleigh (1984a: 24):

> they locate the issue in whether or not it is morally right to restrict the choices of an informed consenting adult athlete in taking drugs for the purpose of enhancing performance while accepting serious risks of harmful side effects.

The justification for paternalism in the case of genetic modification would need to have a quite different basis. It is not so much a concern for harms to the individual, than it is a concern for harms to others (in the sense that also includes non-human others). Admittedly, within Simon's and Brown's formulation of the issue, they consider the importance of issues related to fairness and coercion, thus recognising the harms to others. Yet it is an important distinction to recognise that genetic modification does not respond to the kinds of harm that have built a case against the use of drug taking and doping in sport. Again, it is possible to recognise Mill's (1843/1995) harm principle as constitutive to this ethical approach.

However, the balancing of these harms requires more than Mill's classic utilitarianism for deriving ethical guidelines about genetic modification in sport. The degree of restriction on personal freedoms that is implied through banning genetic modification in sport has far broader implications than does the banning of drug use. At most, a similar claim that may be made of banning genetic modification is paralleled in the issue concerning the prohibition of *recreational* drugs from sport. For example, in 1998 at the Nagano Olympic Winter Games, a controversial case arose in respect of Canadian snowboarder Ross Rebagliati, winner of the first-ever gold medal in the snowboarding giant slalom at Nagano. Only three days after winning the gold, the IOC asked Rebagliati to return the medal after it was discovered that he had tested positive for marijuana.

Further details about Rebagliati's innocence or guilt are not particularly important for our present discussion. Rather, what is most intriguing is that a drug which is not considered to be performance enhancing would be of interest to an anti-doping policy. The example was controversial since it called into question whether the list of banned substances ought to be extended to non-performance drugs. For some, the Rebagliati case entailed an unwarranted violation of the individual's personal freedoms and overstepped the realms of the paternalistic power of sports authorities to restrict what an athlete can and cannot do. Marijuana is a depressant and, arguably, not considered to be enhancing of a snowboarder's performance. As such, it is not clear why it was deemed illegal for specific sports.[3] Houlihan (1999) notes that, for many sports, there is a general concern from sports federations to have their sport associated with illegal drugs and that this is partly why it is illegal. It may also be possible to argue that there is a concern about the heightened risk arising from athletes who are under the influence of hallucinogenics, but this is also a highly contentious position and it could be argued that the infringement on individual freedom is far more harmful than any presumed safety risk.

For genetic modification, there is an even stronger case for considering whether sporting authorities should be entitled to discriminate against genetically modified athletes. In respect of genetic testing and pre-selection, the banning of such technology implies substantial restrictions upon parental freedoms. Currently, parents enjoy a freedom to raise their children as they see fit, excepting some important, fundamental legal requirements on the protection of a child's right to welfare. By comparison, the restrictions in regard to the participation of children in elite sports are few. Kidd and Donnelly (2000: 12) recognise that 'no one has yet taken this approach [a legal means to address human rights violations] to pursue children's rights in sports.' There exist no restrictions to prevent parents of young children from placing them in elite sports training clubs, and it is only recently that age limits are being set to outline the extent to which children should participate in elite sport. In addition, the process of talent identification and competitions that lead to the selection of elite teams is an integral and respected aspect of sport. Again, for these kinds of practices, it is not considered unethical (or something to be prohibited) for parents to place their children in such clubs. Genetic pre-selection and selection involves a similar kind of process and so similar claims to their being accepted can be made, although such a conclusion might beg the question about selection at all.

Nevertheless, there is a significant difference between these two kinds of talent identification process in the way in which they are achieved. The kinds of process that might go into testing a child or embryo for genetic characteristics can be more invasive than traditional scouting methods. For this reason there may be grounds for concern. However, if genetic screening is justified and used on a health-related basis, then such information may already be available to talent scouts. In such circumstances, the child will not have to go through any additional or harmful procedure to that which is medically necessary. Rather, it would simply be a case for the parent to authorise the use of such information as a basis for selection in elite sport. Again, this calls into question who should have access to genetic information, and upon what basis its use is justified. Where the freedom to access such information resides with parents, its use could be immoral in a similar way to how some might consider the use of abortion on account of sex preference as immoral. Consequently, it must be questioned whether parents and other interested parties are entitled to use the genetic information of their children in ways that they see fit or whether such information does not belong to them. Raising doubt for such use implies a substantial rethinking of biomedical ethics. Regardless, the potential for discrimination that can derive from genetic screening is substantial. For example, Harris (1998) considers that, if genetic screening is used, there is a need for legislation to control the potential for discrimination. This could imply a significant restriction of parental liberties.

A similar issue arises out of germ-line genetic modification for sport. In this case, parents would have the authority to restrict modifications to a child's health, but it is not clear whether this is a desirable situation. It raises the question as to whether the prospect of being able to genetically modify prospective children should be a basis for rethinking parental freedom (see Murray, 1986c). Importantly, the freedom that parents enjoy does not imply that they could choose to create a super-athlete should the technology be available. Rather, parents will retain the right to consent to modifications on behalf of their child in relation to their health. Thus the use of genetic modification at all is still governed by the ethical limits of parenting and medicine. This situation presents a significant and controversial barrier to the discussion about genetic modification in sport.

Parental freedom is of crucial importance in bioethics, which has a tradition premised upon the legal definition of *autonomy*, particularly within the USA, which has driven a great deal of biomedical law. Wolpe (1997) recognises that bioethics prioritises individual autonomy and that this must be understood as problematic for resolving discussions about ethics in medicine. This consideration is relevant in the discussion about paternalism and freedoms in sport by critiquing whether individual freedoms should be prioritised. Wolpe (1997) and Platt (1998) suggest that individual rights should not override other kinds of rights, despite the tradition of doing so, and the pragmatic and democratic appeal that such principles imply. Consequently, challenging parental freedoms by restricting what kinds of technology are legal – as has been the case through IVF – conflicts with a significant principle within bioethics: *autonomy*. As Harris (1999: 89–92) explains:

> matters involving the most intimate and personal choices a person may make in a lifetime, choices central to a person's dignity and autonomy, are central to the liberty protected by the Fourteenth Amendment . . . decisions to reproduce in particular ways . . . constitute decisions concerning central issues of value, then, arguably, the freedom to make them is guaranteed by the constitution (written or not) of any democratic society, unless the state has a compelling reason for denying them that control. . . . European Union . . . would have to show that more was at stake than the fact that a majority found the ideas disturbing or even disgusting.

Genetic modification in sport challenges the sanctity of such a premise by raising doubts about the limit of parental freedoms. Parenting in Western societies has enjoyed a relatively loose level of regulation in the past and *informed consent*, which serves as a fundamental tool in healthcare, confers authority upon parents to make decisions on behalf of their children. However, the degree to which this is useful where genetic modification is available can be questioned. The utility of practical ethics here can be to advocate more of a discursive approach that involves a process of deliberation between respective interested parties, rather than appealing to such tools as *informed consent*. While such an instrument has great importance in the ethical provision of medical care, Elliott (1999: 93) recognises that it also has limitations:

we are still left with the problem of what *counts* as that ability [to consent] – whether a person is incompetent by virtue of making a poor decision, or by virtue of making an irrational decision, or by virtue of coming to his decision in an unsystematic, illogical or erratic way . . . we need an account of competence that explains why we sometimes feel that a person can both be competent and make bad, irrational or even unreasonable choices.

In the current medical climate, it is highly unlikely that parents would be permitted to genetically enhance their children for sport, though this does not explain the justification for such a prohibition. Nevertheless, it is less clear whether a similar prohibition could be sustained if the enhancements could legitimately be regarded as health enhancing. Consequently, it is essential that further investigations within sports ethics, particularly from the perspective of sports authorities, recognise this *broader* implication of implementing restrictions upon what kinds of people are allowed to play sport. If genetic enhancement arises out of some health rationale, then there would be no basis on which to prohibit such people from competition.

A further basis on which to discern whether sports federations could limit the freedom of athletes to genetically enhance themselves may require examining the legal relationship between athletes and sports organisations. If athletes are considered as professionals and sport is recognised as a work environment, as is the case for many professional athletes, then this may have a bearing upon what can be asked of the athlete. While it is not possible here to expand upon what kind of human practices sports are, it is a crucial discussion in developing a legal and ethical response to the freedoms of sporting authorities. Such conclusions will also provide greater clarity on the requirements upon athletes to submit to the professional codes that might ensue as a result of such circumstances.

The freedom to use pharmacogenomics or somatic cell genetic modification rests solely with the athlete and the freedom of sports authorities to limit such choices. In this respect, the discussion is conceptually similar to the issue of drug use. Again, recognising that the use of such technology would not imply a detrimental effect upon the athlete's health, the position favouring the paternalism of sporting authorities is relatively weak. Nevertheless, if the intention is also to ensure that an abuse of such technology does not take place, then it is important to consider recent trends within anti-doping discourse which recognise that the athlete is not an isolated human being. In respect of drugs, it requires a significant number of people to bring about a situation where athletes use drugs. As such, anti-doping measures must take into account the potential for the athlete to be influenced by others into using new methods of doping. A stronger claim may be made in respect of genetic modification, where the athlete will be dependent upon medically cognisant professionals for reliable information and advice. Again, isolating the athlete as solely culpable for using genetic modification would be naïve, as it would fail to recognise the complex power relationships between athletes, coaches and significant others.

The arguments from harm and the subsequent discussion on the moral limits of paternalism and individual rights requires further elaboration. Thus far, it is clear that governing bodies of sport are in a rather difficult predicament with genetic modification, where harms will ensue in whichever decision is made about its ethical status. For this reason, it is crucial that the ethical status remains open to the possibility that legalising genetic modification may be more desirable than banning it. It is not sufficient to expect a concise answer to the question of whether genetic modification is appropriate for sports at this stage. Some of its applications are, at most, as harmful as currently *accepted* methods of performance enhancement. Others raise new harms, but their rejection from sport on account of some idealised conception conflicts with the sustaining of individual rights. Further discussion must take place to problematise the relationship of the athlete with the sports organisation and as a human being in society, who is also beholden to ethical decisions made in medical ethics.

One initial response to this harmed group is to question whether one is entitled to expect *not* to be disadvantaged by one's genetic disposition. Such a view is implied by the Unesco (1997) Declaration, though it is not clear that such entitlement is sustainable or that it leads necessarily to legalising genetic modification for sport. Nevertheless, this is where the inconsistency of sporting values becomes a little clearer or, perhaps, where their consistency is put to the test. If sport is valuable because it promotes equality of opportunity and fairness, then the organisation of sports must be committed to making such circumstances possible. Such a commitment would need to entail making elite sports participation open to all kinds of persons, regardless of their genetic predisposition. This already takes place through the provision of sport for people of different kinds of bodily capacity, some of whom might be described as genetically impaired. For the same reason that there is provision for the genetically impaired, it would also be unacceptable to neglect the entitlement of the genetically enhanced to participate in sport. Perhaps this argument speaks more to the rights of the germ-line genetically enhanced, but we might also imagine therapeutic modifications to the somatic cells, which result in some kind of sporting enhancement for the individual. These kinds of people would still be entitled to compete in sport, though they could be said to have an advantage over non-modified competitors.

The responsibility to avoid the 'anti-' gene doping stance

Despite the arguments I make here about the ethical desirability of genetic modification in sport, there is an alarming consequence for how the discussions concerning genetic modification in sport are already evolving in international sport. There is now a tendency to frame genetics by the general terms of reference found within anti-doping organisations. All kinds of genetic modification are being given the generic term *gene doping*. For most, this buzzword is an entirely suitable and unproblematic way to describe the implications of genetic modification for sport. However, the arguments here have demonstrated that such a broad conceptualisation is not possible and, for most of the different forms of genetic modification, they do not resemble conventional forms of doping.

My response to this is not simply that the term *gene doping* is an inaccurate representation of genetic modification, as I have argued throughout this book. There is also a *responsibility* to avoid adopting a principled ethical policy against the use of genetics in sport. This is not an advocation of the free use of all kinds of genetic modification. Rather, it is to recognise that there has been no serious attempt to conceptualise the ethical implications of genetics for sport within policy discussions thus far. For this reason this approach of prohibition is not possible to justify, unless it is accompanied by extensive philosophical, ethical and empirical research concerning the subject of genetics in sport.

I do not suggest that, in order to call genetic technology doping or not, all that is required is for there to be some process of discussion and enquiry which may give rise to *correct* conclusions. It is simply to acknowledge that sporting authorities are not yet in a position to know how best to categorise genetics in sport. There is no clear position about the value of genes in sport, as understood by either *natural* endowment or *modification*. Most importantly, I do not see an interest to conceptualise genetic modification beyond understanding it as another method of doping. It is not simply that I would like to see an effort to question the ethics of genetic modification, but also to engage with the question about what kind of technology genetics is, and how it compares to other kinds of technology in sport.

The responsibility of such policy makers should be less about implementation and pragmatism, and more about endeavouring to identify justifiable and rational bases for drawing distinctions about various methods of performance modification. While this may seem quite straightforward, it conflicts substantially with the process of deliberation within sporting institutions. Houlihan (1999) identifies that the process of anti-doping policy makers rarely dedicates time to the process of conceptualising the ethical issues or trying to navigate through them somehow. Rather, I suggest, the method of ethics employed in sport policy is based upon ill-founded middle principles: performance modifiers are somehow written into or out of ethical codes and, on this basis, the way in which they are perceived is determined before the policies are derived. This is one of the reasons why it is such a significant step in the evolution of the anti-doping Code, that it is being revised through WADA. This process is a very significant development for many sports ethicists because it indicates a willingness to be more reflective about the ethical limits of doping.

In order to take into account fully the value of genetic modification in sport (and outside of it), a further step must be taken by sporting authorities which would necessitate eliminating the *anti* part of anti-doping. Moreover, it might require eliminating *anti-doping* altogether and deriving a more representative description of the issue, such as a *policy on performance enhancement* or perhaps distinguishing what are clearly medical policies on performance enhancement from ethical policies. Currently, anti-doping has very little option but to be against the principle of genetic modification. After all, anti-doping makes its ethical perspective on what it defines as *doping* self-evident. Moreover, as Houlihan reveals, being committed to anti-doping entails being committed to not re-evaluating the initial assumptions of the ethical position. In his book *Dying to Win*, Houlihan explains four main strands of anti-doping policy development:

- *Focus*: refinement of the broad categories and particular examples of drugs and doping practices targeted by policy makers.
- *Generation and maintenance of policy commitment*: stimulation of political support for policy implementation.
- *Technology development*: effective policy implementation depends substantially on the development of testing and analytical techniques and their continuing refinement to match the advances in pharmacology and the deviousness of drug-abusing athletes.
- *Establishment of the necessary resource infrastructure*: includes the provision of money, laboratories, sampling officers and a regulatory framework.

(Houlihan, 1999: 129)

Evidently, this process does not entail *value redefinition* as an integral part of the discussions whereby the legality of certain processes and substances might be re-appraised. This is no reflection on Houlihan's work; rather, it reveals that such discussions have not been a priority. Potentially, the process of re-evaluating just how *anti* is anti-doping fits within Houlihan's *focus* category, though to ensure that anti-doping departs from a coherent framework about performance modification, it must entail the possibility of concluding that the legality of some substances may need changing. Further reason to suppose that this kind of discussion is not held within anti-doping policy meetings is found later in Houlihan, where he notes the following priorities decided at the second conference of European Ministers responsible for sport held in 1978:

- Need to compile and publish accurate and detailed list of substances and tests.
- Need to identify ways of instituting and supporting practical and regular tests between and at events.
- Need to institute stricter sanctions for users (to be applied to trainers, doctors or managers who have encouraged use), and support by publicity campaign on health dangers of doping.

(Houlihan, 1999: 135)

Again, we do not see the possibility that the *anti* of anti-doping may need re-evaluating or, at least, re-problematising. Given that WADA seeks to internationalise policies in anti-doping, one realises that the possibility for reflective evaluation on the moral goodness or badness of doping, sports federations must be understood as mechanisms of implementation rather than for reflecting upon sporting values, even if the latter is preferable. This is a little ironic, since the very basis upon which anti-doping is premised is supposedly a discourse of values. If it is not possible for sports federations to re-evaluate their values and ethical practices, they cannot really aspire to being agents of moral goodness. To elucidate this weakness, a suitable analogy may be the way in which legal systems function. If there were no recognition of the need to re-evaluate laws and question their core values, then ours would be a very primitive and stagnant world. Moreover, if one tried then to apply such laws on an international basis, this stagnant world would soon become a very unstable and conflictive one.

On this view, due to the deeply felt antisocial connotations of drug use (outside of sport), it is not possible for governments to ascribe to any kind of initiative that might lead to the decriminalisation of drugs and other methods of doping. The contradictions of this reaction to drug use, where some drugs are condemned and made illegal and others are tolerated, is less interesting for the current purposes. Nevertheless, it is within these conditions that the manner of managing drug use in sport must be understood. Sports, as practices of moral goodness, are not particularly consistent with the condoning of an activity mostly associated with antisocial behaviour and its consequences. For this reason alone, the non-medical use of drugs is deemed to be, *prima facie*, immoral.

Consequently, adopting a stance *against* doping of any kind is somewhat compulsory in the sports world, if one aspires to win friends and influence people. Yet this has nothing to do with open and reflective dialogue about sporting values. Again, addressing the frustrations and inconsistencies of this situation is a secondary interest of this conclusion. Other places have dealt in far more detail with this ensuing ethical dialogue, if, indeed, there is a dialogue at all, since the discourse is often confined to academic ethicists.[4] For current purposes it is sufficient to identify how, in the present and past climate of anti-doping, all forms of doping are wrong and there is little reason to suppose that this is changing. Anti-doping policy making is less about evaluating what is right or wrong than it is about applying the conclusion that doping reflects moral badness in sport. In this respect it is somewhat dogmatic, particularly when placed in the context of international sport, where the basis for universalism is even weaker.

Nevertheless, sport is one of the few instances of social enterprise where there is an increasing expectation that policies should and can be universally applied, where an expectation for a universal ethics is an aspiration. Even in medicine, there is a growing recognition of this not being possible, despite there being a common recognition of healthcare as being underpinned by a universal code of ethics. If one recognises the challenge of this in other contexts – such as the harmonisation of human rights policies – then one has some indication about how high this expectation is. International sport organisers operate in a homogenising manner. Within sport, dopers cannot and are not treated differently on account of their heritage and country. Rather, an athlete found with an illegal substance in their body is a cheat regardless of his or her contextual circumstances, which may have led him or her innocently to be in such circumstances.

The end of anti-doping

Given this lack of philosophical rigour in anti-doping and the emerging critique of its importance and appropriateness as a statement about sports ethics, there are pragmatic and ideological arguments for concluding that anti-doping is no longer a viable position to take on performance enhancement.

The pragmatic reasons for concluding that anti-doping must become an historical legacy in the context of genetic modification speak to the likely difficulties faced by anti-doping authorities to catch their so-called 'gene cheats'. While much of the discussion is speculative, there is reason to believe that many kinds of genetic alteration will not be detectable by testing, whether it is because the technology is simply not available, or that the procedure would be far too invasive for it to be medically justified. Where such testing becomes regarded as ineffective, there will be even greater reason to seek more useful means of trying to make sports ethical and safe for athletes. The discovery of a designer steroid called tetrahydrogestrinone (THG), which caused scandal throughout the athletic world in 2003, brings into question what other kinds of substance are being used by athletes without the possibility of detection. Arguably, the public's disenchantment with elite sport, provoked by the lack of trust in witnessing 'natural' performances, is being superseded by the public's disenchantment with anti-doping. Where such circumstances arise, it seems foolish to continue with a policy of punishment where a more effective strategy could be to monitor the use of doping to optimise performance safely.

Ideologically, anti-doping is also approaching a threshold, because it no longer makes sense in a society where there exist genetically modified *humans*. As genetic alteration becomes a legitimate way of being human, it is unreasonable to identify such changes as deviant or unacceptably unnatural. For this reason, to claim that genetically modified athletes would be unacceptable in sport would not be meaningful.

As a broader criticism, there has not been a sufficient level of analysis within sports ethics and policy making to derive a *conceptual framework for performance enhancement*. Ethical discussions have focused solely on the drug issue, to the neglect of a vast number of other technologies that confer a similar kind of effect. Only recently have the ethical issues deriving from performance-enhancing technology in sport been given serious attention (Miah and Eassom, 2002), though still this discourse does not enter much into policy discussions in sports federations. For genetic modification specifically, it is not that sports values are insufficient to derive conclusions about whether it is unacceptable, but that bioethics indicates a broader literature that is not dealt with through the current arguments raised against drugs and other enhancements. Such arguments inform and strengthen the claims to what is valued in sport and provide a more substantial basis from which to derive conclusions about the ethical limits of genetic modification in sport.

By considering genetic modification in sport within the context of broader bioethical concerns, it is possible to sharpen the credibility of sporting arguments by drawing out clearer ideas about what gives value to being human. Such analyses allow a clearer articulation of values in sport, as demonstrated by concluding the ethical limits of genetic modification in sport as reliant upon the philosophical limits of *autonomy*, *dignity*, *personhood* and *authenticity*.

Towards a policy on genetic modification in sport

In order to develop a legal instrument on the matter of genetic modification in sport, it is important to consider what theoretical perspectives can be useful. Despite the inadequacy of the initial premises of anti-doping policy – that doping is to be removed from sport – there are some merits that are worthy of attention, notably within recent developments. The ambitions for harmonisation of an anti-doping policy are important, though they omit the crucial consideration of what it is that is being harmonised. What is absent from anti-doping campaigns is the philosophical and ethical groundwork that is necessary to inform the anti-doping argument. This appeal for ethics to be valued by sports organisations does not aspire to some fanciful aspiration for philosophers to be the gatekeepers of what is right or wrong in sport. To consider that the ethicist must be used as a moral expert is both unrealistic and inaccurate. However, the claim that anti-doping must re-engage with its philosophical and ethical origins asserts that anti-doping is fundamentally misconceived because it is unable to take into account the particularities of the circumstances within which performance-enhancing substances and methods are used. Indeed, Houlihan (1999), one of the world's leading theorists on anti-doping policy, recognises that the absence of a clear definition leaves sports authorities reliant upon simple rule violations as a basic rationale for developing anti-doping policy. Such a basis for sport ethics is not sufficient, since it is the very justification of rules – particularly new rules and new doping methods – that is under question. In respect of genetic modification, the primary question is whether the enhancement *should* be against the rules, not how best it may be kept out of sports.

I have argued that being genetically modified (in general) is consistent with being human, and, for this reason, it is unreasonable to conclude that genetic modification should not be a valuable aspect of sporting performance. However, trying to gain an advantage over other competitors does not constitute a reasonable justification for wanting to use such technology. Instead, genetically modified athletes would need to claim that being modified is constitutive of their humanity and that they must be treated with respect for this reason.

Currently, the Ethics and Education Committee of the World Anti-Doping Agency has been involved in discussions concerning the revision of the Anti-Doping Code, the basic instrument for discriminating between different kinds of substances. Thus the definitional work that is suggested as needing to precede harmonisation (or, at least, to accompany it) is being addressed within anti-doping campaigns. A similar process must ensue with respect to genetic modification in sport. However, it is also important that such discussions borrow from the format of deliberations about bioethics outside of sport. Genetic modification in sport is not solely a sports issue in a similar way that it may be argued that drug use in sport is not solely a sports issue. For the latter, it may be argued that the abuse of drugs is inextricable from the broader social concern about how drugs are used. Similarly, the use of genetic modification in sport must be coherent with broader policy decisions in respect of genetics. Moreover, and perhaps more importantly, the format for the discussions about genetics must learn from how such discussions are taking place outside of sport. It is not sufficient for sports organisations to implement a working party that will exist for three or four years to formulate its policy and then reach a conclusion. Applications in genetics are not finite and the issues cannot rely only on generalised medical principles about what is ethical or not in sport, even if such ideas will constitute an important part of the discussion.

Currently, the problem facing world sports authorities is *how to engage* with the problem of genetics in sport. Is it to be treated as another form of doping? If so, then what kind of doping method – or, more broadly, performance enhancer – is genetics? Is it more like a lighter tennis racket, a drug, or something completely new and different? A problematisation of these issues must take place during these defining years, though it is misleading to assume that such discussions will reach conclusive ends or that they are necessary only for a specific amount of time. Rather, the process of policy formation can only be a continual renegotiation of ideas and values. In the case of drug use in sport and other forms of doping, this point is only beginning to gain strength as the credibility of distinctions and theorising within anti-doping policies lacks clarity.

Within WADA, there is a move towards redefining the problem and evaluating the moral and conceptual differences between different substances and methods of performance enhancement. What is most apparent from examining the development of anti-doping policy is that its derivation has been done back to front – the problem of doping in sport preceded the policy making and theorising about its ethical status. Governing bodies have only recently begun to embrace broader expertise in establishing successful policy making and the harmonisation of anti-doping policy is gradually becoming more successful. Supposing that there are particular kinds of genetic intervention that might not be desirable within sports, it will not be sufficient for sports authorities to derive these limits alone. Neither would such prospects be desirable, since it would neglect the inextricable ties between sport and society more broadly. Currently, governing bodies have an opportunity to initiate debate when there is still time to make a decision, before such innovations become widespread. This opportunity should be taken.

Athletes have always harnessed training techniques that are scientifically rigorous and thus ambitiously efficient. Measuring performance and keeping records is characteristic of modern-day sport, though never before has its importance been so acute. Currently, the distinction between winners and losers is so small that the human eye has trouble seeing it, as is testified by the photo finish in sprints and horse-racing. Amidst all this technology, the question remains to be asked: At what point does the technology surpass the influence of the athlete in a performance in a manner that is devaluing of sporting performances?

Yet where human limits in performance are being approached – as would seem to be the case in some track and field events – genetic manipulation presents the possibility of being able to provide further performance enhancement. As long as it is safe to genetically engineer humans, one might expect there to be *engineered* athletes in competition who would succeed, in part, because of this enhancement. Should such enhancements be deemed legal by governing bodies or are they comparable to drug taking and other forms of doping? Doping and drug taking remain high on the agenda for governing bodies seeking to remove any kind of substance or process that confers an unfair advantage on an individual when competing. Indeed, out-of-competition testing is becoming an increasing target for anti-doping measures, indicating the breadth of contempt for any form of drug use in sport at all.

These arguments suggest that genetic enhancement cannot be characterised in the same way as other forms of doping. The ability to enhance muscle repair through genetic manipulation and thus to shorten the recovery period after injury presents a challenging dichotomy for the administration of sports medicine. Presuming that the technology is not deemed illegal at the outset, it is dubious that governing bodies would judge such a *regenerative* procedure as unacceptable. Alternatively, the ability to locate and manipulate, for example, an endurance gene that could promote red blood cell production and prevent the onset of fatigue is clearly a method of performance enhancement. The discovery of and ability to manipulate any such gene could be useful for endurance athletes who seek to increase their running capabilities.

Perhaps one solution to this ethical dilemma is to create distinct, genetically enhanced competitions and to continue voluntary submission to anti-doping testing procedures. This may solve the concerns about fair play, though clearly the ramifications for competitive sport would be immense. Where there exist genetically modified athletes competing at a level that far exceeds the abilities of the non-enhanced, the public interest in the latter might wane immeasurably. After all, it will be the genetically modified athletes who will be breaking human barriers and surpassing known, physical limitations – and isn't this what is exciting about sport?

Notes

Introduction: Why genetics now?

1 It is a little ironic that this hysteria has subsequently transcended into the mere labelling of foods to distinguish between genetic modification and non-genetic modification goods. Indeed, this example reflects how panic about genetics becomes enculturated, normalised and made invisible, something which might also be said of genetically modified athletes in due course.

2 Continually, misunderstandings (and blatant misrepresentations) have arisen about how the process to clone Dolly entailed the wasting of 277 embryos or even sheep that were born with dysfunctional genes. For clarity, the one in 277 attempts so often used to reject cloning as wasteful of life refers to the number of fusions that took place between donor cells and the unfertilised egg before the successful creation of an embryo. From these 277 attempts, only twenty-nine became embryos, all of which were introduced into thirteen ewes. Out of this thirteen, only one ewe became pregnant, giving birth to the ewe we now call Dolly.

3 As an aside, Francis Fukuyama (2002b) also highlights the application of genetics to sport in the Economist magazine *The World in 2003* as the next big test of genetic technology for the world.

1 Why not dope? It's still about the health

1 There seem to be similar assumptions made about the undesirability of genetic modification as are made about drug taking in sport. This can help elucidate how genetic modification in sport might become distorted and rejected on similarly questionable philosophical bases.

2 Thanks to Bruce Jennings for a rather fruitful conversation about the moral athlete and for reminding me how useful is the film *Rocky IV*, even if we partially disagree on the precise characteristics of such athletes.

3 However, it might be argued that public opinion in respect of different kinds of performance enhancements might be more difficult to apprehend. For example, while we might expect clear ideas about how drugs are perceived, it may be more difficult to discern reactions to the use of blood transfusions or altitude chambers. Unfortunately, such methods of enhancement are subsumed into the discourse of doping – e.g. blood doping – which makes it difficult to gauge any clear differences in perception.

4 I would like to stress here that I am not entirely dismissing the work of the anti-doping movement. I have many valued colleagues who are involved with anti-doping in various contexts, who are genuinely seeking to develop coherent and justifiable ethical policies. Even those colleagues who I believe are making fundamental errors in their approach to anti-doping are not operating from an interest to do harm to sport, nor lack sincerity in their decisions and conclusions. My concern (and rejection)

is for the rather stagnant manner in which such discussions are often made, the inconsistency of policies, and the lack of significance that is given to ethical inquiry in relation to doping. After all, misplaced sincerity is not a sufficient justification for the continuance of poor ethical conduct.

5 It is important to note that Schneider and Butcher (2000) are dealing specifically with doping and that genetic modification is not considered explicitly within their argument.

6 It is not possible here to give a thorough articulation of why I consider Schneider and Butcher's (2000) overview is inconsistent. Specifically, I have difficulties with their category of harms and how this fits in relation to other categories. It would seem that, on many occasions, other categories could also be seen as harms. Thus my tendency is to provide an overview of all arguments departing from a central concept of 'harm'. They use harm more to refer to biological harm, though I consider that a more generic term is relevant, where harm may also be to fail to respect the constitutive elements of a sport. More details of this analysis may be found in Miah(2002a).

7 The authors referenced alongside the different harms provide a picture of where these arguments have been considered in some detail, rather than necessarily reflecting the central argument of the author. In many cases the authors consider a variety of viewpoints in the analysis of arguments concerning doping, though it is useful as some form of guide to understand how interests have been focused.

8 For more details about the moral consideration of non-living entities see Elliott (1993).

9 I am unaware of any strong concerns about the social harm of blood doping or of using altitude chambers.

10 The implications of Carr's conclusions are far-reaching and pertinent to the ethical discussion about genetic modification. It may be possible to extend Carr's argument to genetic endowment and conclude that genetic modification would be desirable, if it could eliminate differences between athletes based upon genetic luck. For Carr, this characteristic of sport has no value, since it is beyond the influence of the athlete.

11 Such an example is beginning to emerge in male professional tennis, where bigger balls are being piloted to combat the dominance of the strong serve, which is becoming impossible for a human to retrieve (Miah, 2000, 2002b).

2 Forget drugs and the ideology of harmonisation

1 Currently, the only international federation to not be fully dependent upon WADA is FIFA, which recognises WADA's banned list, but which applies its own sanctions.

2 Wu *et al.* (1999) deals with a similar problem in detecting rhGH, suggesting ways of being able to detect artificial growth hormone that is identical to the host. Their technique may have implications for detecting genetic modifications.

3 For a detailed overview of bioethics in Europe, see Rogers and Durand de Bousingen (1995), particularly Chapter 8. Conversely, to understand more about sport in Europe and the importance of how Europe is particularly well placed to progress in developing policy about genetics in sport, see Gardiner *et al.* (2001).

4 This was the case particularly in relation to Dr Richard Seed, US scientist turned rebel cloner. Indeed, the cloning issue rears its head repeatedly in the media, with numerous people claiming to have cloned the first human being.

3 What is possible? Imminent applications for the genetically modified athlete

1 For a more in-depth historical overview of genetics, see the Genome News Network (2003), which provides useful information and links to landmark publications in the history of genetic science from Darwin to the present day.

2 This notoriety was steeped in controversy over who could claim credit for having identified its *twisted helix* structure. Specifically, at least two other researchers seemed

important in the process of this historic finding, namely Rosalind Franklin and Maurice Wilkins (Hubbard, 2003).
3 The description of genes is more contested than one might expect for such a scientifically rigorous subject. Genetics – indeed, biology – relies upon metaphor and visualisation, which makes for a variety of ways of conceptualising the structures and their relationships. Indeed, the entire subject of genetics uses metaphors such as the 'book of life' and the 'blueprint' of the human genome, which aspire to make the science meaningful for non-scientists. For this reason, the way we talk about genes is a highly disputed subject (Condit and Condit, 2001). For examples describing genes, see Ford (1999) and Ridley (1999).
4 For a comprehensive list of key publications in this recent history, see the Oakridge National Laboratory website at: http://www.ornl.gov/TechResources/Human_Genome/project/journals/journals.html.
5 For extensive details of this work, see the 11 April edition of *Science* and the 24 April edition of *Nature* (2003).
6 The terminology used to describe the alteration of genes is intriguing. In the early 1990s it was commonplace to see the phrase 'genetic engineering', even within scientific texts. Yet such a term, along with 'genetic manipulation', seems to have developed a cultural baggage that appears overly eugenic. In contrast, more recent descriptions of the same technology include the more sanitised 'genetic modification', 'gene therapy' or 'gene transfer technology'. For an insightful exploration of the language of genetics, see Nordgren (2003).
7 Some doubt is cast on the strength of this correlation by Taylor *et al.* (1999).
8 My thanks to Parissa Safai for bringing news of this research to my attention.

4 Interests, politics and ways of reasoning

1 Due to the terrorist attacks on the World Trade Center on 11 September, this meeting did not take place and was rescheduled for March 2002.
2 More may be said about the political context of WADA. While revising the Code has attracted some important praise for its work, it remains to be seen whether WADA really operates independently from the IOC. Given the highly incestuous world of international sport (for both good and bad) – for example, Chair of WADA is former IOC Vice-President Richard W. Pound – it would be wise to be aware of possible conflicts of interest within the organisation.

5 Humanness, dignity and autonomy

1 While it would be interesting to consider the genetic modification of animals for sport, this would demand another monograph and so the present focus will be on human genetics. For a brief article on this topic, see Henderson (2001).
2 It is important to remember that the use of tools does not define human identity, since there are examples of animals that can use natural objects and change their function to become a tool. For example, biological scientist Jane Goodall observed how a particular kind of chimpanzee would use leaves which it crushed together to form a sponge to soak water out of tree stump hollows or would use sticks to crack nuts.
3 It is interesting to note that each of these approaches, and, I suggest, concepts of posthumanness in general, seem to be framed by some technological project, though unnecessarily I think.
4 This is intended in a similar manner to how Frankford (1998: 75) describes policy statements as becoming divorced from their 'context of articulation'.
5 Nevertheless, it might *require* concluding that athletes do have a significant case for claiming their right to enhancement through genetic modification.

6 Personhood, identity and the ethics of authenticity

1 The speciesist limitation is also highlighted in the sporting literature by Brown (1995), who considers that the notion of persons is problematic because it omits to consider animal sports, such as horse-racing, cock-fighting or bear baiting as cases of moral concern.

2 Similar arguments are found in A.J. Ayer's *The Concept of a Person* (1964), where the interest is more to address the mind/body relationship than to identify the moral importance of personhood. This approach seems mistaken, since it need not be necessary that beings are persons simply by virtue of their having a body or even that they can be valued only for being persons.

3 Further details of Locke's explanation of personhood may be found in Doran (1989), as may explanations of other authors considered in this overview.

4 Frankfurt sees this as a way of placing humans in a different category from all other animals.

5 Additional contextual work on Tooley, particularly the associations of his claims and the work of Aquinas, may be found in Doran (1989) and Eberl (2000).

6 Further explanation on Hume's theory of personal identity may be found in Biro (1996).

7 Taylor (1985) makes explicit the connections with Heidegger's *Being and Time* and his concerns for *angst*, which call for a need to seek authenticity. For Heidegger, our embeddedness in cultural contexts leads us towards inauthenticity. Moreover, being authentic involves confronting and contemplating what is the sum value of one's life.

8 In addition, Honnefelder (1996) draws upon Locke, arguing that a concern for identifying what constitutes personhood is actually a concern for identity, though it is important to be careful with Honnefelder, as he appears to conflate these terms at times.

9 Fleming also makes such desires a precondition to the entitlement of rights, which will be discussed in more depth later.

10 There seems no reason to base a position about human dignity on where humans are located in relation to other living entities. Indeed, I would be more comfortable with concluding that our concept of dignity must logically be applied to some animals, than to some humans. Similarly, the concept of liberty is more tied to social freedoms than to individual ones, the former requiring a quite different basis for evaluation than is pertinent to an inquiry into human dignity.

11 Bayertz (1996) actually notes the three concepts of rationality, perfectibility and autonomy as the grounding for human dignity.

12 Specifically, Flanagan highlights a distinction in Taylor, noting that 'the overall picture is best understood as one in which weak evaluators range from the simple wanton who makes no motivational assessments at all to persons who do make motivational assessments along a wide variety of dimensions, so long as these dimensions are not ethical' (1990: 40–41).

13 Taylor notes that his use of this concept is informed by George Herbert Mead.

7 Virus, disease, illness, health, well-being . . . and enhancement

1 Very little has yet been written about the klapskate, though forthcoming work by Ivo van Hilvoorde (2003) speaks to the ethical implications of this innovation. Additional information about the science of the skates can be found in Houdijk *et al.* (2001).

2 The challenge for the physician in sport is explored in Murray (1984b), which outlines the potential for conflicts of interest to arise.

3 The incidence of asthma medication use among athletes increased from 1.7 per cent at the 1984 Los Angeles Olympics to 6.1 per cent at the Salt Lake Winter Olympics (Mackay, 2002).

4 Parens (1998) considers that a continuum for enhancement technologies is misleading, and it would be wise to take this on board before trying to posit some continuum of health ranging from disease to *enhanced health*.

5 The *Journal of Medicine and Philosophy* has been particularly important in considering in depth this definitional problem and the misuse and misunderstanding of various terms related to health, particularly elucidating the distinction between disease. In 1995, an entire issue (Vol. 20, no. 5) and in 2000 (Vol.25, no. 5) were dedicated to conceptualising health and disease.

6 Glannon (2001) identifies three kinds of genetic disease (monogenic, polygenic, and multifactorial), the latter two of which are best explained as being the product of an interaction of biology and environment. However, he does note that this remains a scientific combination rather than understanding environment as value laden.

7 Barilan and Weintraub (2001) provide an engaging articulation of the problems with notions of the *artificial* and the *natural*, where the latter tend to reflect what is acceptable, and the former, usually pertaining to new technology, are considered bad, dangerous or inhuman. Such arguments may be seen to support the earlier, historical overview of humanness and the implicit and explicit connotations of the stories of *The Nightingale* and *Frankenstein*.

8 Caplan (1992) provides an outline of the various key authors supporting each perspective in bioethics.

9 Boyd (2000: 9) considers that, in one very important sense, the meaning of disease is quite literally, dis-ease, or simply 'an impediment to free movement'.

10 Drawing on Illich (1990), Hedgecoe (1998) is concerned that medical practice is instilling an unhealthy culture of dependency of individuals upon medicine.

11 Currently, concerns of this kind are arising in respect of the medical diagnosis of female sexual dysfunction, contested by some as a misappropriation of medical terminology, and feared for its promoting of the treatment of this 'condition' with drugs, as has taken place in respect of male sexual dysfunction with sildenafi (Viagra) (Moynihan, 2003).

12 Again, it is useful to remember Juengst's (1998) argument here about the medicalisation of the wrong problems.

13 In the context of Silvers (1998), Parens considers that it may be necessary to introduce an additional term of 'prevention' to mediate therapy and enhancement, since, she argues, 'it is not helpful to refer . . . to vaccinations as enhancements; such interventions would fall directly into the prevention category if we could agree that we need a third category in addition to treatment and enhancement' (1998: 9–10).

14 For a discussion on the importance of 'social acceptability' in the definition of disease, and for further debate on the issue of defining disease more generally, see Cooper (2002).

15 This challenge to Boorse's view is also raised by Hare (1986).

16 While I concur with many of Erde's (2000) criticisms of Rudnick (2000), he does not develop much of a response to Rudnick's theory of health as a process or regulative idea, which is the specific argument I seek to develop.

17 While the evolutionary biological approach to this might be at odds with such conclusions, it is a far greater battle to challenge individualism in healthcare and it will not be my task here to challenge such an approach.

18 This approach builds upon the work by Clouser *et al.* (1981), later developed in Culver and Gert (1982) and Culver (1996).

19 The concept of an open future has been discussed by a number of authors, though notably by Joel Feinberg (1980/1992).

8 Unfair advantages and other harms

1 This idea of a contract-like situation in competitive sport was detailed in Chapter 1, making reference to Butcher and Schneider (1998), Eassom (1998), Feezell (1986), Loland (1998a), Morgan (1994) and Simon (1991).

2 That said, it is useful to consider this point in the context of the earlier discussion about the distinctions between health, well-being and so on. Such conclusions might

suggest that my articulation of harm is also approaching a similar broadness within the medical sphere.

3 It is important not to confuse this as simply making an ethical distinction between repair or enhancement, as is sometimes expressed within sport ethical debates. It is *not* the case that non-therapeutic applications of genetic modification are similar to what might be termed genetic enhancements.

4 A further ethical issue arises about the requirement to undergo antenatal genetic testing, once new tests for genetic conditions are made available. Bennett (2001) is concerned that being required to take such tests would challenge the right to remain in ignorance.

5 For a response to this *slippery-slope argument*, see Resnik (1994).

6 It is interesting to note that Macer also acknowledges that, perhaps, the more determining factor for why such requirements were not maintained was the financial cost of the testing.

7 This point is partially reflective of the current controversy surrounding the use of stem-cells, themselves not lives, but having the potential to construct life. The moral or ethical status of such cells has been crucial in setting policy on the acceptable limits of gene therapy in the past three years and continues to be debated. For information on the stem-cell debate see Caplan and McGee (1999), Lovell-Badge (2001), McLachlan (2002), National Bioethics Advisory Commission (1999), Nuffield Council on Bioethics (2000) and Singer (2000).

8 As an aside, it is entertaining to read Varzi and Coen (2001) as some indication of what does not seem to count as valid experimental research!

10 Sport needs genetic modification

1 A further argument might moreover problematise the value of athletes as role models, questioning whether such persons are good role models, regardless of whether they use illegal performance enhancements.

2 The importance of results in sport has not always been so clear. Even within some non-Western sports, where the importance of winning is significant, the emphasis on results is secondary to the ritual and spectacle of the event. Indeed, Allen Guttmann writes in his 1978 text *From Ritual to Record* about the peculiarity of modern Western sport to place so much importance in recording sporting achievements. Guttmann is puzzled by the modern obsession with results and measurement, which, he argues, is born out of the seventeenth-century scientific revolution. Thus an initial retort to excellence as performance is to recognise that there are other ways of valuing sport.

3 A further complication to this recommendation might entail questioning whether one can really reason by adopting the perspective of a foetus or, indeed, whether the process of such reasoning should make some *person-based* assumptions. However, it is not possible to develop these ideas further here.

11 Conclusions and implications

1 The Court of Arbitration was established by the International Olympic Committee, National Olympic Committees and the International Sports Federations in 1983 (Kidd and Donnelly, 2000: 10).

2 There are other roots to this argument, which include gaining an unfair advantage through deceptive means. This argument is not applicable to the present discussion, since our question is whether or not genetic modification should be banned. I am not disputing the unfairness of deception in this case. Rather, I am interested in understanding whether genetic modification should be illegal at all. If the technology is permitted, then there would be no concern about unfair advantage arising from deception, since all athletes will be aware that their competitors may have been modified.

3 It is relevant to note that it would seem the infraction was an oversight. It was not clear that marijuana was on any prohibited substance list due to the unusual organisation of the snowboarding events. Rather than be under the auspices of a snowboarding federation, the International Skiing Federation adopted the role of organising the competition. However, unlike the snowboarding federation, the ISF included marijuana on its prohibited substances list, thus rendering some confusion about its acceptability.

4 Numerous references could be given here detailing articles in relation to doping, ethics and sport. Rather than list each of them, it is a useful basis to depart from readings within the *Journal of the Philosophy of Sport* from 1980. In addition, Morgan and Meier's (1988/1995) renowned edited volume includes a number of classic articles about ethical perspectives on drugs and sport, and one of the most recent publications dealing with this problem is edited by Wilson and Derse (2001).

Bibliography

Allen, D.B. and Fost, N.C. (1990) 'Growth Hormone for Short Stature: Panacea or Pandora's Box?', *Journal of Pediatrics*, **117** (1): 16–21.

American Association for the Advancement of Science Annual Meeting (2003) 'Bigger, Faster, Stronger: Genetic Enhancement and Athletics', Online. Available: <http://health.ucsd.edu/news/2003/02_18_Friedmann.html> (accessed 15 March).

Anderson, O. (2000) 'Now Science is Getting to the Long and the Short of how Genes Influence Performance', Peak Performance, Online. Available: http://www.pponline.co.uk/encyc/0524.htm (accessed 8 July 2001).

Anderson, S. (1998) *The Cloning of Human Beings*. Twentieth World Congress of Philosophy, Boston. Online. Available: <http://www.bu.edu/wcp/Papers/Bioe/Bioe/Ande.htm> (accessed January 2004).

Anderson, W.F. (1994) 'Genetic Engineering and our Humanness', *Human Gene Therapy*, **5** (6): 755–759.

Annas, G.J. and Grodin, M.A. (1992) *The Nazi Doctors and the Nuremberg Code: Human Rights in Human Experimentation*, New York: Oxford University Press.

Appleyard, B. (1999) *Brave New Worlds: Staying Human in the Genetic Future*, London: HarperCollins.

Arnold, P.J. (1992) 'Sport as a Valued Human Practice: A Basis for the Consideration of Some Moral Issues in Sport', *Journal of Philosophy of Education*, **26** (2): 237–255.

Arnold, P.J. (1997) *Sport, Ethics and Education*, London: Cassell Education.

Aschwanden, C. (2000) 'Gene Cheats', *New Scientist*, **2221**: 24–29. Online. Available: <http://nasw.org/users/christie/genecheats.html> (accessed 12 May 2003).

Associated Press (2001) 'Sports Threat: Gene Transferring', Wired 25 January. Online. Available: <http://www.wired.com/news/technology/0,1282,41428,00.html> (accessed 22 April 2002).

Australian Law Reforms Commission (2001) *Issues Paper 26 Protection of Human Genetic Information – 12. Other Services and Contexts*. Sydney: Australian Law Reforms Commission, Online. Available: <http://www.austlii.edu.au/au/other/alrc/publications/issues/26/> (accessed 9 September).

Australian Law Reforms Commission (2003) *ALRC 96: Essentially Yours*.

Ayabe, S. and Tan, S.Y. (1995) 'Entering the Age of the New Genetics with Eyes Wide Open', *Hawaii Medical Journal*, **54** (April): 460–463.

Ayer, A.J. (1964) *The Concept of a Person*, London: Macmillan.

Bailey, C.I. (1975) 'Sport and the Element of Chance', *Journal of Sport Behaviour*, **3** (2): 69–75.

Baker, A. and Hopkins, W.G. (1998) 'Altitude Training for Sea-Level Competition', *Sportscience: Training & Technology*. Internet Society for Sport Science: http://sportsci.org/traintech/altitude/wgh.html.

Barilan, Y.M. and Weintraub, M. (2001) 'The Naturalness of the Artificial and Our Concepts of Health, Disease and Medicine', *Medicine, Health Care and Philosophy*, **4** (3): 311–325.

Barton-Davis, E.R., Shoturma, D.I., Musaro, A., Rosenthal, N. and Sweeney, H.L. (1998) 'Viral Mediated Expression of Insulin-like Growth Factor I Blocks the Aging-related Loss of Skeletal Muscle Function', *Proceedings of the National Academy of Sciences, USA*, **95** (December): 15603–15607.

Battin, M.P. (1994) *The Least Worst Death*, Oxford and New York: Oxford University Press.

Bayertz, K. (ed.) (1996) *Sanctity of Life and Human Dignity*, Dordrecht, Boston and London: Kluwer Academic.

Bayertz, K. and Engelhardt Jr., H.T. (eds) (1994) *The Principles of Menschenwürde and Sanctity of Life in Bioethics*, Dordrecht: Kluwer Academic.

Beauchamp, T.L. (1997) 'Informed Consent', in R.M. Veatch (ed.) *Medical Ethics*, London: Jones and Barlett.

Beauchamp, T.L. and Childress, J.F. (1994) *Principles of Biomedical Ethics* (4th edn), New York and Oxford: Oxford University Press.

Benn, P. (2001) 'The Sex Selection Question', *Spiked-Online*. London, Online. Available: <http://www.spiked-online.com/Articles/00000002D2D1.htm> (accessed 15 November).

Bennett, R. (2001) 'Antenatal Genetic Testing and the Right to Remain in Ignorance', *Theoretical Medicine*, **22**: 461–471.

Birnbacher, D. (1994) 'Ambiguities in the Concept of Menschenwürde', in K. Bayertz and H.T. Engelhardt Jr. (eds) *The Principles of Menschenwürde and Sanctity of Life in Bioethics*, Dordrecht: Kluwer Academic, pp. 107–122.

Birnbacher, D. (1998) *Embryo Research as a Paradigm of Ethical Pragmatics*. Twentieth World Congress of Philosophy, Boston, Online. Available: <http://www.bu.edu/wcp/Papers/Bioe/BioeBirn.htm> (accessed 10 December).

Biro, J. (1996) 'Hume's New Science of the Mind', in D. Fate Norton (ed.) *The Cambridge Companion to Hume*, Cambridge: Cambridge University Press, pp. 33–63.

Blake, A. (1996) *The Body Language: The Meaning of Modern Sport*, London: Lawrence & Wishart.

Boorse, C. (1975) 'On the Distinction Between Disease and Illness', *Philosophy and Public Affairs*, **5**: 49–68.

Boorse, C. (1977) 'Health as a Theoretical Concept', *Philosophy of Science*, **44**: 542–573.

Bostrom, N. (1998) What is Transhumanism?, Online. Available: <http://www.nickbostrom.com/old/transhumanism.html> (accessed 23 July 1999).

Bouchard, C., Malina, R.M. and Perusse, L. (1997) *Genetics of Fitness and Physical Performance*, Champaign, IL: Human Kinetics.

Boyd, K.M. (2000) 'Disease, Illness, Sickness, Health, Healing and Wholeness: Exploring some Elusive Concepts', *Journal of Medical Ethics: Medical Humanities*, **26** (1): 9–17.

Breivik, G. (1987) 'The Doping Dilemma – Game Theoretical Consideration', *Sportwissenschaft*, **17** (1): 83–94.

Breivik, G. (2000) 'Against Chance: A Causal Theory of Winning in Sport', in T. Tännsjö and C. Tamburrini (eds) *Values in Sport: Elitism, Nationalism, Gender Equality, and the Scientific Manufacture of Winners*, London: E & FN Spon, pp. 141–156.

Brewer, B.D. (2002) 'Commercialization in Professional Cycling 1950–2001: Institutional Transformations and the Rationalization of Doping', *Sociology of Sport Journal*, **19**: 276–301.

British Medical Association (2002) 'Boxing and the brain: revisiting chronic enceptalopathy', *British Journal of Sports Medicine*, **36** (11).

Brock, D.W. (1998) 'Enhancements of Human Function: Some Distinctions for Policymakers', in E. Parens (ed.) *Enhancing Human Traits: Ethical and Social Implications*, Washington, DC: Georgetown University Press, pp. 48–69.

Brown, W.M. (1980) 'Ethics, Drugs and Sport', *Journal of the Philosophy of Sport*, **7**: 15–23.

Brown, W.M. (1984a) 'Comments on Simon and Fraleigh', *Journal of the Philosophy of Sport*, **11**: 33–35.

Brown, W.M. (1984b) 'Paternalism, drugs and the nature of sport', *Journal of the Philosophy of Sport*, **XI**: 14–22.

Brown, W.M. (1990) 'Practices and Prudence', *Journal of the Philosophy of Sport*, **17**: 71–84.

Brown, W.M. (1995) 'Personal Best', *Journal of the Philosophy of Sport*, **22**: 1–10.

Bruce, D. and Bruce, A. (eds) (1998) *Engineering Genesis: The Ethics of Genetic Engineering in Non-Human Species*. London: Earthscan Publications.

Brull, D., Dhamrait, S., Myerson, S., Erdmann, J., Regitz-Zagrosek, V., World, M., Pennell, D., Humphries, S.E. and Montgomery, H. (2001) 'Bradykinin B2BKR receptor polymorphism and left-ventricular growth response', *The Lancet*, **358** (October): 1155–1156.

Buchanan, A., Califano, A., Kahn, J., McPherson, E., Robertson, J. and Brody, B. (2002) 'Pharamacogenetics: Ethical Issues and Policy Options', *Kennedy Institute of Ethics Journal*, **12** (1): 1–15.

Burke, M.D. (1997) 'Drugs in Sport: Have they Practiced too Hard? A Response to Schneider and Butcher', *Journal of the Philosophy of Sport*, **24**: 47–66.

Burley, J. (1999) 'Bad Genetic Luck and Health Insurance', in J. Burley (ed.) *The Genetic Revolution and Human Rights*, Oxford: Oxford University Press, pp. 54–60.

Busch, A. (1998) *Design in Sport: The Cult of Performance*, London: Thames and Hudson.

Butcher, R. and Schneider, A. (1998) 'Fair Play as Respect for the Game', *Journal of the Philosophy of Sport*, **25**: 1–22.

Butryn, T. (2002) 'Cyborg Horizons: Sport and the Ethics of Self-Technologization', in A. Miah and S.B. Eassom (eds) *Sport Technology: History, Philosophy and Policy*, Oxford: Elsevier Science, pp. 111–133.

Caplan, A.L. (1992) 'If Gene Therapy is the Cure, What is the Disease?', in G. Annas and S. Elias *Gene Mapping*, Oxford: Oxford University Press. Also Online. Available: <http://www.med.upenn.edu/%7Ebioethic/02/GeneticsEthicsArticle01.shtml> (accessed 30 October 1999).

Caplan, A.L. and McGee, G. (1999) 'The Ethics and Politics of Small Sacrifices in Stem Cell Research', *Kennedy Institute of Ethics Journal*, **9**: 151–158.

Carr, D. (1999) 'Where's the Merit if the Best Man Wins?', *Journal of the Philosophy of Sport*, **26**: 1–9.

Carter, M.A. (1998) *Synthetic Model of Bioethical Inquiry*. Twentieth World Congress of Philosophy, Boston, USA. Online. Available: <http://www.bu.edu/wcp/Papers/Bioe/BioeCart.htm> (accessed 12 June 1999).

Catlin, D.H. and Murray, T.H. (1996) 'Performance-enhancing Drugs, Fair Competition, and Olympic Sport', *Journal of American Medical Association*, **276** (3): 231–237.

Celera Genomics Sequencing Team (2001) 'The Sequence of the Human Genome', *Science*, **291** (5507): 1304–1351.

Chadwick, R.F. (ed.) (1987) *Ethics, Reproduction and Genetic Control*, London: Routledge.

Chadwick, R.F. and Levitt, M. (1998) 'Genetic Technology: A Threat to Deafness', *Medicine, Health Care and Philosophy*, **1** (3): 209–215.

Cheng, H-Y.M. and Penninger, J.M. (2003) 'When the DREAM is Gone: From Basic Science to Future Prospectives in Pain Management and Beyond', *Expert Opinion on Therapeutic Targets*, **7** (2): 249–263.

Cheng, H-Y.M., Pitcher, G.M., Laviolette, S.R., Whishaw, I.Q., Tong, K.I., Kockeritz, L.K., Wada, T., Joza, N.A., Crackower, M., Goncalves, J., Sarosi, I., Woodgett, J.R., Oliveira-dos-Santos, Antonio J., Ikura, M., van der Kooy, D., Salter, M.W. and Penninger, J.M. (2002) 'DREAM Is a Critical Transcriptional Repressor for Pain Modulation', *Cell*, **108**: 31–43.

Cherry, M.J. (2000) 'Polymorphic Medical Ontologies: Fashioning Concepts of Disease', *Journal of Medicine and Philosophy*, **25** (5): 519–538.

Clarey, C. (2001) 'Chilling New World: Sports and Genetics', *International Herald Tribune*, 26 January.

Clouser, K.D., Culver, C.M. and Gert, B. (1981) 'Malady: A New Treatment of Disease', *Hastings Center Report*, **11**: 29–37.

Coe, A. (2000) 'The Balance Between Technology and Tradition in Tennis', in S.A. Haake and A.O. Coe (eds) *Tennis, Science, Technology*, London: Blackwell Science, pp. 3–40.

Cole-Turner, R. (1998) 'Do Means Matter?', in E. Parens (ed.) *Enhancing Human Traits: Ethical and Social Implications*, Washington, DC: Georgetown University Press, pp. 151–161.

Condit, C.M. and Condit, D.M. (2001) 'Blueprints and Recipes: Gendered Metaphors for Genetic Medicine', *Journal of Medical Humanities*, **22** (1): 29–39.

Connor, S. (2002) 'Warnock: No Ethical Reason to Ban Cloning', *Independent*.

Cooper, R. (2002) 'Disease', *Studies in History and Philosophy of Science*, **33**: 263–282.

Crouch, R.A. (1999) 'Letting the Deaf be Deaf: Reconsidering the Use of Cochlear Implants in Prelingually Deaf Children', in H. Lindemann Nelson and J. Lindemann Nelson (eds) *Meaning and Medicine: A Reader in the Philosophy of Health Care*, New York and London: Routledge, pp. 360–370.

Culver, C.M. (1996) 'Morality and the New Genetics: A Guide for Students and Health Care Providers', in B. Gert, E.M. Berger, G.F. Cahill Jr., K.D. Clouser, C.M. Culver, J.B. Moeschler and G.H.S. Singer (eds) *Jones and Bartlett Series in Philosophy*, Sudbury, MA: Jones and Bartlett.

Culver, C.M. and Gert, B. (1982) *Philosophy in Medicine*, Oxford: Oxford University Press.

D'Agostino, F. (1981) 'The Ethos of Games', *Journal of the Philosophy of Sport*, **8**: 7–18.

Daniels, N. (1992) 'Growth Hormone Therapy for Short Stature', *Growth: Genetics and Hormones* 8 (Supplement): 46–48.

DeLattre, E.J. (1975) 'Some Reflections on Success and Failure in Competitive Athletics', *Journal of the Philosophy of Sport*, **2**: 133–139.

Delegation (1999) *Lausanne Declaration on Doping in Sport*, Lausanne: World Conference on Doping in Sport. Online. Available: <http://www.nodoping.olympic.org/Declaration_e.html>.

de Melo-Martin, I. (2002) 'On cloning human beings', *Bioethics*, **16** (3): 246–265.

Denham, B.E. (1997) 'Sports Illustrated, the "War on Drugs," and the Anabolic Steroid Control Act of 1990', *Journal of Sport and Social Issues*, **21** (3): 260–273.

Denham, B.E. (1999) 'On Drugs in Sports in the Aftermath of Flo-Jo's Death, Big Mac's Attack', *Journal of Sport and Social Issues*, **23** (3): 362–367.

Denham, B.E. (2000) 'Performance-enhancing Drug Use in Amateur and Professional Sports: Separating the Realities from the Ramblings', *Culture, Sport, Society*, **3** (2): 56–79.

Dennett, D.C. (1976) 'Conditions of Personhood', in A.O. Rorty (ed.) *The Identities of Persons*, Berkeley: University of California Press, pp. 175–196.

Dennett, D.C. (1988) 'Conditions of Personhood', in M.F. Goodman (ed.) *What is a Person?* Clifton, NJ: Humana Press, pp. 145–167.

De Simone, B. (2002) 'Drug Talk Hits a Higher Level: Lance Armstrong's and Other Cyclists' Use of Sleeping Tents that Simulate High Altitude Stirs a Controversy', *Chicago Tribune*, Chicago. Online. Available: <http://www.chicagotribune.com/sports/printedition/chi-0207280247jul28.story> (accessed 28 July).

Diekema, D.S. (1990) 'Is Taller Really Better? Growth Hormone Therapy for Short Children', *Perspectives in Biology and Medicine*, **34** (1): 109–123.

Dixon, N. (2001) 'Boxing, Paternalism and Legal Moralism', *Social Theory and Practice: An International and Interdisciplinary Journal of Social Philosophy*, **27** (2): 323–344.

Doran, K. (1989) *What is a Person? The Concept and the Implications for Ethics*, Lewiston, NY: The Edwin Mellen Press.

Downie, R.S. and Telfer, E. (1969) *Respect for Persons*, London: George Allen & Unwin.

Downie, R.S., Tannahill, C. and Tannahill, A. (1996) *Health Promotion: Models and Values*, Oxford: Oxford University Press.

Eassom, S.B. (1995) 'Playing Games with Prisoners' Dilemmas', *Journal of the Philosophy of Sport*, **22**: 26–47.

Eassom, S.B. (1998) 'Games, Rules and Contracts', in M.J. McNamee and S.J. Parry (eds) *Ethics and Sport*, London and New York: E & FN Spon, pp. 57–78.

Eberl, J.T. (2000) 'The Beginning of Personhood: A Thomistic Biological Analysis', *Bioethics*, **14** (2): 134–157.

Egonsson, D. (1998) *The Importance of Being Human*. Twentieth World Congress of Philosophy, Boston, USA. Online. Available: <http://www.bu.edu/wcp/Papers/OApp/OAppEgon.htm> (accessed 11 September).

Elliott, C. (1998a) 'The Tyranny of Happiness: Ethics and Cosmetic Pharmacology', in E. Parens (ed.) *Enhancing Human Traits: Ethical and Social Implications*, Washington, DC: Georgetown University Press, pp. 177–188.

Elliott, C. (1998b) *What's Wrong with Enhancement Technologies?*, CHIPS Public Lecture. Online. Available: <http://www.gene.ucl.ac.uk/bioethics/writings/Elliott.html> (accessed 24 February 1999).

Elliott, C. (1999) *A Philosophical Disease: Bioethics, Culture and Identity*, London: Routledge.

Elliott, C. (2001) 'Pharma Buys a Conscience', *The American Prospect*, **12** (17). Online. Available: <http://www.prospect.org/print/V12/17/elliott-c.html> (accessed October 2002).

Elliott, R. (1993) 'Environmental Ethics', in P. Singer *A Companion to Ethics*, Oxford: Blackwell, pp. 284–293.

Engelhardt Jr., H.T. (1974/1999) 'The Disease of Masturbation: Values and the Concept of Disease', in H. Lindemann Nelson and J. Lindemann Nelson (eds) *Meaning and Medicine: A Reader in the Philosophy of Health Care*, New York and London: Routledge, pp. 5–15.

Entine, J. (2000) *Taboo: Why Black Athletes Dominate Sports and Why We're Afraid to Talk About It*, Public Affairs.

Erde, E.L. (2000) 'On Values, Professionalism and Nosology: An Essay with Late Commentary on Essays by DeVito and Rudnick', *Journal of Medicine and Philosophy*, **25** (5): 581–603.

Fairchild, D.L. (1989) 'Sport Abjection: Steroids and the Uglification of the Athlete', *Journal of the Philosophy of Sport*, **16**: 74–88.

Farrey, T. (2000) 'Genetic Testing Beckons', ESPN. Online. Available: <http://espn.go.com/otl/athlete/monday.html> (accessed 20 January).

Feezell, R.M. (1986) 'Sportsmanship', *Journal of the Philosophy of Sport*, **13**: 1–13.

Feezell, R.M. (1988) 'On the Wrongness of Cheating and why Cheaters Can't Play the Game', *Journal of the Philosophy of Sport*, **15**: 57–68.

Feinberg, J. (1980/1992) *The Child's Right to an Open Future. Freedom and Fulfilment: Philosophical Essays*, Princeton, NJ: Princeton University Press, pp. 76–97.

Fields, S. (2001) 'Proteomics in Genomeland', *Science*, **291** (5507): 1221–1224.

Fitzsimons, P. (2000) 'Drop the Speed Togs and Let Best Win', *Sydney Morning Herald*, Sydney. Online. Available: <http://www.smh.com.au/news/0003/17/sport/sport10.html> (accessed October).

Flanagan, O. (1990) 'Identity and Strong and Weak Evaluation', in O. Flanagan and A.O. Rorty (eds) *Identity, Character, and Morality: Essays in Moral Psychology*, Cambridge, MA: The MIT Press, pp. 37–66.

Fleming, L. (1987) 'The Moral Status of the Foetus: A Reappraisal', *Bioethics*, **1** (1): 15–34.

Fletcher, J. (1979) *Humanhood: Essays in Biomedical Ethics*, New York: Prometheus Books.

Ford, B.J. (1999) *Genes: The Fight For Life*, London: Cassell.

Ford, N.M. (1986) *When Did I Begin? Conception of the Human Individual in History, Philosophy and Science*, Cambridge: Cambridge University Press.

Fotheringham, W. (1996a) 'Cycling: Hour of Pain, Shame or Glory', *Guardian*, London: 14.

Fotheringham, W. (1996b) 'Cycling: Obree Outraged at "Superman" Ban', *Guardian*, London: 23.

Fraleigh, W. (1982) 'Why the Good Foul is not Good', *Journal of Physical Education, Recreation and Dance*, **January**: 41–42.

Fraleigh, W.P. (1984a) 'Performance Enhancing Drugs in Sport: The Ethical Issue', *Journal of the Philosophy of Sport*, **11**: 23–29.

Fraleigh, W.P. (1984b) *Right Actions in Sport: Ethics for Contestants*, Champaign, IL: Human Kinetics.

Frankford, D.M. (1998) 'The Treatment/Enhancement Distinction as an Armament in the Policy Wars', in E. Parens (ed.) *Enhancing Human Traits: Ethical and Social Implications*, Washington, DC: Georgetown University Press, pp. 70–94.

Frankfurt, H.G. (1971/1988) 'Freedom of the Will and the Concept of a Person', in M.F. Goodman (ed.) *What is a Person?* Clifton, NJ: Humana Press, pp. 127–144.

Friedmann, T. and Roblin, R. (1972) 'Gene Therapy for Human Genetic Disease?', *Science*, **17** (5): 402.

Friedmann, T. and Koss, J.O. (2001) 'Gene transfer and athletics: an impending problem', *Molecular Therapy*, **3** (6): 819–820.

Fukuyama, F. (2002a) *Our Posthuman Future: Consequences of the Biotechnology Revolution*, London: Profile Books.

Fukuyama, F. (2002b) 'The Quandary of Progress', in *The Economist: The World in 2003*, p. 136.

Fulford, K.W.M. (1989) *Moral Theory and Medical Practice*, Cambridge: Cambridge University Press.

Galli, C., Lagutina, I., Crotti, G., Colleoni, S., Turini, P., Ponderato, N., Duchi, R. and Lazzari, G. (2003) 'A Cloned Foal Born to its Dam Twin', *Nature*, **424**: 635.

Gardiner, S., James, M., Welch, R. and O'Leary, J. (eds) (2001) *Sports Law* (2nd edn), London: Cavendish.

Gardner, R. (1989) 'On Performance-enhancing Substances and the Unfair Advantage Argument', *Journal of the Philosophy of Sport*, **16**: 59–73.

Gardner, W. (1995) 'Can Human Genetic Enhancement Be Prohibited?', *Journal of Medicine and Philosophy*, **20**: 65–84.

Gayagay, G., Yu, B., Hambly, B., Boston, T., Hahn, A., Celermajer, D.S. and Trent, R.J. (1998) 'Elite Endurance Athletes and the ACE I Allele – The Role of Genes in Athletic Performance', *Human Genetics*, **103** (1): 48–50.

Gaylin, W. (1990) *Adam and Eve and Pinocchio: On Being and Becoming Human*, New York: Viking Press.

Gelberg, J.N. (1996a) 'Technology and Sport: The Case of the ITF, Spaghetti Strings, and Composite Rackets', *North American Society for Sports History, NASSH Proceedings*, pp. 77–78.

Gelberg, J.N. (1996b) 'The Rise and Fall of the Polara Asymmetric Golf Ball: No Hook, No Slice, No Dice', *Technology in Society*, **18** (1): 93–110.

Gelberg, J.N. (1998) 'Tradition, Talent and Technology: The Ambitious Relationship Between Sports and Innovation', in A. Busch *Design in Sport*, London: Thames and Hudson, pp. 88–110.

Genome News Network (2003) Timeline. Online. Available: <http://gnn.tigr.org/timeline/timeline_home.shtml> (accessed June 2002).

Gillon, R. (ed.) (1994) *Principles of Health Care Ethics*, Chichester: John Wiley.

Glad, B. (1986) 'The Technical Scene and the New Javelin', *New Studies in Athletics*, **1** (2): 13–16.

Glannon, W. (2001) *Genes and Future People: Philosophical Issues in Human Genetics*, Oxford: Westview Press.

Glover, J. (1984) *What Sort of People Should There Be?*, Harmondsworth: Penguin.

Glover, J. (1999) 'Eugenics and Human Rights', in J. Burley (ed.) *The Genetic Revolution and Human Rights*, Oxford: Oxford University Press, pp. 101–124.

Goldspink, G. (2001) 'Gene Expression in Skeletal Muscle', *Biochemical Society Transactions*, **30**: 285–290.

Goodman, M.F. (1988) 'Introduction', in M.F. Goodman (ed.) *What is a Person?*, Clifton, NJ: Humana Press, pp. 1–27.

Gordijn, B. (1999) 'The Troublesome Concept of the Person', *Theoretical Medicine and Bioethics*, **20**: 347–359.

Gorner, P. (2000) 'Parents Suing over Patenting of Genetic Test', *Chicago Tribune*. Online. Available: <http://chicagotribune.com/news/metro/chicago/article/0,2669,ART-48233,FF.html> (accessed 19 November).

Gray, C.H. (ed.) (1995) *The Cyborg Handbook*, London: Routledge.

Gray, C.H. (1997) 'The Ethics and Politics of Cyborg Embodiment: Citizenship as a Hypervalue', *Cultural Values*, **1** (2): 252–258.

Gray, C.H. (2002) *Cyborg Citizen: Politics in the Posthuman Age*, London: Routledge.

Guttmann, A. (1978) *From Ritual to Record: The Nature of Modern Sports*, New York: Columbia University Press.

Haig, D. (1993) 'Genetic Conflicts in Human Pregnancy', *Quarterly Review of Biology*, **68** (4): 495–532.

Hailer, M. and Ritschl, D. (1996) 'The General Notion of Human Dignity and the Specific Arguments in Medical Ethics', in K. Bayertz (ed.) *Sanctity of Life and Human Dignity*, Dordrecht, Boston and London: Kluwer Academic, pp. 91–106.

Hamlyn, P. (2001) 'Gene Genie Casts Ominous Shadow', *Telegraph*, London. Online.

Haraway, D. (1985) 'A Manifesto for Cyborgs: Science, Technology, & Socialist Feminism in the 1980s', *Socialist Review*, **80**: 65–108.

Hare, R.M. (1986) 'Health', *Journal of Medical Ethics*, **12**: 174–181.

Harris, J. (1998) *Clones, Genes, and Immortality*, Oxford: Oxford University Press.

Harris, J. (1999) 'Clones, Genes, and Human Rights', in J. Burley (ed.) *The Genetic Revolution and Human Rights*, Oxford: Oxford University Press, pp. 61–94.

Hayles, N.K. (1999) *How We Became Posthuman: Virtual Bodies in Cybernetics, Literature, and Informatics*, London: University of Chicago Press.

Häyry, H. and Lehto, T. (1998) *Who Should Know About our Genetic Makeup and Why?*. Twentieth World Congress of Philosophy. Online. Available: <http://www.bu.edu/wcp/Papers/Bioe/BioeHay1.htm> (accessed September).

Häyry, H. and Takala, T. (2001) 'Genetic Information, Rights, and Autonomy', *Theoretical Medicine*, **22**: 403–414.

Hedgecoe, A. (1998) 'Geneticization, Medicalisation and Polemics', *Medicine, Health Care and Philosophy*, **1** (3): 235–243.

Henderson, C. (2001) 'A Winning Creation', *Horse & Hound*, 31 May: 24–27.

Henderson, M. (2000) 'Insurers to Check for Genetic Illness', *The Times*, London: 17.

Hendriks, A. (1997) 'Genetics, Human Rights and Employment: American and European Perspectives', *Medicine and Law*, **16**: 557–565.

Hilvoorde, I. van (2003) 'Flopping, Klapping and Gene Doping: Shifting Dichotomies Between "Natural" and "Artificial" in Elite Sport', Paper presented at *Extreme Bodies* Meeting, Maastricht, Netherlands (working paper).

Hintz, R.L. (2004) 'Editorial: Growth hormone – uses and abuses', *British Medical Journal*, **328**: 907–908.

Ho, M. (1998) *Genetic Engineering – Dream or Nightmare?: The Brave New World of Bad Science and Big Business*, Bath: Gateway Books.

Hoberman, J.M. (1988) 'Sport and the Technological Image of Man', in W.J. Morgan and K.V. Meier (eds) *Philosophic Inquiry in Sport*, Champaign, IL: Human Kinetics, pp. 319–327.

Hoberman, J.M. (1992) *Mortal Engines: The Science of Performance and the Dehumanization of Sport*, New York: The Free Press (republished in 2001 by Blackburn Press).

Hofmann, B. (2001a) 'The Technological Invention of Disease', *Journal of Medical Ethics: Medical Humanities*, **27** (1): 10–19.

Hofmann, B. (2001b) 'On the Value-ladenness of Technology in Medicine', *Medicine, Health Care and Philosophy*, **4**: 335–346.

Hofmann, B. (2002) 'Technological Medicine and the Autonomy of Man', *Medicine, Health Care and Philosophy*, **5**: 157–162.

Holowchak, M.A. (2000) 'Aretism and Pharmacological Erogenic Aids in Sport: Taking a Shot at the Use of Steroids', *Journal of the Philosophy of Sport*, **27**: 35–50.

Honnefelder, L. (1996) 'The Concept of a Person in Moral Philosophy', in K. Bayertz (ed.) *Sanctity of Life and Human Dignity*, Dordrecht, Boston and London: Kluwer Academic, pp. 139–160.

Houdijk, H., Wijker, A.J., De Konig, J.J., Bobbert, M.F. and De Groot, G. (2001) 'Ice Friction in Speed Skating: Can Klapskates Reduce Ice Frictional Loss?', *Medicine & Science in Sports & Exercise*, **33** (3): 499–504.

Houlihan, B. (1999) *Dying to Win: Doping in Sport and the Development of Anti-Doping Policy*, Strasbourg: Council of Europe Publishing.

Hubbard, R. (2003) 'Science, Power, Gender: How DNA Became the Book of Life', *Signs: Journal of Women in Culture and Society*, **28** (3): 791–799.

Hume, D. (1739) *A Treatise of Human Nature*. Online. Available: <http://www2.canisius.edu/~gallaghr/hume.html> (accessed August 2002).

Huxley, A. (1932/1994) *Brave New World*, London: Flamingo.

Illich, I. (1990) *Limits to Medicine: Medical Nemesis: the Expropriation of Health*, London: Penguin.

International Human Genome Sequencing Consortium (2001) 'Initial Sequencing and Analysis of the Human Genome', *Nature*, **409** (6822): 860–921.

International Olympic Committee (IOC) (2001) Press Release: 'IOC Gene Therapy Working Group – Conclusion', Lausanne: *International Olympic Committee*. Online. Available: <http://www.olympic.org/uk/news/publications/press_uk.asp?release=179> (accessed August).

Johnson, W.O. (1976) 'From Here to 2000', in A. Yiannakis, R.D. McIntyre, M.J. Melnick and D.P. Hart (eds) *Sport Sociology: Contemporary Themes*, Dubuque, Iowa: Kendall/Hunt.

Jonsen, A.R. (1991) 'Casuistry as Methodology in Clinical Ethics', *Theoretical Medicine*, **12**: 295–307.

Jonsen, A.R. and Toulmin, S. (1988) *The Abuse of Casuistry: A History of Moral Reasoning*, Berkeley: University of California Press.

Juengst, E.T. (1998) 'What Does *Enhancement* Mean?', in E. Parens (ed.) *Enhancing Human Traits: Ethical and Social Implications*, Washington, DC: Georgetown University Press, pp. 29–47.

Kahn, A. (1997) 'Clone Mammals . . . Clone Man', *Nature*, **386**: 119.

Kant, I. (1785) *Fundamental Principles Of The Metaphysic Of Morals*, translated by T.K. Abbott. Online. Available: <http://www.knuten.liu.se/~bjoch509/works/kant/princ_morals.txt> (accessed June 2002).

Keyley, J. (1996) 'Using Genetic Information: A Radical Problematic for an Individualistic Framework', *Medicine and Law*, **15**: 715–720.

Kidd, B. and Donnelly, P. (2000) 'Human Rights in Sports', *International Review for the Sociology of Sport*, **35** (2): 131–148.

Knoppers, B.M. (1999) 'Who Should Have Access to Genetic Information?', in J. Burley (ed.) *The Genetic Revolution and Human Rights*, Oxford: Oxford University Press, pp. 39–53.

Kramer, P. (1994) *Listening to Prozac*, London: Fourth Estate.

Kretchmar, R.S. (1992) 'Nagging Questions About the Pursuit of Excellence as a Justification for Enhancing Performance in Sport', in R.W. Christina and H.M. Eckert (eds) *Enhancing Human Performance in Sport, New Concepts and Developments, The American Academy of Physical Education*, Champaign, IL: Human Kinetics, pp. 136–150.

Lamsam, C., Fu, F.H., Robbins, P.D. and Evans, C.H. (1997) 'Gene Therapy in Sports Medicine', *Sports Medicine*, **25** (2): 73–77.

Lavin, M. (1987) 'Are the Current Bans Justified?', *Journal of the Philosophy of Sport*, **14**: 34–43.

Ledley, F.D. (1994) 'Distinguishing Genetics and Eugenics on the Basis of Fairness', *Journal of Medical Ethics*, **20**: 157–164.

Lee, S., Barton, E.R., Sweeney, H.L. and Farrar, R.P. (2004) 'Viral expression of Insulin-Like Growth Factor-I enhances muscle hypertrophy in resistance-trained rats', *Journal of Applied Physiology*, **96**: 1097–1104.

Leiden, J.M. (2000) 'Human Gene Therapy: The Good, the Bad, and the Ugly', *Circulation Research*, **86**: 923.

Leist, A. (1996) 'Persons as "Self-Originating Sources of Value"', in K. Bayertz (ed.) *Sanctity of Life and Human Dignity*, Dordrecht, Boston and London: Kluwer Academic, pp. 177–199.

Levine, B.D. and Stray-Gunderson, J. (1997) '"Living High – Training Low": Effect of Moderate-altitude Exposure Simulated with Nitrogen Tents', *Journal of Applied Physiology*, **83** (1): 102–112.

Levy, N. (2002) 'Deafness, Culture, and Choice', *Journal of Medical Ethic*, **28**: 284–285.

Lin, J., Wu, H., Tarr, P.T., Zhang, C., Wu, Z., Boss, O., Michael, L.F., Puigserver, P., Isotani, E., Olson, E.N., Lowell, B.B., Bassel-Duby, R. and Spiegelmann, B.M. (2002) 'Transcriptional Co-activator PGC-1 Drives the Formation of Slow-twitch Muscle Fibres', *Nature*, **418**: 797–801.

Lippman, A. (1992) 'Led (Astray) by Genetic Maps: The Cartography of the Human Genome and Health Care', *Social Science and Medicine*, **35** (12): 1469–1476.

Little, M.O. (1998) 'Cosmetic Surgery, Suspect Norms, and the Ethics of Complicity', in E. Parens (ed.) *Enhancing Human Traits: Ethical and Social Implications*, Washington, DC: Georgetown University Press, pp. 162–176.

Locke, J. (1690) *An Essay Concerning Human Understanding*. Online. Available: <http://www.infidels.org/library/historical/john_locke/human_understanding.html> (accessed July 2002).

Lockwood, M. (1985) 'When Does a Life Begin?', in M. Lockwood (ed.) *Moral Dilemmas in Modern Medicine*, Oxford: Oxford University Press, pp. 9–31.

Loland, S. (1998a) 'Fair Play: Historical Anachronism or Topical Ideal?', in M.J. McNamee and S.J. Parry (eds) *Ethics and Sport*, London and New York: E & FN Spon, pp. 79–103.

Loland, S. (1998b) *The Record Dilemma*. Twentieth World Congress of Philosophy, Boston. Online. Available: <http://www.bu.edu/wcp/Papers/Spor/SporLola.htm> (accessed September).

Loland, S. (2000) 'The Logic of Progress and the Art of Moderation in Competitive Sports', in T. Tännsjö and C. Tamburrini (eds) *Values in Sport: Elitism, Nationalism, Gender Equality, and the Scientific Manufacture of Winners*, London: E & FN Spon, pp. 39–56.

Loland, S. (2002a) 'Sport Technologies – A Moral View', in A. Miah and S.B. Eassom (eds) *Sport Technology: History, Philosophy and Policy*, Oxford: Elsevier Science, pp. 157–171.

Loland, S. (2002b) *Fair Play in Sport: A Moral Norm System*, London and New York: Routledge.

Loland, S. and McNamee, M. (2000) 'Fair Play and the Ethos of Sports: An Eclectic Philosophical Framework', *Journal of the Philosophy of Sport*, **27**: 63–80.

Longman, J. (2001) 'Pushing the Limits: Getting the Athletic Edge May Mean Altering Genes', *New York Times*. Online. Available: http://www.nytimes.com/2001/05/11/sports/11GENE.html.

Lovell-Badge, R. (2001) 'Stem Cell Therapy and Research', *Mill Hill Essays*. Online. Available: <http://www.nimr.mrc.ac.uk/MillHillEssays/2001/stemcells.htm> (accessed July 2002).

MacIntyre, A. (1979) 'Medicine Aimed at the Care of Persons Rather Than What . . . ?', in E.J. Cassell and M. Siegler (eds) *Changing Values in Medicine*, New York: University Publications of America, pp. 83–96.

MacIntyre, A. (1985) *After Virtue: A Study in Moral Theory* (2nd edn), London: Duckworth.

Mackay, D. (2002) 'Whitlock and Wilkins Face Drug Bans on Eve of Games', *Guardian*.

Martinek, V., Fu, F.H. and Huard, J. (2000) 'Gene therapy and tissue engineering in Sports Medicine', **28** (2). Online. Available: <http://www.physsportsmed.com/issues/2000/02_00/huard.htm>

McCarthy, A. (2000) 'Pharmacogenetics: Implications for Drug Development, Patients and Society', *New Genetics and Society*, **19** (2): 135–143.

McCrory, P. (2001) 'Ethics, molecular biology and sports medicine', *British Journal of Sports Medicine*, **35** (3): 142–143.

McCrory, P. (2003) 'Super athletes or gene cheats: the threat of gene transfer technology to elite sport', *British Journal of Sports Medicine*, **37** (3): 192–193.

McIntosh, P. (1979) *Fair Play: Ethics in Sport and Competition*, London: Heinemann.

McKnight, C. (1998) 'On Defining Illness', *Journal of Applied Philosophy*, **15** (2): 195–198.

McLachlan, H.V. (2002) 'Bodies, Persons and Research on Human Embryos', *Human Reproduction and Genetic Ethics*, **8** (1): 4–6.

McLean, S.A.M. (2002) 'Genetic Screening of Children: The U.K. Position', *Journal of Contemporary Health Law and Policy*, **12** (1): 113–130.

McMillan, J. (2002) 'Sex Selection, in the United Kingdom', *Hastings Center Report*, **32** (1): 28–31.

McNamee, M.J. (1992) 'Physical Education and the Development of Personhood', *Physical Education Review*, **15** (2): 13–28.

McNamee, M.J. (1995) 'Sporting Practices, Institutions, and Virtues: A Critique and a Restatement', *Journal of the Philosophy of Sport*, **22**: 61–82.

Macer, D.J. (1990) 'Shaping Genes: Ethics, Law and Science of Using New Genetic Technology in Medicine and Agriculture: Eubois Ethics Institute'. Online. Available: <http://zobell.biol.tsukuba.ac.jp/~macer> (accessed July 2001).

Magdalinski, T. (2000) 'Performance Technologies: Drugs and Fastskin at the Sydney 2000 Olympics', *Media International Australia*, **97** (November): 59–69.

Magnay, J. (2002) 'Pack Up Your Altitude Tent And Move On: World Anti-Doping Agency Prepares To Tackle Becks', *Sydney Morning Herald*, Sydney, Australia, 16 May. Online.

Mann, P.S. (1998) *Meanings of Death*. Twentieth World Congress of Philosophy, Boston, USA. Online. Available: <http://www.bu.edu/wcp/Papers/Bioe/BioeMann.htm> (accessed September).

Martinek, V., Fu, F.H. and Huard, J. (2000) 'Gene Therapy and Tissue Engineering in Sports Medicine', *The Physician and Sports Medicine*, **28** (2). Online. Available: http://www.physsportsmed.com/issues/2000/02_00/huard.htm.

Mazlish, B. (1993) *The Fourth Discontinuity*, London: Yale University Press.

Mendel, G. (1866) 'Versuche über Pflanzen-Hybriden'. Verhandlungen des naturforschenden Vereines in Brünn [Proceedings of the Natural History Society of Brünn].

Miah, A. (2000) '"New Balls Please": Tennis, Technology, and the Changing Game', in S.A. Haake and A.O. Coe (eds) *Tennis, Science, and Technology*, London: Blackwell Science, pp. 285–292.

Miah, A. (2002a) *Philosophical and Ethical Questions Concerning Technology in Sport: The Case of Genetic Modification*, Department of Sport Science, Leicester: De Montfort University.

Miah, A. (2002b) 'Is Bigger Better? A Response to the International Tennis Federation's "Bigger Balls" Proposal', *International Sports Studies*, **24** (2): 19–32.

Miah, A. (2003a) 'Dead Bodies for the Masses: The British Public Autopsy and the Aftermath', *CTHEORY*, **E119**. Online. Available: <http://www.ctheory.net/text_file.asp?pick=363> (accessed October).

Miah, A. (2003b) 'Patenting Human DNA', in B. Almond and M. Parker (eds) *Ethical Issues in the New Genetics*, Aldershot: Ashgate, pp. 111–117.

Miah, A. and Eassom, S.B. (eds) (2002) *Sport Technology: History, Philosophy and Policy*, Oxford: Elsevier Science.

Mill, J.S. (1843/1995) *On Liberty. Classics of Western Philosophy* (4th edn), ed. S.M. Cahn, Indianapolis: Hackett, pp. 1171–1244.

Moldrup, C. (2002) 'When Pharmacogenomics Goes Public', *New Genetics and Society*, **21** (1): 29–37.

Montgomery, H., Marshall, R., Hemingway, H., Myerson, S., Clarkson, P., Dollery, C., Hayward, M., Holliman, D.E., Jubb, M., World, M., Thomas, E.L., Brynes, A.E., Saeed, N., Barnard, M., Bell, J.D., Prasad, K., Rayson, M., Talmud, P.J. and Humphries, S.E. (1998) 'Human Gene for Physical Performance', *Nature*, **393** (21 May): 221–222.

Montgomery, H., Clarkson, P., Barnard, M., Bell, J., Brynes, A., Dollery, C., Hajnal, J., Hemingway, H., Mercer, D., Jarman, P., Marshall, R., Prasad, K., Rayson, M., Saeed, N., Talmud, P., Thomas, L., Jubb, M., World, M. and Humphries, S. (1999) 'Angiotension-converting-enzyme Gene Insertion/Deletion Polymorphism and Response to Physical Training', *The Lancet*, **353** (13 February): 541–545.

Moore, A.D. (2000) 'Owning Genetic Information and Gene Enhancement Techniques: Why Privacy and Property Rights May Undermine Social Control of the Human Genome', *Bioethics*, **14** (2): 97–110.

Morgan, N. (2001) *Sports Facing Next Problem After Drug-takers – Gene Cheats*, London: Bloomberg Press.

Morgan, W.J. (1994) *Leftist Theories of Sport: A Critique and Reconstruction*, Urbana: University of Illinois Press.

Morgan, W.J. and Meier, K.V. (eds) (1988/1995) *Philosophic Inquiry in Sport*, Champaign, IL: Human Kinetics.

Moynihan, R. (2003) 'The Making of a Disease: Female Sexual Dysfunction', *British Medical Journal*, **326**: 45–47. Online. Available: <http://bmj.com/cgi/content/full/326/7379/45?etoc> (accessed June).

Munthe, C. (2000) 'Selected Champions: Making Winners in an Age of Genetic Technology', in T. Tännsjö and C.M. Tamburrini (eds) *Values in Sport: Elitism, Nationalism, Gender Equality, and the Scientific Manufacture of Winners*, London and New York: E & FN Spon, pp. 217–231.

Murray, T.H. (1983) 'The Coercive Power of Drugs in Sports', *Hastings Center Report*, August: 24–30.

Murray, T.H. (1984a) 'Drugs, Sports, and Ethics', in T.H. Murray, W. Gaylin and R. Macklin (eds) *Feeling Good and Doing Better*, Clifton, NJ: Humana Press, pp. 107–126.

Murray, T.H. (1984b) 'Divided Loyalties in Sports Medicine', *The Physician and Sportsmedicine*, **13** (8): 134–140.

Murray, T.H. (1986a) 'Guest Editorial: Drug Testing and Moral Responsibility', *The Physician and Sportsmedicine*, **14** (11): 47–48.

Murray, T.H. (1986b) 'Human Growth Hormone in Sports: No', *The Physician and Sportsmedicine*, **14** (5): 29.

Murray, T.H. (1996) 'The Worth of a Child', Berkeley, California: University of California Press.

National Bioethics Advisory Commission (1999) *Ethical Issues in Human Stem Cell Research*, Washington, DC: http://bioethics.gov.

Neese, R.M. (2001) 'On the Difficulty of Defining Disease: A Darwinian Perspective', *Medicine, Health Care and Philosophy*, **4** (1): 37–46.

Nelkin, D. and Lindee, M.S. (1995) *The DNA Mystique: The Gene as a Cultural Icon*, New York: W.H. Freeman & Co.

Nordenfelt, L. (1998) 'On Medicine and Health Enhancement – Towards a Conceptual Framework', *Medicine, Health Care and Philosophy*, **1** (1): 5–12.

Nordgren, A. (2003) 'Metaphors in Behavioural Genetics', *Theoretical Medicine*, **24**: 59–77.

Nuffield Council on Bioethics (1993) *Genetic Screening: Ethical Issues*, London: Nuffield Council on Bioethics, 120.

Nuffield Council on Bioethics (2000) *Stem Cell Therapy: The Ethical Issues*, London: Nuffield Council on Bioethics, 20.

Orwell, G. (1949/1983) *1984*, New York: The New American Library.

Palmer, C.A. (1992) 'Drugs vs. Privacy: The New Game in Sports', *Marquette Sports Law Journal*, **2** (2): 175–209.

Parens, E. (ed.) (1998) *Enhancing Human Traits: Ethical and Social Implications*, Washington, DC: Georgetown University Press.

Parfit, D. (1971/1976) 'Personal Identity', in J. Glover (ed.) *The Philosophy of Mind*, Oxford: Oxford University Press, pp. 142–162.

Parfit, D. (1984) *Reasons and Persons*, Oxford: Clarendon Press.

Parker, M. (2001) 'Genetics and the Interpersonal Elaboration of Ethics', *Theoretical Medicine*, **22**: 451–459.

Parry, S.J. (1987) 'The Devil's Advocate', *Sport & Leisure*, November–December: 34–35.

Perry, C. (1988) 'Blood Doping and Athletic Competition', in W.J. Morgan and K.V. Meier (eds) *Philosophic Inquiry in Sport*, Champaign, IL: Human Kinetics, pp. 307–312.

Perusse, L., Rankinen, T., Rauramaa, R., Rivera, M.A., Wolfarth, B. and Bouchard, C. (2003) 'The Human Gene Map for Performance and Health-related Fitness Phenotypes: The 2002 Update', *Medicine & Science in Sports & Exercise*, **35** (8): 1248–1264.

Philpott, M. (1996) 'Not Guilty, by Reason of Genetic Determinism', in H. Tam (ed.) *Punishment, Excuses and Moral Development*, Aldershot: Avebury Press, Chapter 5. Also Online. Available: <http://www.med.upenn.edu/~bioethic/genetics/articles/4.philpott.not.guilty.html> (accessed April 2003).

Plata, R., Cornejo, A., Arratia, C., Anabaya, A., Perna, A., Dimitrov, B.D., Remuzzi, G. and Ruggenenti, P. (2002) 'Angiotensin-converting-enzyme Inhibition Therapy in Altitude Polycythaemia: A Prospective Randomised Trial', *The Lancet*, **359** (9307): 663–666.

Platt, T. (1998) *Medicine, Metaphysics and Morals*, Twentieth World Congress of Philosophy, Boston. Online. Available: <http://www.bu.edu/wcp/Papers/Bioe/BioePlat.htm> (accessed September).

Post, S.G. (1991) 'Selective Abortion and Gene Therapy: Reflections on Human Limits', *Human Gene Therapy*, **2** (3): 229–233.

Powell, D. (2001) 'Spectre of Gene Doping Raises its Head as Athletes see Possibilities', *The Times*, London.

Pullman, D. (2002) 'Human Dignity and the Ethics and Aesthetics of Pain and Suffering', *Theoretical Medicine*, **23**: 75–94.

Putnam, H. (1999) 'Cloning People', in J. Burley (ed.) *The Genetic Revolution and Human Rights*, Oxford: Oxford University Press, pp. 1–13.

Rabilloud, T. (2001) *Protéomique et Bioéthique*. Eighth Session of the International Bioethics Committee, Paris: Unesco, pp. 43–46.

Rachels, J. (1986) 'Active and Passive Euthanasia', in P. Singer (ed.) *Applied Ethics*, Oxford: Oxford University Press, pp. 29–35.

Rawls, J. (1971) *A Theory of Justice*, Cambridge, MA: Harvard University Press.

Reiss, M.J. and Straughan, R. (1996) *Improving Nature?: The Science and Ethics of Genetic Engineering*, Cambridge: Cambridge University Press.

Rendtorff, J.D. (1998) *Basic Principles in Bioethics and Biolaw*, Twentieth World Congress of Philosophy, Boston. Online. Available: <http://www.bu.edu/wcp/Papers/Bioe/BioeRend.htm> (accessed September).

Resnik, D.B. (1994) 'Debunking the Slippery Slope Argument against Human Germline Gene Therapy', *Journal of Medicine and Philosophy*, **19** (1): 23–40.

Resnik, D.B. (2001) 'Regulating the Market for Human Eggs', *Bioethics*, **15** (1): 1–25.

Rhodes, R. (1995) 'Clones, Harms, and Rights', *Cambridge Quarterly of Health Care Ethics*, **4** (1): 285–290.

Ridley, M. (1999) *Genome: The Autobiography of a Species in 23 Chapters*, London: Fourth Estate.

Roberts, M.A. (1996) 'Human Cloning: A Case of No Harm Done?', *Journal of Medicine and Philosophy*, **21**: 537–554.

Robertson, S. and Savulescu, J. (2001) 'Is There a Case In Favour of Predictive Genetic Testing in Young Children?', *Bioethics*, **15** (1): 26–49.

Rogers, A. and de Bousingen, D. (1995) *Bioethics in Europe*, Strasbourg: Council of Europe.

Rosas, A. (2002) 'Psychological and Evolutionary Evidence for Altruism', *Biology and Philosophy*, **17** (1): 93–107.

Rose, A. (1988) 'Mandatory Drug Testing of College Athletes: Are Athletes Being Denied their Constitutional Rights?', *Pepperdine Law Review*, **16**: 45–75.

Rosenberg, D. (1995) 'The Concept of Cheating in Sport', *International Journal of Physical Education*, **32** (2): 4–14.

Rothstein, M.A. and Knoppers, B.M. (1996) 'Legal Aspects of Genetics, Work and Insurance in North America and Europe', *European Journal of Health Law*, **3**: 143–161.

Rudnick, A. (2000) 'The Ends of Medical Intervention and the Demarcation of the Normal from the Pathological', *Journal of Medicine and Philosophy*, **25** (5): 569–580.

Sandberg, P. (1995) 'Genetic Information and Life Insurance: A Proposal for Ethical European Policy', *Social Science Medicine*, **40** (11): 1549–1559.

Savulescu, J. (2001) 'Procreative Beneficence: Why we Should Select the Best Children', *Bioethics*, **15** (5/6): 413–426.

Schjerling, P. (2001) 'Genetic Manipulation in Sports: "Gene Doping"', Proceedings of the one-day seminar, *Genes in Sport*, University College London.

Schneider, A.J. and Butcher, R.B. (1994) 'Why Olympic Athletes Should Avoid the Use and Seek the Elimination of Performance Enhancing Substances and Practices from the Olympic Games', *Journal of the Philosophy of Sport*, **21**: 64–81.

Schneider, A.J. and Butcher, R.B. (2000) 'A Philosophical Overview of the Arguments on Banning Doping in Sport', in T. Tännsjö and C.M. Tamburrini (eds) *Values in Sport: Elitism, Nationalism, Gender Equality, and the Scientific Manufacture of Winners*, London: E & FN Spon, pp. 185–199.

Scott, C. (1984) 'Heidegger, Madness, and Well-Being', in R. Shahan and J. Mohanty (eds) *Thinking about Being: Aspects of Heidegger's Thought*, Norman, OK, University of Oklahoma Press.

Shapiro, M.H. (1991) 'The Technology of Perfection: Performance Enhancement and the Control of Attributes', *Southern California Law Review*, **65**: 11–113.

Silvers, A. (1998) 'A Fatal Attraction to Normalizing: Treating Disabilities as Deviations from "Species-typical" Functioning', in E. Parens (ed.) *Enhancing Human Traits: Ethical and Social Implications*, Washington, DC: Georgetown University Press, pp. 95–123.

Simon, R.L. (1984) 'Good Competition and Drug-enhanced Performance', *Journal of the Philosophy of Sport*, **11**: 6–13.

Simon, R.L. (1985) *Sports and Social Values*, Englewood Cliffs, NJ: Prentice-Hall.

Simon, R.L. (1991) *Fair Play: Sport, Values, and Society*, Boulder, CO: Westview Press.

Simpson, J.L., Ljungqvist, A., Ferguson-Smith, M.A., de la Chapelle, A., Elsas, L.J., Erhardt, A.A., Genel, M., Ferris, E.A. and Carlson, A. (2000) 'Gender Verification in the Olympics', *Journal of the American Medical Association*, **284** (12): 1568–1569.

Singer, P.A. (1993) *Practical Ethics* (2nd edn), Cambridge: Cambridge University Press.

Singer, P.A. (1999) 'Genetics and Ethics: Spare us the Hysteria', *The Age*. Online. Available:<http://www.theage.com.au/daily/990630/news/specials/news3.html>(accessed 30 June).

Singer, P.A. (2000) 'Clinical Review: Recent Advances – Medical Ethics', *British Medical Journal*, **321** (28): 282–285.

Slater, L. (1998) *Prozac Diary*, London: Hamish Hamilton.

Smith, K.C. (2001) 'A Disease by any Other Name: Musings on the Concept of a Genetic Disease', *Medicine, Health Care and Philosophy*, **4** (1): 19–30.

Sneddon, R. (2000) 'The Challenge of Pharmacogenetics and Pharmacogenomics', *New Genetics and Society*, **19** (2): 145–164.

Spriggs, M. (2002) 'Lesbian Couple Create a Child Who is Deaf Like Them', *Journal of Medical Ethics*, **28** (5): 283.

St Louis, B. (2003) 'Sport, Genetics and the "Natural Athlete": The Resurgence of Racial Science', *Body and Society*, **9** (2): 75–95.

Stock, G. (1993) *Metaman: The Merging of Humans and Machines into a Global Superorganism*, London: Simon & Schuster.

Stock, G. (2002) *Redesigning Humans: Choosing our Children's Genes*, London: Profile Books.

Sturbois, X., Maier, E., Schamasch, P., Cummiskey, J. and de Merode, Prince A. (2002) 'Gene therapy or doping of the future', Concerted action in the fight against doping in sport, online. Available: <http://www.cafdisantidoping.net/en/print/preview.asp?articleid=285.

Suits, B. (1973) 'The Elements of Sport', in R.G. Osterhoudt (ed.) *The Philosophy of Sport: A Collection of Original Essays*, Illinois: Charles C. Thomas.

Suits, B. (1978) *The Grasshopper: Games, Life, and Utopia*, Toronto: University of Toronto.

Suits, B. (1988) 'Tricky Triad: Games, Play and Sport', *Journal of the Philosophy of Sport*, **XV**: 1–9.

Svensson, E.C., Black, H.B., Dugger, D.L., Tripathy, S.K., Goldwasser, E., Hao, Z., Chu, L. and Leiden, J.M. (1997) 'Long-term Erythropoietin Expression in Rodents and

Non-human Primates Following Intramuscular Injection of a Replication-defective Adenoviral Vector', *Human Gene Therapy*, **8** (15): 1797–1806.

Tamburrini, C.M. (1998) 'Sports, Facism, and the Market', *Journal of the Philosophy of Sport*, **25**: 35–47.

Tamburrini, C.M. (2000a) 'What's Wrong with Doping?', in T. Tännsjö and C.M. Tamburrini (eds) *Values in Sport: Elitism, Nationalism, Gender Equality, and the Scientific Manufacture of Winners*, London: E & FN Spon, pp. 200–216.

Tamburrini, C.M. (2000b) *The 'Hand of God'? Essays in the Philosophy of Sports*, Göteborg: Acta Universitatis Gotoburgensis.

Tamburrini, C.M. (2002) 'After Doping What? The Morality of the Genetic Engineering of Athletes', in A. Miah and S.B. Eassom (eds) *Sport Technology: History, Philosophy and Policy*, Oxford: Elsevier Science, pp. 253–268.

Tännsjö, T. (1998) 'Is Our Admiration for Sports Heroes Fascistoid?', *Journal of the Philosophy of Sport*, **25**: 23–34.

Taylor, C. (1985) *Human Agency and Language: Philosophical Papers 1*, Cambridge: Cambridge University Press.

Taylor, C. (1991) *The Ethics of Authenticity*, Cambridge, MA: Harvard University Press.

Taylor, R.R., Mamotte, C.D.S., Fallon, K. and van Bockxmeer, F.M. (1999) 'Elite Athletes and the Gene for Angiotensin Converting Enzyme', *Journal of Applied Physiology*, **87**: 1035–1037.

Tenner, E. (1996) *Why Things Bite Back: Predicting the Problems of Progress*, London: Fourth Estate.

Thompson, P.B. (1982/1988) 'Privacy and the Urinalysis Testing of Athletes', in W.J. Morgan and K.V. Meier (eds) *Philosophic Inquiry in Sport*, Champaign, IL: Human Kinetics, pp. 313–318.

Tollefsen, C. (2001) 'Embryos, Individuals, and Persons: An Argument Against Embryo Creation Research', *Journal of Applied Philosophy*, **18** (1): 65–77.

Tooley, M. (1983) *Abortion and Infanticide*, Oxford: Clarendon Press.

Tooley, M. (1986) 'Abortion and Infanticide', in P. Singer (ed.) *Applied Ethics*, Oxford: Oxford University Press, pp. 57–85.

Turney, J. (1998) *Frankenstein's Footsteps: Science, Genetics and Popular Culture*, New Haven and London: Yale University Press.

Tuxill, C. and Wigmore, S. (1998) '"Merely Meat?" Respect for Persons in Sports and Games', in M.J. McNamee and S.J. Parry (eds) *Ethics and Sport*, London and New York: E & FN Spon, pp. 104–115.

Tymowski, G. (2001) 'Rights and Wrongs: Children's Participation in High-performance Sports', in I.R. Berson, M.J. Berson and B.C. Cruz (eds) *Research in Global Child Advocacy, Vol. 1*, Greenwich, CT: Information Age Publishing.

Unesco (1997) *Universal Declaration on the Human Genome and Human Rights*, Online. Available: <http://www.unesco.org/ibc/genome/projet/index.html> (accessed 2001).

US President's Council on Bioethics (2002) 'Human Cloning and Human Dignity: An Ethical Inquiry', Washington, DC: *The President's Council on Bioethics*, Online. Available: <http://www.bioethics.gov/reports/cloningreport/fullreport.html> (accessed July).

van Hooft, S. (1998) 'Suffering and the Goals of Medicine', *Medicine, Health Care and Philosophy*, **1** (2): 125–131.

Varzi, A. and Coen, L. (2001) 'That Useless Time Machine', *Philosophy*, **76** (298): 581–583.

Vehmas, S. (2001) 'Just Ignore it? Parents and Genetic Information', *Theoretical Medicine*, **22**: 473–484.

Wadler, G.I. (1998) 'Doping in Sport: From Strychnine to Genetic Enhancement, It's a Moving Target', *The Duke Conference on Doping in Sport*, R. David Thomas Executive Conference Center, Online. Available: <http://www.law.duke.edu/sportscenter/wadler.pdf> (accessed 1999).

Wallace, S. (2001) 'Drugs in Sport: Cheats Could Inject Genes to Beat System', *The Daily Telegraph*, Lausanne, 3 December.

Walsh, D. (2001) 'New Crisis Facing Sport', *The Times*, London, 19 November.

Warnock, M. (1985) *A Question of Life: The Warnock Report on Human Fertilisation & Embryology*, Oxford: Blackwell.

Warnock, M. (1987) 'Do Human Cells Have Rights?', *Bioethics*, **1** (1): 1–14.

Watson, J.D. and Crick, F.H.C. (1953) 'Molecular Structure of Nucleic Acids. A Structure for Deoxyribose Nucleic Acid', *Nature*, **171**: 737–738.

Wertz, S.K. (1981) 'The Varieties of Cheating', *Journal of the Philosophy of Sport*, **8**: 19–40.

Whitfield, J. (2001) 'Exercising Your Genes, Nature – Science Update', Online. Available: <http://www.nature.com/nsu/011206/011206–5.html> (accessed 4 December).

Wilkie, T. and Graham, E. (1998) 'Power without responsibility: media portrayals of Dolly and Science', *Cambridge Quarterly for Healthcare Ethics*, **7**: 150–159.

Williams, A.G., Rayson, M.P., Jubb, M., World, M., Woods, D.R., Hayward, M., Martin, J., Humphries, S.E. and Montgomery, H. (2000) 'The ACE Gene and Muscle Performance', *Nature*, **403** (10 February): 614.

Williams, B. (1970) 'The Self and the Future', *Philosophical Review*, **79** (2): 161–180.

Williams, B. (1973) *Problems of the Self*, Cambridge: Cambridge University Press.

Wilmut, I., Schnieke, A.E., McWhir, J., Kind, A.J. and Campell, K.H.S. (1997) 'Viable Offspring Derived from Foetal and Adult Mammalian Cells', *Nature*, **385**: 810–813.

Wilson, J. (2002) 'The Accidental Altruist: Biological', *Biology and Philosophy*, **17** (1): 71–91.

Wilson, S. (2001) 'Doping Experts Wary Of Gene Manipulation', *The Associated Press*, 26 January.

Wilson, W. and Derse, E. (eds) (2001) *Doping in Elite Sport: The Politics of Drugs in the Olympic Movement*, Champaign, IL: Human Kinetics.

Wolpe, P.R. (1997) *The Triumph of Autonomy in American Bioethics: A Sociological View*, Online. Available: <http://www.med.upenn.edu/~bioethic/library/papers/paul/Triumph.html> (accessed June 2002).

World Anti-Doping Agency (WADA) (2002) *Press Release: WADA Conference Sheds Light on the Potential of Gene Doping*, New York: World Anti-Doping Agency, Online. Available: <http://www.wada-ama.org> (accessed April).

World Anti-Doping Agency (WADA) (2003) *International Standard for the Prohibited List 2004*: <http://www.wada-ama.org/docs/web/standards_harmonization/code/list_standard_2004.pdf> (accessed June).

World Health Organisation (1948) *Constitution*, United Nations, Online. Available: <http://www.who.int> (accessed 2003).

World Medical Association (2000) 'The World Medical Association Declaration of Helsinki: Ethical Principles for Medical Research Involving Human Subjects', Online. Available: <http://www.wma.net/e/policy/17c.pdf> (accessed July 2002).

Wu, Z., Bidlingmaier, M., Dall, R. and Strasburger, C.J. (1999) 'Detection of Doping with Human Growth Hormone', *British Medical Journal*, **353** (9156): 895.

Yang, N., MacArthur, D.G., Gulloin, J.P., Hahn, A.G., Beggs, A.J., Eusteal, S. and North, K. (2003) 'ACTN3 Genotype is Associated with Human Elite Athletic Performance', *American Journal of Human Genetics*, **73**: 627–631.

Index